The SharePoint Shepherd's Guide for End Users: 2013

Robert L. Bogue

AVAILTEK

www.availtekllc.com

(This page was intentionally blank before we decided to put this message on it about it being intentionally blank. Now it's just mostly blank, except for this message. Carry on there is nothing to see here.)

The SharePoint Shepherds Guide for End Users: 2013
By Robert L. Bogue

Editor: Kathi Anderson
Technical Editor: Amy Dehmer
Cover Design: Arnel Reynon

While every precaution has been taken in the preparation of this book, the publisher and author assume no responsibility for errors or omissions, or for damages resulting from the use of the information contained herein.

ISBN-13: 978-0-9824198-1-6

Printed in the United States of America

For more information about this book including frequently asked questions and corporate licensing please visit us at http://www.sharepointshepherd.com/2013.

Get the SharePoint Shepherd's Guide for End Users

Wiki Version

Make the book more accessible to you and your users. The Wiki edition of *The SharePoint Shepherd's Guide for End Users: 2013* is a searchable productivity aid for all of the users in your organization. Get answers when you need them without carrying another book.

Visit www.SharePointShepherd.com/2013 for more information.

About the Author

Robert Bogue is a thought leader on all things SharePoint and an engaging presenter who speaks at events around the world. Rob has been awarded the Microsoft MVP designation ten times, and earned recognition as a Microsoft Patterns and Practices Champion. Rob holds certifications from Microsoft: MCPD, MCITP, MCTS, MCSA: Security, MCSE as well as CompTia: A+, Network+, Server+, I-Net+, IT Project+, E-Biz+, CDIA+. Rob also served as a team member for the Microsoft SharePoint Guidance (http://www.microsoft.com/spg).

He is the author of 22 books including, The SharePoint Shepherd's Guide for End Users series which is also available in a Wiki version as *The SharePoint Tutor*. Robert is committed to "making the complicated, simple." Find out more about SharePoint made simple at, http://www.SharePointShepherd.com or follow Rob's blog at http://www.ThorProjects.com/blog/. You can also email Rob at Shepherd@SharePointShepherd.com.

About the Technical Editor

Amy Newton Dehmer is a SharePoint consultant with Allegient, LLC with more than 13 years of Information Technology experience. Her passion is in helping companies maximize their SharePoint value by leveraging out of the box functionality. Her unique understanding of software, business, and people enables her to deliver excellence in the SharePoint solutions she provides. Amy specializes in SharePoint technologies with a focus on implementation and configuration, publishing infrastructure, and SharePoint Designer workflows, and has worked with SharePoint technologies since the 2001 version.

Dedication

It's been 5 years since I wrote the first version of the Shepherd's Guide. I've received so many compliments on the work that I've done on the previous guides. I cannot say how grateful I am for all of the feedback.

Over the past 5 years I've continued to rebuild my relationship with my father. There are many reasons why our paths separated for a while and more for why our paths are coming together.

As I raise my own son, I realize how incredibly important the role of fathers is. I know that my father made mistakes along the way – but as I go through the process myself, I realize both that there is no manual for how to be a father and that he did a lot more right than he did wrong.

I simply could not have become the man that I've become without the support of my father.

Acknowledgements

I've been reflecting lately about the diverse backgrounds and the number of people who have contributed to my professional career over the years. I realize that there have been quite literally thousands and thousands of individuals who have written me emails or with whom I've had conversations that have enriched my understanding of the market and technology. It's startling to me to reflect over the more than 20 years of work in the IT industry and realize how many people I've touched and how many people have touched me.

There's no possible way that I could list every person who has contributed to my professional growth. The task for listing those who have directly impacted the book is less daunting – but still daunting.

It's easy to thank Brian Proffitt again, as he's once again slaved over the task content of the book to make sure that it's right and meets everyone's needs. Since Brian moved a few hours away years ago we've not had the opportunity to spend as much time with each other. So I'm deeply grateful that he chose to work with me again on this project so that we can continue to work together even if we can't socialize as much as we would like.

Amy Dehmer once again joined this project to do technical editing. That's a monumental task for any project – but with SharePoint it seems particularly so. Amy has helped us juggle all of the loose ends of the project without pulling her hair out – that's no small feat.

This time around I have to also thank Kristin Sheibley who has served as my office manager, project manager, and drill sergeant on this book. She came in to help to ensure that the project would get done when it seemed like every part of the project was off track in one way or another.

I also need to thank my friend, Arnel Reynon, who was kind enough to work on the cover art again this time. I'm so happy with how he can take ideas and breathe life into them. Often he extends my original ideas to make them stunning.

Finally, I need to thank the great number of people that I call friends. They've become accustomed to my odd questions at odd times. I appreciate their continued patience.

Contents

What is The SharePoint Shepherd's Guide for End Users: 2013?

In the old days, being a shepherd meant having the responsibility for the care and guidance of a flock of sheep. Sheep need a relatively large area to graze to sustain the flock. Protecting a flock might mean the difference between life and death for the family or social unit who depended upon them. Shepherds guided the sheep into safe meadows and protected them from predators.

The book you hold in your hands (or read on your screen) is designed to provide the same sort of protection that a shepherd of old would provide. It's designed to help guide you to green pastures. You'll not only learn some of the tasks that you can do with SharePoint, but also exactly how to accomplish those tasks. You'll get the core skills needed to be successful with the immensely powerful platform that is SharePoint.

The book will also guide you away from bad practices or simple problems that can be inadvertently created by missing a simple step, accidentally including a space in a name, or generally just making a mistake.

Information in this book is presented in a simple, step-by-step style. Need to do something in SharePoint? Find the specific task to guide you and follow the easy to understand, illustrated steps. We'll walk through the process of doing nearly everything that an end user might want to do in SharePoint. We'll point out along the way how different fields are used and what might go wrong if you try the process.

To a new user, SharePoint may seem daunting and confusing. With this book to guide you, you will see that the way to a greener pasture of SharePoint knowledge is not as difficult as you think.

Introduction and Decision Trees

Although the *SharePoint Shepherd's Guide for End Users* is specifically designed to deliver direct how-tos for accomplishing many things in SharePoint 2013, it is also recognized that there are times when background information is needed to better plan your SharePoint deployment. What are SharePoint's capabilities, and more importantly, what are the decisions you need to make when working with SharePoint resources?

In this section, you will learn about:

- **What is SharePoint?:** Fully understanding what SharePoint is can be challenging, but there are many things that are easy to understand about SharePoint and how it can be a part of how you work.

- **What is a Content Type?:** The real magic of content types isn't in the ability to define fields and processes. The real magic is in the idea that you can put multiple content types in the same document library (or list).

- **How Do I Manage Versions?:** SharePoint supports versioning for both list items and for files. You don't have to rename the file to know which version is which.

- **How Do I Get Notified of Changes?:** There are three basic ways that SharePoint can notify you of changes.

- **Choosing the Right Site Template:** SharePoint Server 2013 Enterprise Edition offers 13 site templates out of the box. Trying to figure out which template is the right template to create is more than a bit challenging, particularly if you've not seen the templates in use.

- **Create a List or Library App:** With SharePoint's document libraries having so many features that are similar to lists – particularly the ability to store additional metadata with the file – it can be confusing to decide whether you should be creating a list or a library.

- **Organize with Folders or Metadata:** The decision of whether to organize data with folders or with metadata is a classic problem that's been with SharePoint for many versions.

- **Create a Page or Site:** The decision is essential because migrating data from one site or page to another site or page can be challenging with out-of-the-box tools.

- **Create a Subsite or Site Collection:** A frequent question is whether a subsite or a site collection should be created when trying to address some new need in SharePoint.

- **Managing Permissions with Active Directory Groups or SharePoint Groups:** A common question about managing security in SharePoint is how to control the users who have – or do not have – access to the system.

- **Creating a Word Form or an InfoPath Form:** Should you recreate all of your forms in InfoPath? Well, if your users know Word, there's no compelling reason why you should make extra work for yourself. They're comfortable with the existing forms. What can you get by changing the forms over to InfoPath?

What is SharePoint?

An old skit from *Saturday Night Live* (Season 1, Episode 5) talks about a fake product called Shimmer that is both a floor wax and a dessert topping. This idea, that a product can be more than one thing, has often been used to talk about SharePoint. Because SharePoint is such a versatile tool, it's often quite hard to describe. Consider for a moment how you might explain a Swiss Army knife to someone who's only ever seen a regular three-blade pocket knife. How would you explain eating utensils on a pocket knife? The situation with SharePoint is much the same – it's pretty hard to describe until you're using it.

Let me offer another analogy before we get into the meat of what SharePoint is and does. When you were very young, you didn't know how to ride a bicycle. You saw older kids doing it, but you had never done it yourself. No amount of explanation from your parents or your friends could help you understand what riding a bike feels like.

Fully understanding what SharePoint is can be challenging, but there are many things that are easy to understand about SharePoint and how it can be a part of how you work. At the most basic level, SharePoint is a Web-based system. That means all you need is a Web browser to access SharePoint. The information you get from the Web browser will vary somewhat, depending upon how SharePoint is being used. Let's first look at SharePoint as a collaboration tool, and from there, we can move on to how SharePoint can be a communication tool.

Collaboration Tool

One of my favorite things to ask is: What does the word "collaboration" mean to you?" The term is often used and rarely understood. Most people think it means "working together," which is somewhat odd because collaboration tools often allow you to work together – while being apart. The next time you hear the word collaboration, you might want to ask, "Do you mean to conspire with the enemy?" That is one of the dictionary definitions.

For the most part, there are two kinds of collaboration. The first kind is real-time, collaboration interactions that happen immediately or at the same time. This is the kind of collaboration that happens in a face-to-face meeting; that is, if any collaboration happens at all in the meeting. Real-time collaboration is all about the dialog, people interacting at the same time for a common goal.

The second kind of collaboration is – stunningly – non-real time. That is to say, the collaboration doesn't happen at the exact same moment for both parties but, rather, occurs after some elapsed time. The best example of this is email. You and a friend or colleague can be working together to plan a party or create a response to a request for proposal. Even though you are working together, it's unlikely that you're doing it at the exact same moment.

Microsoft (and others) offers solutions to the real-time communication problem. Microsoft Lync, Microsoft Live Messenger, Skype and Microsoft Live Meeting are all examples of real-time communication offerings from Microsoft. While SharePoint integrates with Lync or Live Messenger to show on a SharePoint page whether someone is available or not (called presence information) on a SharePoint page, SharePoint is not, itself, a real-time collaboration tool. SharePoint activates Lync or Live Messenger and displays an icon next to a person's name, indicating their status using the same iconography and coloring provided in the real-time communications tool.

In the non-real-time category of collaboration, SharePoint is like that Swiss Army knife – there are numerous tools that are available inside SharePoint to help you work with others, whether they're in the next office over or halfway around the world. There are really two key ways to think about the kinds of things on which users collaborate.

Document Collaboration

The first key type of collaboration is documents, such as working together to create a final output document. It could be a policy, a proposal, a PowerPoint presentation, or an Excel spreadsheet. Whatever the document is, you need to get the input from multiple people into the same single document. Historically, this has been handled through file shares, or more popularly through email. The problem with email is that it's difficult to find the right version and it consumes a lot of mailbox storage to keep pushing back and forth different versions of the same file.

SharePoint has a set of tools designed to manage the process of collaborating on documents. First, SharePoint offers version control. You can keep different versions of the same file on the system. This eliminates the problems associated with trying to manually track the file by incrementing a version number and prevents accidental overwriting of other users' work. The versioning feature, like most other features in SharePoint, is configurable so that you can turn it off or on, and even control how it works. SharePoint allows you to limit the number of versions, as well as to control the type of versioning – either simple versioning or using major and minor versions.

Major and minor versions opens up the concept of publishing – or approving – documents so that everyone can see the latest published version, but contributors – those with write access – can also see up-to-date working copies. This allows documents to be worked on in the same place that users consume them – if you want. Also, SharePoint allows you to require that documents be checked out before editing and can, by using out-of–the-box and custom workflows, even help to facilitate the approval process for a document.

You also have a set of records management functions that enable you to declare documents as official records for the organization – and therefore subject to a more restrictive set of policies for deleting or changing the record. SharePoint also has the ability to apply rights-management policies so that, even if a user downloads the document, it can still be protected from unauthorized access.

The final thing to know about how SharePoint manages documents is that SharePoint allows you to hold additional metadata for a document. Metadata literally means data about data. In this case, it's the properties associated with the document. There are some automatic properties that all documents have, including those stored on your local computer. Files have names, sizes, creation dates, modification dates, etc. With the exception of the names, other automatic file properties are considered automatic metadata. It's information that the system added to the file for you. SharePoint supports automatic metadata, but in contrast to a regular file system, you can add your own metadata to a file.

This custom metadata can be anything you want. Perhaps you want to store the customer's name, the lead referral source, the type of products being sold, or nearly anything else. Once the data is stored, you can then view the list of documents, not just by name and folder as you could on a hard drive, but you can also view them sorted, grouped, and filtered by any of the metadata that you've entered. This makes it easier to navigate large volumes of information easily. It also means that you can treat metadata about documents just like any other list of data.

Data Collaboration

Document collaboration is what we do when we push documents back and forth via email, but there is other data that we collaborate on – or use to collaborate – that doesn't fit easily in documents. Consider for the moment a group that's working across the world. It might be useful to know what time zone each participant is in, what office they're located in, and perhaps their mobile telephone number. SharePoint allows you to create any kind of list data you want – very much like you would create columns in an Excel spreadsheet.

In the case of team members, it might be a matter of creating a new contacts list – one that has the kinds of fields that you would expect in an Outlook contact – and add fields for time zone, office, and mobile phone number. The list could then be accessible with these additional fields on the Web to be sorted, grouped, and filtered.

Contacts may or may not seem like an obvious kind of data list with which you work. There are numerous others, though. Tasks lists are simply lists of tasks to be done. Calendars are simply a list of appointments. Announcements to communicate with the group are simply notes. However, there are two key differences between SharePoint and using a more traditional method, like storing the data in a spreadsheet.

The first is that SharePoint has a much richer set of options for the fields. Because a spreadsheet is designed to be rows and columns, it's sometimes hard to include pictures, or large blocks of formatted text. Since SharePoint treats each entry as a separate record and automatically generates a data entry form for you, it's easier to add fields that would be difficult to do in a spreadsheet.

Second, and perhaps more important, when you put a list of items in an Excel spreadsheet, only one person can work on that list at any given time. So Suzi and Fred can't both be completing their tasks at the same time. SharePoint, however, stores these as individual items in a collection and allows both Suzi and Fred to make updates to different items in the same collection at the same time.

Going further, SharePoint allows you to apply version control to an item. This allows you to keep older versions of the item for review. Consider the case where you have task items for a project. SharePoint can automatically track when updates were made and by whom, by keeping versions of the same record. This means that contributors don't have to be as focused on what each other is doing. They can simply do their work and allow SharePoint to do its job coordinating the activity.

Communications Tool

The ability to work on information together is just one piece of the puzzle. What about how to disseminate that information to the appropriate parties inside the organization? That's a fundamentally different problem than tracking revisions and enabling collaboration. As a communications tool, SharePoint has a set of key features that allow you as the user to control its appearance and how the data is displayed to the consumers.

Building Pages from Parts

Rarely does the user get to create his or her own Web page. While some online portals allow users to select their components and the order that they appear, in most corporate environments, everything is pre-assigned and rigid. That isn't the case in SharePoint. One of SharePoint's key features is the ability for anyone to build a page from a set of components – called Web Parts. Even more impressive is that SharePoint allows you to configure these Web Parts to suit your needs.

Web Parts have what are called properties. These are settings that you – the user – can control; these properties make the Web Part behave the way you want it to. In some cases, the properties allow you to control which view is displayed in the Web Part. Other properties control the title and location of the Web Part on the page.

SharePoint ships with numerous Web Parts, including Web Parts for showing the members of a site, for allowing you to add static content, to insert other pages as a part of your page, etc. Developers in your organization and at third-party companies can write Web Parts, which are added to the gallery of available Web Parts that you can then add to a page.

Creating Your Own Pages and Sites

Your control of SharePoint isn't limited to adding parts to pages – you can add pages themselves. You can select from a template or create your own pages. These new pages can have Web Parts placed on them, as well. The benefit of being able to create your own pages is that it allows you a way to show different contents to different people – or to contain different types of content that may not belong on the same page.

For truly separate topics, SharePoint allows you to create your own containers, called apps, which were formerly known as libraries or lists. Sites can have different security, navigation menus, and pages. Sites are like folders except more powerful. While SharePoint allows you to secure folders, sites allow you to change how users are grouped and assigned security. This allows you to tailor the experience of different groups of consumers based on varying sets of criteria.

Quick Wiki

Wikis derive their name from the Hawaiian word for "quick." The Wiki concept is designed to be quick and easy. There are several implementations of wiki – perhaps the most popular is Wikipedia, which rivals the information held by traditional encyclopedia companies. Wikis themselves are designed to allow untrained users to quickly create and connect information. Instead of the <A HREF="http://sharepointshepherd.com">SharePoint Shepherd</A> notation that a Web page would require, a wiki allows you to build links by simply specifying the title that you want for the target. For instance, [[SharePoint Shepherd]] creates a link to a page titled SharePoint Shepherd.

What's better is that wikis included in a SharePoint implementation will automatically allow you to create the page after you've created (stubbed out) the link. By clicking on the link to SharePoint

Shepherd, you'll be given the opportunity to create the page if it doesn't already exist. The net effect is that it takes very little effort to create knowledge repositories that are connected to one another.

SharePoint extends this model by allowing you to add Web Parts to a wiki page. This means that the content and links that you've created can sit side-by-side with a Web Part, showing the results of a query, the temperature in Alaska, or status from some third-party system.

The benefit of a wiki is plain in terms of speed to get content into the system. The negative to wikis is that pages tend not to have the same look and feel, nor does the navigation seem to have any structure to it.

Structuring Web Content

In communication environments, particularly where you're communicating with the public, the key concern isn't always how quick the content can be generated but is, instead, how easy it is for the consumers to consume. This means that the pages should have a consistent page layout and that the navigation should be created in a planned way – that is architected. SharePoint allows you to publish structured content through a set of features called publishing features. These features allow for the creation of page layouts – page templates – into which content can be added. The page layouts are varied by content type so that some of the pages can have more fields than others. Users can create new pages by selecting a new page and the layout they want to use. The content is added into the entry boxes in the layout and, when completed, the output is merged into a single page that the user can see.

The beauty of this arrangement is that the page is stored relatively pre-built in the database so it can be returned quickly, but it's also stored in its component parts so that it's easy to change the appearance of the page when the company changes its name or its branding. Power users can create the page layouts themselves so it's easy to create new types of content and layouts for it. It leaves the power of managing the appearance of the site to the user.

In addition to the ability to control – and change – the appearance of content, SharePoint includes several components designed to dynamically build the menus. By dynamically building menus to match the content that has been created, SharePoint minimizes the amount of effort that must be spent considering how to create the navigation and how to keep menus up-to-date. Further, SharePoint includes a page for Manage Content and Structure that allows you to move the content around, thereby changing the structure and menus which are dynamically generated. With all these tools, it's probable that your site will seem navigable. Of course, some users won't know how to navigate through your site's structure and will need another way to find the information they're looking for – that is where search comes in.

Leveraging the Power of Search

Unlike older systems that allowed you to only search for things within special fields, SharePoint includes a full-text search capability that can extract the text from documents and allow you to search that content for information. SharePoint ships with support for several of the most popular file formats, including text, xml, the Microsoft Office suite of applications, and Adobe's Acrobat PDF file format. There is also extensibility support to allow third-party vendors to plug their own search apps into SharePoint.

Beyond being able to search content stored in SharePoint, the search engine can be configured to index information in File Shares, Exchange, and nearly every kind of system that you can imagine if you're willing to build the XML file that specifies how to get to that content. The result is that SharePoint can be an enterprise-level tool for finding information.

SharePoint's full-text search capability can even reach out to other systems through federation. This allows you to run the same search on your intranet that you run on the Internet – at the same time. SharePoint also allows for the use of faceted search, using the metadata that SharePoint stores on a document or list or library item to further refine the result sets.

Consider that you're looking for a specific presentation on the topic of wind power that you know was given to the ABC Corporation in May. You can search for "wind power abc corporation" and receive a relatively large set of results and then click on a link on the set to limit your results to the PowerPoint presentation type. You can further refine the results to those where the client is identified as ABC Corporation by clicking on the dynamic list of customers that was generated from the results. Ultimately, you can even click into a date range to shrink the scope of the search results to a more manageable level. Often, one, two, or three facets will quickly reduce the number of results to a handful (less than a page). The impact of this is that it is easier to find the results that you're looking for – quickly.

Faceted search relies upon the correct metadata being filled out by users as they upload content to the system. That's something that is facilitated by the upload process – and by the Microsoft Office clients themselves.

Adding Office Client Applications

One of the key challenges in any content management system is getting users to apply metadata or storage location consistently. SharePoint is different than most other content management systems because SharePoint leverages the Office client applications to facilitate the addition of the metadata by the users when they're creating the document.

One feature is QuickParts, which allows the user to enter data into the document directly and have that data promoted to metadata properties automatically. Another is the document information panel (DIP), with an InfoPath form that appears at the top of the document to specify properties. Both aid in the capture of metadata in the document. SharePoint promotes the properties in the documents to metadata in the SharePoint document library. This can dramatically simplify the process of capturing the metadata necessary to route documents (SharePoint's Content Organizer can move documents to new locations based on metadata).

Office client integration also includes the ability to take SharePoint data off-line and to synchronize calendars and contacts to Outlook. This means that SharePoint can be your storage repository for your data even if the primary way that you access that data is to leverage office tools like Microsoft Office and Outlook.

A Tale of Two SharePoints

It's important to realize that most, but not all, of the features ascribed to SharePoint are available in any version. There are two different SharePoint products. There's the SharePoint Foundation product, whose license is included as a part of your Windows Server license, and SharePoint Server, which is a separate for-pay product.

SharePoint Foundation has all of the Office integration, document management, and list management features, as well as basic search capabilities. SharePoint Server includes the Web content management features for publishing. SharePoint Server itself comes in two versions: Standard and Enterprise. Enterprise includes services like Visio Services, InfoPath Form Services, and others. Refer to your Microsoft licensing expert for more specific details.

The key here is that there is a great deal that can be done with SharePoint Foundation. When you need features like Web Content Management, you'll want to upgrade to SharePoint Server Standard edition. When you want to use enhanced services like Visio services, you'll need to get SharePoint Server Enterprise edition.

What is SharePoint Designer and Do I Need It?

For the most part, SharePoint is a Web-based system. Most of the changes that you do for SharePoint are done from a Web browser. There are some cases where you will use a free tool called SharePoint Designer. SharePoint Designer also allows you to create your own workflows so that you can create your own automatic responses to how data flows.

If you're allowed to install software and you're going to use SharePoint, then you should install SharePoint Designer and see if it can help you out.

Conclusion

There are dozens of features not mentioned in this brief introduction to SharePoint. The point here is to give you a flavor – not enumerate every feature. An enumerated feature list can be found at http://www.microsoft.com/sharepoint.

If you have a better way to explain what SharePoint is, please drop me a line at Shepherd@SharePointShepherd.commailto:Rob.Bogue@ThorProjects.com.

What is a Content Type?

Content types are mentioned more than occasionally in the SharePoint documentation that you see online and hear from experts speaking at conferences. It's one of those things that makes SharePoint very powerful – but in some ways equally confusing.

Let's start with the problem that content types are designed to solve. You have a set of different kinds of documents that you may want to work with that might really be best if stored in the same place. Consider the idea that you are in a sales role and that you work with customers on a variety of projects. Each time you need to do a proposal there are several different kinds of documents that are needed. For instance, you might need to do a PowerPoint file as a face-to-face presentation to the customer. You might also need to develop a pro-forma profit and loss (P&L) analysis for approval by management. Further, you might also need to develop a formal offer letter.

The fact is, the files themselves are different, needing different approval processes and perhaps they differ in the amount and type of metadata that is required. For instance, doing a presentation to the customer may not require any approvals. The P&L might require approval by finance. The formal offer letter might require both financial and sales management approval.

On the metadata side, you might require that all the different documents require the customer ID number of the customer for the proposed project. You might require a projected one-year and three-year profit from the P&L. The formal offer letter might require an offer date and an offer expiration date.

SharePoint handles the need for different metadata and different approval processes with a content type. A content type collects a set of rules, including the fields and the processes around the content. The formal offer letter might include the fields as well as an approval workflow that includes both finance and sales management.

Content types form a hierarchy; that is, a content type can derive from another content type. So in our example, we might create a content type called customer document, which includes the field for the customer ID. The formal offer letter could derive from the customer document type and pick up the customer ID field. In this way, you can make changes to a whole set of content types by modifying their shared parent content type.

The real magic of content types isn't in the ability to define fields and processes. The real magic is in the idea that you can put multiple content types in the same document library app. In the management of a list or library app, there's an option to enable content types. Once enabled, you can connect a library to an existing content type – in other words, to an existing definition. When you add the content type to the library, SharePoint automatically adds the fields of the content type to the library. Then when a user saves a document as a specific content type, SharePoint displays the fields that apply to that content type on the edit form.

One benefit of the content type approach is that if you create lists in different subsites, you can ensure that all of the libraries have the same definition for the data – because they're using the same content type. Without content types, the creator would have to manually verify the creation of each field and ensure that the processes including workflows are assigned correctly.

With a basic understanding of what content types are, it would be natural to be curious when you might want to use them. Certainly one common scenario was laid out here – where there are several different kinds of documents in the same library with different data storage and processing needs; in other words, when you want to store dissimilar things in the same place. However, the opposite reason is also true.

Consider the idea of forms on your Intranet. Some forms come from IT. Some forms come from HR. Some forms come from Accounting. However, when someone wants a form, they don't want to have to know whether the form is a HR form or an IT form or an Accounting form. They want to be able to get the form they're looking for. By using the same content type in IT, HR, and Accounting, it's possible to leverage search to look only for items matching that content type. The net result is that you can get a searchable list of forms regardless of their source location. In this case, content types are good because they provide a way to bring together the same data located in different areas of the organization.

Content types aren't limited to just the columns, templates, and workflows we've discussed above. Content types are also a way to give developers a way to extend functionality in SharePoint. Some examples are customizing forms used for creating list or library items (New/Display/Edit forms), adding custom actions to a list or library app item (event receiver), or detailing specialized permissions (Information Rights Management).

How Do I Manage Versions?

Most people have struggled with version management at some point in their career. There's been some sort of a snafu where the wrong version of a letter, a presentation, or a spreadsheet was used. Many of us have gone back into email to try to find the "latest" version of some important document. Those of us with battle scars have taken to adding identification to the file itself in the form of a "V1" appendix to the regular file name. Others have settled on adding a suffix of the date to the name of the file. These strategies work when you have multiple versions to look at side-by-side but fail miserably when you can't remember what the last version was and you don't have time to hunt down all of the versions.

Luckily, SharePoint can save you from these challenges. SharePoint supports versioning for both list items and for files. You don't have to rename the file to know which version is which. Once enabled, SharePoint will automatically keep previous versions of the file – up to the limit you set – without any further action from you. This prevents the user errors that sometimes overwrite good versions of the file with bad changes, and makes it easier to be certain that you have the latest version.

Let me sidestep the conversation of document versioning for a moment, since that conversation is more detailed – and more understood. I have said that SharePoint supports versions of list items. This means that you can see who changed what in each item in a list. This can be very handy when you're trying to piece together what happened with a task, issue, or other item. Items support a simple versioning where each new version gets a new, incremental whole number. So the first version of an item is version 1, the second version is version 2, and so on.

The versioning settings are on the list or library settings page. They're important enough to get the second link from the top-left of the settings page. Enabling versioning for the list is as simple as turning on the *Enable version* option. On libraries, the versioning information allows for enhanced features beyond the basic incremental versioning supported on lists.

In addition to basic versioning, files can have major/minor versioning enabled. This versioning takes each draft (non-approved) version and assigns it a new partial number. For instance, the first version of a draft document is 0.1 and the next non-published version is 0.2. Once published, the version number is converted to a whole number. So 0.2 could be come 1.0 if the version is approved.

The implication of major/minor versioning is that the public (those with read permissions) can see the approved versions (whole numbers). Users with contribute access have access to see both the approved version as well as the current draft version.

Consider the scenario of an employee handbook. Most employees in the organization get to see the most recent approved version – and might be allowed to even see the previously approved versions. The HR department can work on the draft versions of the document in the same place that users are getting the previous approved version. When HR approves the latest draft, it immediately becomes available to all of the employees of the organization.

In some cases simply managing versions isn't enough. There are times when it's possible to overwrite the changes of another user. If all the users are connected online to SharePoint when making changes, SharePoint will prevent a second user from opening a file up for edit if another user is editing it. This is very useful because it prevents most situations where there might be problems because of users overwriting each other's work. (If both users have Office 2010 or 2013, they may be given the option to co-edit the document.)

However, consider for a moment a user who is using Office to take files offline. They make changes while they are disconnected on an airplane. When they synchronize back, their changes may conflict with changes made on the server while they weren't connected. While Word has a very good set of conflict resolution tools, PowerPoint and Excel – as well as non-Office files – don't have the same benefit. In this case, SharePoint does allow a user to formally check out a file. Once a file is checked out, no other user can modify the file until the file is checked in or someone discards the check out.

It's possible to require checkout on an entire document library so all files must be checked out to be edited. In practice, this is rarely used because it's generally not worth the extra hassle to have to check out the document to edit it; again, SharePoint will handle letting folks know that a document is being edited if everyone is online.

SharePoint is good at notifying users that the file is checked out. It adds a small arrow marker over the bottom right of the document icon to indicate the file is checked out. Additionally, there's a Checked Out To field that will show the name of the user who has the file checked out. Finally, if you attempt to edit a document that is checked out, you'll receive a dialog prompt indicating that the file is checked out and isn't available for edit.

With all these features, it can be hard to decide how to best handle your situation. As a general rule, basic versioning is used in all collaborative cases where you just want to protect yourself from accidentally overwriting someone else's changes. Major/Minor versioning is used when the documents are public documents that are revised by a small group of people. As already mentioned, the require check-out feature is used for special cases where there is zero tolerance for accidentally overwriting things. Finally, every user should check out a document they intend to edit before they go offline to indicate to other users that they're intending to modify it.

The one thing that you won't have to do is append the version number to the file or a date to manually manage the versions yourself.

How Do I Get Notified of Changes?

Knowing when something changes is a trick in any organization. Of course, the person making the change can let you know that they've done it – if they know that you need to know about the change. SharePoint can help, if you're interested; even if neither the data nor the person who updates the data knows that you want to know about the changes. There are three basic ways that you can be notified of changes.

First, you can use the Newsfeed feature. The Newsfeed solves the problem of being notified about changes in the most expedient and, in some ways, least elegant way possible. The Newsfeed on a page can notify users in a group about actions that are taken on various documents.

Another facility has become popular and can get the same effect without additional pressure on your inbox – that technology is Really Simple Syndication, more frequently referred to by the acronym RSS.

SharePoint apps and searches are capable of providing an RSS feed via a specially formatted link. This becomes a summary of the latest data in the app. It's also possible for search to provide RSS. RSS feeds, as these links are called, can be displayed directly in Internet Explorer, in Microsoft Outlook, or in dedicated news reader software.

The benefit of getting information as an RSS feed is that you can have the immediacy of an immediate alert with the efficiency of a daily or weekly alert. Immediate alerts are sent – surprisingly – immediately. That means that multiple changes will mean multiple emails. It also means that each individual change is found in a separate message. There is no summary view that can show you all of the recent changes together, as would happen with a daily or weekly alert message. An RSS feed allows you to see the summary of changes like those delayed emails with the ability to hit refresh and get immediately updated data.

Internet Explorer and Outlook allow you to track the same feeds in a shared space called the Windows Common Feed list. This means that Outlook can periodically check the RSS feeds and provide access to them offline like you would have with emails.

In short, the Newsfeed is a simple, fast way to get updates on activity performed by members of your team. However, once you get comfortable with RSS and how it can be used in Outlook and Internet Explorer, it's likely that you'll migrate to using RSS feeds to manage rapidly changing information.

In addition to SharePoint Newsfeed and RSS feeds, there are other techniques you can use to get notified that something is changing. You can create workflows in SharePoint Designer that are designed to notify you only when certain criteria are met. For instance, let's say that you're a manager who has given your employees purchase order request signing authority for $1,000, but you want to know any time they submit a purchase order request for more than $250. You can create a workflow on the purchase order request document library. You can set a criterion of amounts more than $250 and have a special email sent to you. That email could contain additional information from the purchase request, including the requestor, the cost center, the vendor, etc. Anything that is promoted to the properties of the file/item can be used to form the message to you. The benefit of this is that you'll be able to better control the information you want to see without looking at the items themselves.

Whatever option you choose, SharePoint makes it easy to be notified of changes.

Choosing the Right Site Template

SharePoint Server 2013 Enterprise Edition offers 18 site templates out of the box. Making a decision on which one to use for your site isn't exactly straight forward. However, by asking a set of yes/no questions you can quickly walk through the key criteria for picking the right site template for you.

First, there are four templates that don't even make the decision tree. They're so specialized and designed for administrators that you'll probably never create them. They are:

- Developer – This template is used by developers who are creating solutions with Visual Studio for SharePoint.

- My Site Host – This is used by IT administrators who are setting up profiles on SharePoint.

- Community Portal – Used by IT administrators to create a place where users can find community sites on SharePoint.

- Product Catalog – A starting point for creating a product catalog on SharePoint for Internet publishing.

The decision tree has three basic sections. First, you get a set of screening questions to handle special use cases, second there's a less-common section that handle less-common use cases, and finally the last block of questions handle the most common use cases. They're handled by first eliminating the odd and less common templates then making the decision among the core templates that you're likely to use most often.

In the screening group there are three key questions and site templates:

- Journal or Blog – If the primary purpose of the site is a blog – or a running journal of information, then the blog template may be the best choice. It's specifically designed for this purpose.

- Business Intelligence – If you're building a site for reporting on information and helping the business to make better decisions then the business intelligence center is the way to go.

- Flowchart Library – If you are going to be creating a library for process flows in your organization using Visio, the Visio Process Repository may be the answer.

In the less common -- but still important -- category there are two key questions: Is the site for formal document management or will its primary purpose be for search?

The first question in this group is whether the site will be for formal document management – that doesn't mean simple version control of documents, but rather a large scale document management or knowledge management initiative with or without regulatory compliance needs.

If you're doing formal document management, the next question is whether the site will be an official repository for records. In this case, the right answer is the record center template which is setup to handle records management. If not, you need to consider if you're creating the site to manage eDiscovery requests. eDiscovery are electronic discovery requests that are caused by legal cases or regulatory requests. You'll know if you need to create an eDiscovery center for compliance events. If not, you'll probably want to start with the standard Document Center template.

The second major decision in the less common block is whether the site will be used primarily for search. If so you'll have to decide whether you need multiple search interfaces in the same site – in other words a tabbed interface. If yes, then you'll need to use the Enterprise site template which includes the built in capability to include multiple search and result pages. If a simple site – without tabs – will do then you can use the basic search center.

The final block includes the most common templates. In this block the major questions are whether the site will be used primarily for communication (vs. collaboration), whether the site will be project specific, and finally whether you anticipate more than 100 users.

Communication sites are different than collaboration sites. If the site will be primarily intended for a small number of people to communicate with a large number of people then it is a communication site. If it's a communication site the next question is whether the information will be unstructured – in other words a collection of random notes. If that's the case, an Enterprise Wiki – with its less structured approach may be ideal.

If it's for structured communication, you simply need to decide whether you're going to have a formal approval workflow. Of the Publishing Site and Publishing Site with Workflow templates the Publishing Site with Workflow template is used for more formal approval situations.

If the site won't be for communication, the next question is whether it is project related. That is, will the site be associated with a single specific project – in that case you'll probably want to use the project site template.

The last question is the basis of the site. Are you building a site to have conversations or manage documents? If you're doing a conversation based site, you'll want to leverage the community site template. If, instead you're focused around management of documents, you'll want to use the Team Site template.

With those questions you should have determined which of the 18 site templates that may work best for your situation.

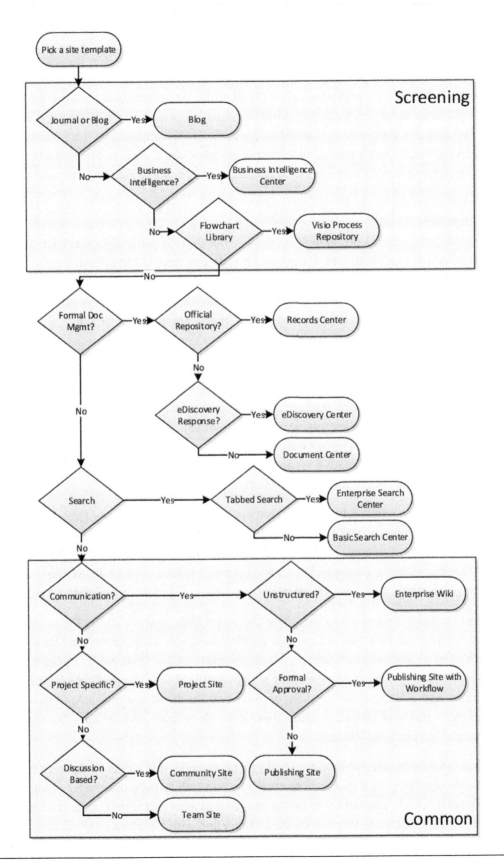

Create a List or Library App

In SharePoint 2013, the constructs of lists and document libraries have been merged into one unified name, known as Apps. At their heart, though, it is still possible to distinguish between library apps – which work with documents and list apps – which work with items. SharePoint's document apps have many features that are similar to list apps – particularly the capability to store additional metadata with the file. It can be confusing to decide whether you should be creating a list or a library app. There are certainly some limitations with creating a Library app – but there are extra features as well.

The key decision to make is the number of files that a given set of data may need. You can often structure the way you look at a problem several ways, but there is generally a way that is more natural than others. In that most natural way possible, do you have situations where you need metadata without an attachment – or a need to associate multiple files with a set of metadata? In either case you'll want to use a list app, since only a list can handle a situation which has data and no files – or more than one file. Library apps always store metadata with a single file.

Since SharePoint 2010 we've had a workaround for wanting zero or more than one attachment by thinking of the problem in terms of a document set. Consider that you have some sort of an approval process which needs some information and perhaps some supporting documentation. In this case, even though there may be zero or more than one attachment it may be possible to continue to use a library app – by leveraging the document set. A document set is really a folder that has properties – and the ability to have a customized start page to change the way the "folder" looks – different from the default metadata a list app has. Utilizing this approach it's possible to work around the idea of having zero or more than one attachment.

The next set of questions pertains to features that are only available on library apps. WebDAV, often referred to as Explorer view, is only available for library apps. Similarly, if you want major and minor versions – so that visitors can only see approved versions – you'll need to use a library app, since lists support only basic versioning. Similarly, library apps support folders, and while list apps can have folders, this is rarely done. If you need folders, you're likely going to want to create a library app.

The final considerations are related to the Office client and XML. SharePoint has the capability of promoting properties in a Word document or in an XML document to properties in SharePoint automatically. This process even allows you to edit the metadata in SharePoint and have that metadata pushed back into the document. This is a powerful set of features. These features only work with library apps. Also, the Office client applications like Word, are only able to open library apps and not lists – this is, of course, because there is no file to open on a list app. The exception to this is Outlook, which can open list apps.

Since InfoPath can now be used to modify list edit forms directly, there's little reason to create a library app for InfoPath forms. If you want to create an InfoPath form to use the rules, validation, and other features of InfoPath, you can try to create the form as a list edit form first, and if the capability isn't available as a list edit form, you can create a library app with a custom InfoPath form.

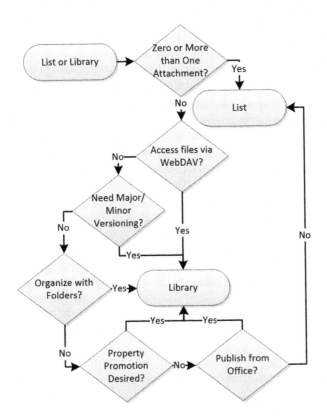

Organize with Folders or Metadata

The decision of whether to organize data with folders or with metadata is a classic problem that's been with SharePoint for years. The problem with this decision is that there are key limitations to both approaches, some of which require a difference in the way you think about the problem.

For instance, in the past, using metadata for storing information in SharePoint meant that you couldn't open the files in the Office client applications because they only understood the folder hierarchy. With Office 2010 and SharePoint 2010, it's possible to see a metadata view of the files – but only if metadata navigation is turned on in SharePoint.

On the other side, there are key limitations which cause issues with file names, including folders and host names that exceed 260 characters. In those cases, the Office client applications will refuse to open the files directly; they'll have to be saved locally then opened in the Office client application – and then re-uploaded to SharePoint. Obviously, this isn't the most efficient way to operate.

The good news is that SharePoint's features – and the capability for Office to view metadata navigation when enabled – make it less difficult to find a balance between the two approaches.

The first deciding factor for whether you need to use folders for organization is whether you're using a method of access to the library app that doesn't support metadata navigation. The most common reason for this is using the Explorer view of a folder. This simply doesn't support viewing the files by metadata; it only supports a folder concept. Similarly, if users are often opening files from Office client applications directly, folders may be necessary – unless all the locations they navigate to support metadata based navigation and you can train users how to use that in the Office clients – some pretty big ifs.

The second key factor that might lead you to folders is the need to have individual security on files. Often documents in a library app have one set of security, but in some cases, it's necessary to have different permissions for different groups of documents. In this case, it's important to create folders. Performance with large numbers of access control lists for each folder falls off quickly. By organizing contents with similar security into folders, the number of unique access control lists is minimized. This can be critical for larger libraries.

There are two factors that might lead to the decision that metadata is required. The first is that not all users navigate to the data in the same way. For instance, assume you're a clothing manufacturer that makes shirts in different colors and in different sizes and styles. If some of your users navigate first by size and others navigate first by style, you'll need something other than a folder structure to allow them to navigate in ways that they're comfortable with – and that's metadata based navigation. Similarly, if you have a folder structure that would lead to more than 260 characters in the web address (URL) for the folder, you'll need to use metadata, since several problems happen once path lengths – including the host name – exceed 260 characters. Specifically, you won't be able to directly open the file in an Office client application.

If none of these criteria apply to you, then selecting either folders or metadata based navigation should work fine. The bias is that metadata based navigation is better from an information architecture perspective – but it's not enough to pull you away from a folder based structure if that's what your users are able to work with.

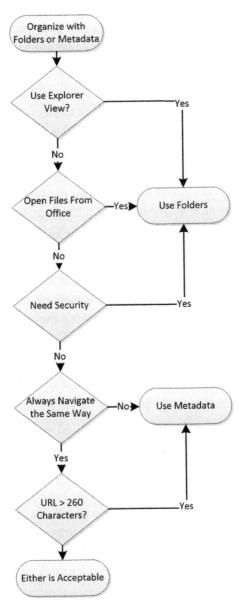

Create a Page or Site

SharePoint offers so many different ways to do things that it's often confusing to pick. This is particularly true of the question of whether to create a new page or a whole new site for something. It doesn't help that creating a page and creating a site can be done from the same page in SharePoint. However, there is a distinct difference between the results of creating a page versus creating a site. The decision is also essential because migrating data from one site or page to another site or page can be challenging with out-of-the-box tools.

The first question to ask is whether you're looking for a page to help provide a different view of the same data or whether the data that the page will operate on will be separate from the data in existing sites. SharePoint can easily query and display data in the same site and less easily show data in other sites in the same site collection, and even less easily show data in different site collections on the same server farm. As a result, if you're looking for the page to display in a different way some data that already exists, then it's likely you want a page.

Next up is considering the navigation. Inside a site, there are two sets of navigation settings. That is, the top navigation and the left navigation (Quick Launch) can have the same content, but they can each be changed. Inside a page, there is just one set of navigation tools. As a result, if you're looking for customized and more robust navigation on the new thing that you're creating, you'll need to create a site.

It's possible to secure both a site and a page if you want, but securing the page doesn't secure the content. If there are situations that require that you have a different security structure with different groups, you'll want to create a subsite within you site collection – more specifically a separate site collection. (See the decision tree for selecting a subsite versus a site collection for more information.)

The final consideration is a bit more difficult to quantify. That consideration is whether what you're trying to create is independent. That is, should the item be on its own because it's different enough. For instance, you might want to create a space for accounts payable inside the accounting department. If you're just listing contacts for accounts payable, it's fine to leave that in the accounting department site. However, if you want to have independent business processes like invoice payment approval, then what you're doing is probably independent enough that it should have its own site because it's going to have a lot of its own data.

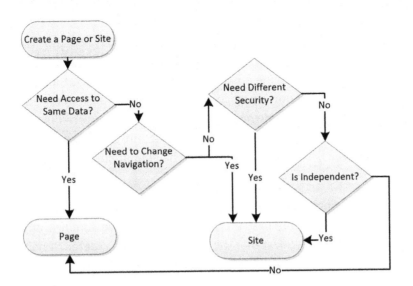

Create a Subsite or Site Collection

A frequent question is whether a subsite or a site collection should be created when trying to address some new need in SharePoint. The answer is often confusing since there are advantages to keeping everything in one site collection – particularly for querying information – but there are also disadvantages, such as the amount of time necessary to backup and restore the site collection. Often you'll find that requirements will lead you to a new site collection, but there are other reasons for having unified navigation, which isn't possible when you have multiple site collections (without custom code).

The first decision to make is whether you can even choose to create a site collection. Because creating site collections requires an administrator, you'll need to have administrative rights on the server or you'll need to be able to request that the site collection be created. If neither of these is true, you'll need to use a site (subsite) within an existing site collection instead of a completely separate site collection. It doesn't matter whether it is the "right" answer or not if you can't do the alternative.

The next set of considerations is whether you need to have the separation that a site collection affords. If you need to have the chargeback for the new entity done separately, you'll need to have a separate site collection since chargebacks are nearly always accomplished at the site collection level. If your organization doesn't do chargebacks, you can answer no and proceed to answering whether you need to have separate quotas (either storage or processing) for the new site. Quotas can only be assigned at a site collection level, so if you need to have quotas set for the new site, you'll have to do a site collection.

The next two questions are about the visibility of other groups and users. In SharePoint all users of a site collection can see all of the user groups in the site collection – and all of the users. So in situations where even knowing what the other groups are or who the other users are is a problem, you'll need separate site collections. For instance, it's common to create separate site collections for different customers so that your customers can't see your other customers or your company's employee names.

The next key question is whether the new site will be large. "Large" is relative, but certainly a site that's expected to consume more than about 50GB of storage would be considered large. Because the smallest unit of backup is the site collection, large sites shouldn't be clumped together; rather, they should remain separated as much as possible to improve recovery performance.

The next question is whether the site is independent. In other words, is the site really related? For instance, accounts payable would potentially be a sub-site of accounting (depending upon the organization's requirements), where manufacturing shouldn't be a sub-site of accounting. In general, smaller sites should be sub-sites and thereby related to the parent.

The final question is whether you need universal – that is consistent – navigation between the site you have and the new site you want to create. Each site collection has its own navigation, and synchronizing navigation across site collections can be challenging. If you need universal navigation, you're more likely to use a sub-site than a new site collection.

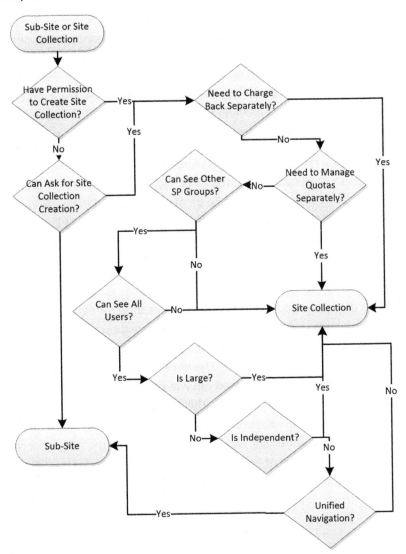

Managing Permissions with Active Directory Groups or SharePoint Groups

A common question about managing security in SharePoint is how to control the users who have – or do not have – access to the system. Obviously, individually managing permissions for individual users can be time consuming and tedious – especially if the users all fall into one or two permission levels. It is much easier to add a user to a group that has the right permissions in the right places than to establish security individually for each user. While this is clear, the question about whether or not site administrators should use SharePoint Groups or Active Directory groups isn't so clear.

It's first important to review the types of groups that SharePoint supports. The first type of group that SharePoint supports is a SharePoint group; that is to say, SharePoint knows the precise membership of the group because every user has to be manually added in SharePoint. The obvious limitation to this approach is that the group is scoped to SharePoint – it can't be used for any other purpose except for security in SharePoint. Less obvious is the fact that a SharePoint group is scoped to the SharePoint site collection it was created in. That means the group cannot be used in another site collection on the same farm.

The second type of group that SharePoint supports is an active directory group, an identity management framework inherent in Windows servers. The active directory group looks to SharePoint to be just another user during the setup of security. The group is added to permissions – or to a SharePoint group – just like any other user. The benefit of an active directory group is that it can be used across site collections and can be used outside of SharePoint. The disadvantage of an Active Directory group is that it's not easy to display the membership of the group to a user who is curious about who is in the group. Similarly, in most organizations, not everyone can add/remove members of a group; that is to say, generally, the IT administrators or the help desk must make changes to group membership. Because of this, managing Active Directory groups is generally harder for an end user than managing a SharePoint Group. However, the consistency in being able to use the group in every site collection, and by non-SharePoint applications, may mean that the extra hassle is worth it.

Making the decision between an Active Directory group and a SharePoint group isn't always as simple as it could be. The following decision tree can help you decide between an active directory group or a SharePoint Group.

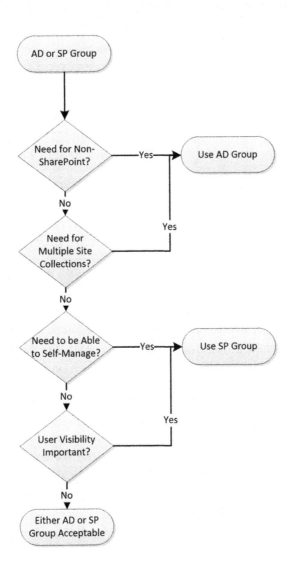

Create a Word form or an InfoPath Form

Let's face it. Most forms in your organization are Microsoft Word forms or modified Excel files. They were created by someone to solve a need. That person, however, may not have been the most skilled in creating forms. They may not have been trained in data structures. However, they knew Word and they created a form that worked. But you may heard that InfoPath is a much better forms tool. However, should you convert all of the Word forms that exist in your organization into InfoPath forms? In a word, no.

Why shouldn't you recreate all of your forms in InfoPath? Well, because if there's no compelling reason, why you should make extra work for yourself? Your users know Word. They're comfortable with the existing forms. What can you get by changing the forms over to InfoPath?

Of course, one of the benefits of InfoPath is that you can promote fields to SharePoint – but Word has the ability to promote these properties, too. The reality is that most forms aren't using the technology that's already in Word to promote properties – and that's quicker to fix than creating a new form to promote properties in InfoPath. If you want to learn how to promote Word properties into SharePoint and how to make those properties easy to enter, see the whitepaper "Managing Enterprise Metadata with Content Types." (You can search for it on the Microsoft site. Despite the fact it was written for SharePoint 2007, it's still relevant today.) Don't worry; you don't have to know content types to be able to promote properties from Word.

So let's address the opposite question: "Are there reasons to recreate forms as InfoPath forms?" In a word, yes. While Word supports basic property promotion, there are a lot of things that Word doesn't support. Chief among the benefits of InfoPath support is that Word doesn't handle one-to-many relationships in the form data. In other words, InfoPath can handle rows of data on the form. For instance, expense reports have multiple expenses, and invoices have multiple lines. Sure, you won't be able to extract all of those individual lines into SharePoint – but you will be able to summarize them.

In addition, Word property promotion relies on the fields being present in the SharePoint library. This isn't an issue most of the time, but when you have a large amount of data you want to capture from the form—arbitrarily, let's say 30 fields—you may not want to publish all those fields to SharePoint. InfoPath allows you to determine which fields are published to SharePoint. Additionally, InfoPath saves its forms in the industry standard XML file format. That means many different systems can reach in and extract data from the InfoPath form – much more easily than fetching the data. If you're going to need the data from the form in another system, InfoPath may be the way to go.

What about validation and formulas? Word isn't setup to do validation – nor is it set up to do calculated values. However, InfoPath can perform these tasks. From conditionally formatting fields based on their values, to blocking values that are out of range, requiring values, etc., InfoPath can help validate the information is right – if you need that.

Another situation where InfoPath may be the right answer is when you need to tie the form data to external data. Consider, for instance, that you are doing an expense report and you want to tie the expenses to a customer. It would be great to be able to make sure that the customer name entered on the form exactly matches the customer name in the sales management system. InfoPath can do this by reaching out and getting data from other systems.

There may be other factors in your decision to create an InfoPath form versus creating a Word form. However, all-in-all, if you don't have any of these specialized needs, you may be better off just creating a quick Word form.

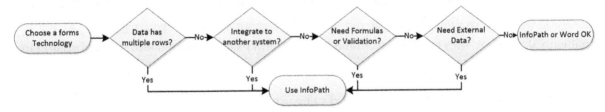

Collaborate on Projects

In any business organization, public or private, the need to effectively communicate and collaborate in a timely manner is very important. Gone are the days of paper memos, and even group email has proved to be a cumbersome method of sharing information. Today, with mobile workers and shifting schedules, the tools of the Internet are the way to go. That's the overall function of SharePoint 2013: to allow users within organizations to collaborate and share work within a commonly accessed Web site framework. These Web sites are no different than any other Web site you might visit, except that with SharePoint, they can be custom-made to perform exactly the functions you and your team need to get the job done.

The sites that SharePoint creates are designed to be used by workgroups, committees, or a whole department of workers—the choices are entirely flexible to your own organization's needs, and you can organize SharePoint sites however you wish.

Sites can hold lists of things to do, libraries of documents that need work, and discussion boards to share ideas...among other tools.

In this section, you will learn how to handle the basics of collaboration:

- **Create a Place for Teams to Work:** Build a Team Site with which users can work.

- **Share Your Site:** Once a new site is created, you need to allow users access to that site.

- **Create a New Group:** While SharePoint provides some basic user groups to which you can assign your users, there may be instances where you will want to create new groups with very specific permissions.

- **Assign Users to a Group:** After groups have been created, users will need to be assigned to these groups.

- **Remove Users from a Group:** In the case of an in-company move or task reassignment, you will need to quickly remove the user from their old group.

- **Edit Group Settings:** Occasionally your group will need certain changes, such as who receives requests to join or leave.

- **Create a Project Site:** Include a Calendar, Task List, Document Library, and other basic lists to get things done. It can be best used as a temporary project site within a Team or company site.

- **Remove a Group:** To prevent site clutter from occurring, you can simply remove obsolete groups from SharePoint.

Task: Create a Place for Teams to Work

Purpose: In any business organization, public or private, the need to effectively communicate and collaborate in a timely manner is very important. That's the overall function of SharePoint 2013: to allow users within organizations to collaborate and share work within a commonly accessed Web site framework. These Web sites are no different than any other Web site you might visit, except that with SharePoint, they can be customized to perform exactly the functions you and your team need to get the job done.

Sites can hold lists of things to do, libraries of documents that require work or action, discussion boards to share ideas ... or one of several other lists, as well.

Before any of these tools can be put to use, you will need to start with the basics: creating a Team Site where users can start working. If you have the appropriate permissions, you can create a new site very easily in SharePoint.

Steps:

1. Start Internet Explorer and type the URL for your organization's SharePoint server. The Start page will open. If you want your new site located as a subsite of another site, navigate to that site.

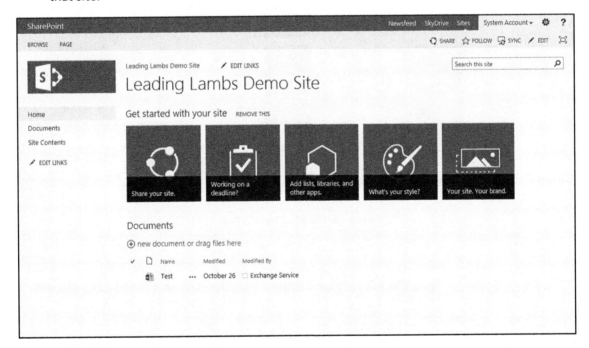

Figure 1: A Start Page for a SharePoint Site

2. Click the **Settings** menu drop-down control, which resembles a gear. The Settings menu will appear.

Figure 2: The Site Actions Menu

3. Click **Site Contents**. The Site Contents page will appear. If you do not see the new subsite option, you do not have the proper authorization. Please contact your administrator.

Figure 3: The Site Contents Page

4. At the bottom of the page, click the **new subsite** link. The New SharePoint Site page will open.

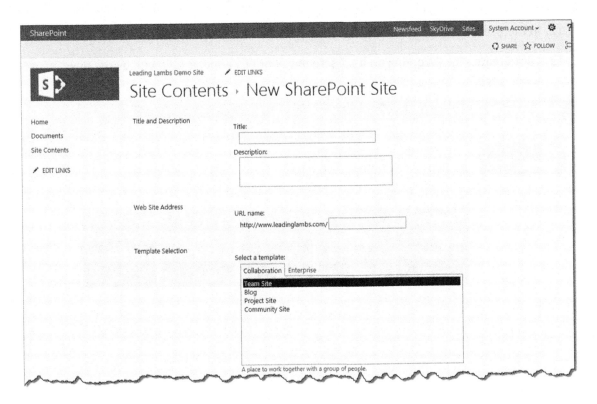

Figure 4: The New SharePoint Site Page

5. In the Title field type a title for your site. The title of your site should be descriptive and can be up to about 50 letters before becoming intrusive. It will appear on the top of your new site.

6. In the Description field type a description for your site. The description is like a sub-title that will be displayed on some of the pages. It should further clarify the title so that anyone can understand the site's purpose.

7. In the URL name field type a short, descriptive name for your team. This will become part of the full Web Site Address for your new Team site. Some features don't work with long URLs, so keeping the name in the URL short but descriptive is recommended.

8. In the Template Selection section, click the Team Site option.

9. In the User Permissions field, select the **Use same permissions as parent site** option. You can change to unique permissions later as shown in "Assign Users to a Group."

    Note: If the publishing feature is activated for your site, the **Display this site on Quick Launch** and **Display this site on the top link bar of the parent site** are not options on the Advanced Create Site page.

10. In the Display this site on the Quick Launch of the parent site field, select the **Yes** option.

11. In the Display this site on the top link bar of the parent site field, select the **Yes** option.

12. In the Use the top link bar from the parent site field, select the **Yes** option.

13. Click **Create**. The "Working on it …" screen will briefly appear, followed by the new Team Site home page.

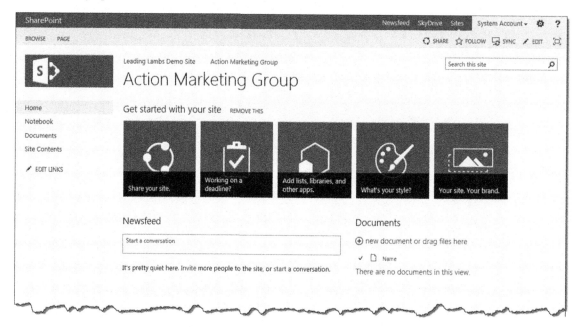

Figure 5: The New Team Site Home Page

Exception: If the **Site Contents** option or **new subsite** link don't appear, you do not have specific permissions to create subsites. Check the permissions settings to ensure you have the appropriate access rights.

Task: Share Your Site

Purpose: Once a new site is created, you need to allow users access to that site. You can do this by individually assigning permissions or by using groups. By default, SharePoint creates four groups:

> Owner: Users who can control and administrate all aspects of a team site
> Member: Users who can contribute to the site by viewing or editing its content
> Visitor: Users who can only read a site's content
> Viewers: Users who can only view a site

You can create other groups of users in SharePoint, however, these groups provide a good starting point. For the most part, you will want new users to have Member status; they can create new entries, or read and change existing entries, but they will not be able to change the layout of the pages. Nor will they be able to create new lists.

Example: Once you have created the Action Group team site, the next order of business is to grant access to the site for team members.

Steps:

1. Start Internet Explorer and type the URL for your organization's SharePoint server. The Start page will open.

2. Navigate to the site where you want to add users to edit your site. The site's home page will open.

Figure 1: Your Team's Home Page

3. Click the **Share** link on the top right. The Share dialog box will open.

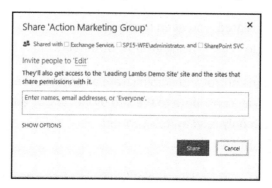

Figure 2: The Share Dialog Box

4. In the **Invite people** field type the name or email address of the people you want to have on the Team Site. A list of matching personnel will appear after three characters are entered as you type the name. You can click on the name to complete the entry.

5. New shares are always added as Members. If you want to give the person more or less capabilities, click the **Show Options** link. The Select a Group or Permission Level section will appear.

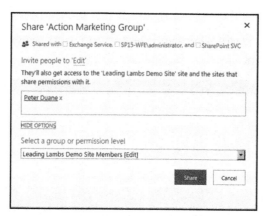

Figure 3: The Expanded Share Dialog Box

6. Choose one of the available options from the drop-down list.

7. Click **Share**. The person(s) will be added to the Team Site.

Task: Create a New Group

Purpose: While SharePoint provides some basic user groups to which you can assign your users, there may be instances where you will want to create new groups that will have different permissions.

An example of this type of group would be for team members who can only read and edit existing contWhen these kinds of access issues crop up, it is a big timesaver to create a unique group with specific capabilities and then assign users to that group as needed. You can even add your own permission levels, as demonstrated in "Create a Custom Permission Level."

Example: A few of your team members need to be assigned to a specific group for web development while working with the new team site. But before they can be assigned to this group, it needs to be created.

Steps:

1. Start Internet Explorer and type the URL for your organization's SharePoint server. The Start page will open.

2. Navigate to the site where you want to add a group. The site's home page will open.

3. On the **Settings** menu gear icon, click the **Site settings** option. The Site Settings page will open.

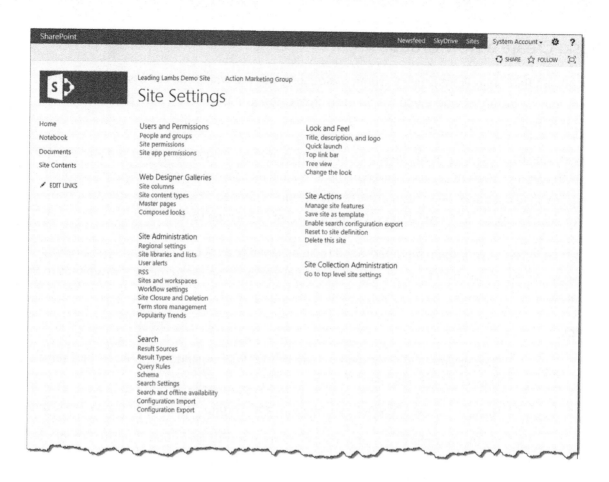

Figure 1: The Site Settings Page

4. In the Users and Permissions section click the **Site permissions** link. The Permissions page will open.

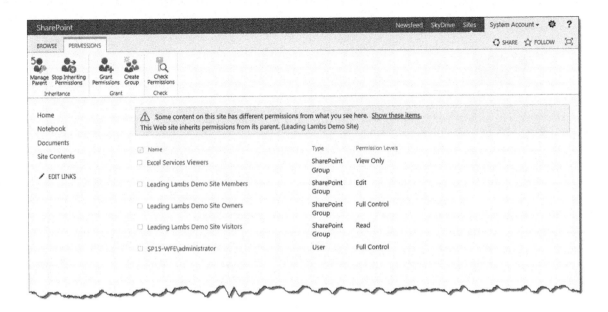

Figure 2: The Permissions Page

5. Click **Create Group** button. The Create Group page will open.

Figure 3: The Create Group Page

6. In the Name field, type a name for the group. When naming the group, consider the people that will be added, not necessarily the permissions that you'll be assigning to them.

7. In the About Me field, type a description for the group. Note that rich text editing tools are present, giving you the capability to format the description however you wish.

8. If the owner of the group is not going to be you, delete your user name and enter the appropriate one in the Group Owner field. The owner will always be able to manage group membership. By changing the owner to someone else, you can allow them to modify the group. Users, such as Site Collection administrators, will also be able to modify the group membership.

9. Click the **Everyone** radio button for the Who can view the membership of the group field, if you want all people with permissions to view your site to see who's in this group,. Otherwise, leave **Group Members** selected. You might want to make the members private if the confidentiality of the members should be maintained.

10. Indicate who can edit members in the group by clicking the **Group Owner** or **Group Members** radio button for the Who can edit the membership of the group field. Typically only the group owner can edit group membership. However, if all of the members are highly trusted, you have the opportunity to allow any of them to modify membership.

11. Click the appropriate option to allow requests to join or leave the group. You may want to allow requests to join or leave the group if you're setting up a volunteer team to support an initiative.

12. Click the appropriate option to auto-accept requests. It is recommended that you keep this option set at **No**. Auto-accepting could make it difficult to manage the comings and goings of your group. However, if you are working with a volunteer group, such as those helping with the company picnic, auto-accepting requests may be appropriate.

13. If you chose to allow requests, enter the appropriate email address to which users can send membership requests. Warning: not every server is properly configured to accept inbound email messages.

14. Click **Create**. The new group will appear in the People and Groups page. You can now add users, as explained in "Assign Users to a Group."

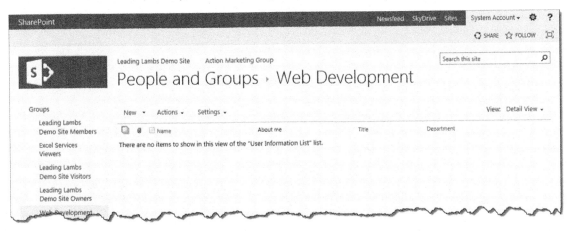

Figure 4: The New Web Development Group

Exception: If you can't add a group name, either the group name already exists or you do not have specific permissions to add groups. Check the permissions settings to ensure you have the appropriate access rights.

Task: Assign Users to a Group

Purpose: After groups have been created, users will need to be assigned to these groups. Unless you have chosen to allow your group to auto-accept requests to join or leave the group, someone will need to quickly add or remove users from the group as the need arises.

Even though this might seem a bit tedious, it's a good idea for someone to act as the "gatekeeper" for a group, if only to make sure the appropriate people are allowed in.

Example: The new Web Development group has been added to the Action Marketing Group's team site, and now you need to assign users to that group.

Steps:

1. Start Internet Explorer and type the URL for your organization's SharePoint server. The Start page will open.

2. Navigate to the site where you want to manage a group's users. The site's home page will open.

3. Click the **Settings** menu gear icon and then the **Site Settings** option. The Site Settings page will open.

4. In the Users and Permissions section, click the **People and groups** link. The People and Groups page will open.

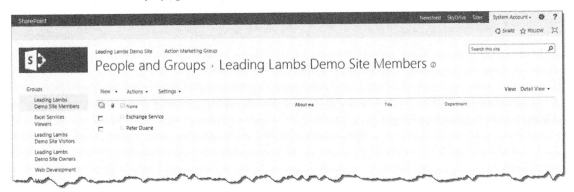

Figure 1: The People and Groups Page

5. In the Quick Launch, click the link for the group to which you want to add users. That group's list will open.

6. Click the arrow beside **New**. The New menu will appear.

7. Click **Add Users**. The Share dialog box will open.

Figure 2: The Share Dialog Box

8. In the Add People field, type in the name of the user. As the name is typed, a list of matching results will appear.

9. Click on the correct name when it appears in the list. The name will be added.

10. Add additional names as needed.

11. Click **Share**. The Share dialog box will close and the users will appear in the group list on the People and Groups page.

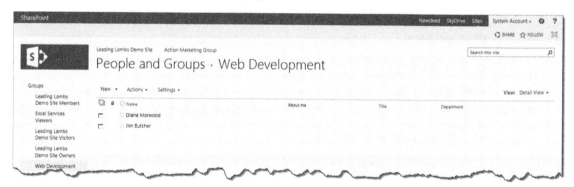

Figure 3: The New Group Members

Exception: If a red squiggly line appears under user names added in the Share dialog box, this indicates the user cannot be found.

Task: Remove Users from a Group

Purpose: Change is present in every work environment. As new people come in, veterans to an organization may find themselves moving on to different assignments, or even different jobs within the company.

When a user leaves a company altogether, their account will be removed from the various systems by the IT department. In that case, their removal from SharePoint's user roles will be automatic. But in the case of an in-company move or task reassignment, you will need to remove a user from their old group.

Example: One of the members of the Web Development group has transferred to a new team, and will need to be removed from the Action Marketing Group's Team Site.

Steps:

1. Start Internet Explorer and type the URL for your organization's SharePoint server. The Start page will open.

2. Navigate to the site where you want to manage a group's users. The site's home page will open.

3. Select the **Settings** menu gear icon, then the **Site Settings** menu option. The Site Settings page will open.

4. In the Users and permissions section, click the **People and groups** link. The People and Groups page will open.

5. In the Quick Launch **Groups** list, click the group from which you want to remove a user. The Group page will open.

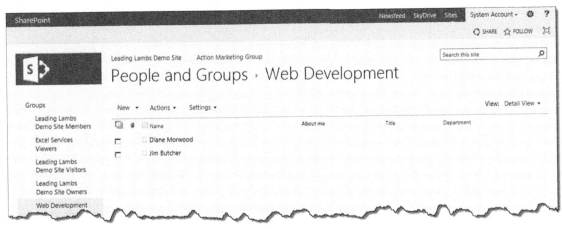

Figure 1: The Group Page

6. Click the checkbox of the user(s) you want to remove. The user is selected.

7. Click the arrow beside the **Actions** menu and select **Remove Users from Group**. A confirmation dialog box will open.

Figure 2: The Actions Menu

Figure 3: The Remove Users from Group Confirmation Dialog Box

8. Click **OK**. The user(s) will be removed from the group.

Task: Edit Group Settings

Purpose: Occasionally your group will need to have changes made, such as changing the group owner who gets requests to join or leave the group. This doesn't happen very often, but SharePoint's flexibility allows you to make such changes easily.

Example: You have been asked to provide a description to the Web Development group in the team site, to differentiate them from other Web Development groups within the company.

Steps:

1. Start Internet Explorer and type the URL for your organization's SharePoint server. The Start page will open.

2. Navigate to the site where you want to manage a group's settings. The site's home page will open.

3. Select the **Settings** menu gear icon, then the **Site Settings** option. The Site Settings page will open.

4. In the Users and Permissions section, click the **People and groups** link. The People and Groups page will open.

5. In the Quick Launch **Groups** list, click the group you want to edit. The Group page will open.

6. Click the arrow beside the **Settings** menu and select the **Group Settings** option. The Change Group Settings page will open.

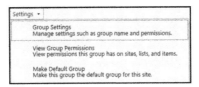

Figure 1: The Settings Menu

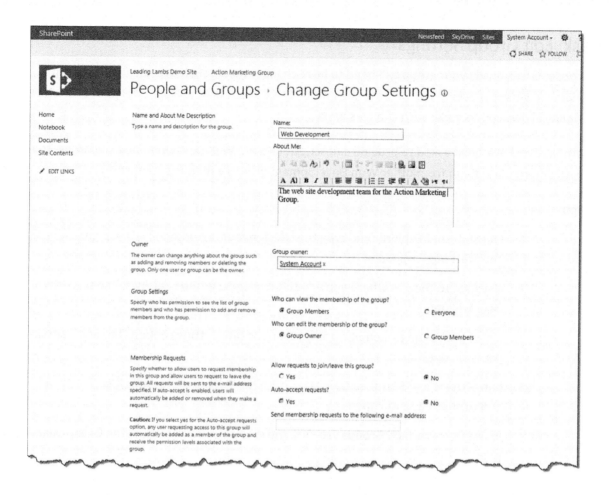

Figure 2: The Change Group Settings Page

7. Make the changes you need, then click **OK**. The changes will be applied to the group. You'll find more information about the fields on this page and what they do in the task "Create a New Group."

Task: Create a Project Site

Purpose: One of the useful templates within SharePoint 2013 is the Project Site. At first glance, this may look and feel very much like a Team Site, and there are similarities. The Project Site includes a Calendar, Task List, Document Library, and other basic lists to get things done. It can be best used as a temporary project site within a Team or company site.

Example: The Action Marketing Group has been tasked to put together a marketing campaign for Leading Lambs' newest product. A Project Site will allow team members as well as other Leading Lambs employees to collaborate on the project.

Steps:

1. Start Internet Explorer and type the URL for your organization's SharePoint server. The Start page will open. If you want your Group Work Site located as a subsite to another site, navigate to that site.

2. Click the **Settings** menu gear icon and click the **Site Contents** option. The Site Contents page will appear.

3. In the Subsites section, click the **new subsite** link. The New SharePoint Site page will open.

4. In the Title field, type a title for the Project Site. The title of your site should be descriptive and can be up to about 50 letters before becoming intrusive.

5. In the Description field, type a description for your site. The description is like a sub-title that will be displayed on some of the pages. It should further clarify the title so that anyone can understand the site's purpose.

6. In the URL Name field, type a short, descriptive name for your group. This will become part of the full Web Site Address for your new Project Site. Some features don't work with long URLs, so keeping the name in the URL short but descriptive is recommended.

7. In the template field, select **Project Site** as the template.

8. In the User Permissions field, select the **Use same permissions as parent site** option. You can change to unique permissions as shown in the task "Assign Users to a Group."

9. In the Display this site on the Quick Launch of the parent site field, select the **Yes** option.

10. In the Use the top link bar from the parent site field, select the **Yes** option.

11. Click **Create**. The "Working on it..." screen will briefly appear, followed by the new Project Site page.

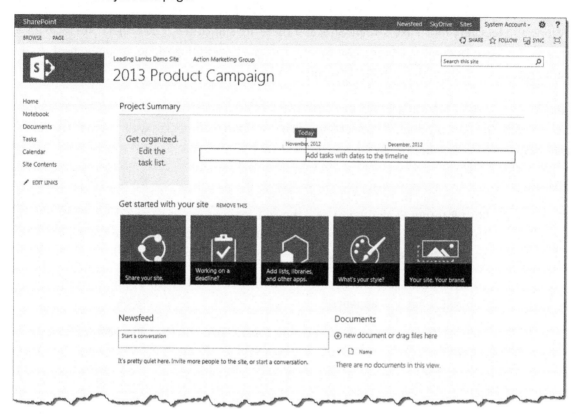

Figure 1: The New Project Site Home Page

Exception: If the desired site template is not listed, you do not have specific permissions to access the correct site templates. Check the permissions settings to ensure you have the appropriate access rights for creating project sites.

Task: Remove a Group

Purpose: In SharePoint, adding groups is so simple that you might forget to keep old, unused groups from filling up your team site. To prevent such clutter from occurring, you can simply remove obsolete groups from SharePoint.

Example: The Web Development group within the Action Marketing Group has been folded into another team within Leading Lambs. Moving forward, there's no need to identify these employees as Web Developers in SharePoint, so the group will be removed.

Steps:

1. Start Internet Explorer and type the URL for your organization's SharePoint server. The Start page will open.

2. Navigate to the site from which you want to remove the group. The site's home page will open.

3. Select the **Settings** menu gear icon, then the **Site Settings** menu option. The Site Settings page will open.

4. In the Users and Permissions section, click the **People and groups** link. The People and Groups page will open.

5. In the Quick Launch **Groups** list, click the group you want to remove. The Group's page will open. If your group does not appear in the list, click **More...** to see all groups, then click the group you want to remove.

6. Click the **Settings** menu drop-down control, and select the **Group Settings** option. The Change Group Settings page will open.

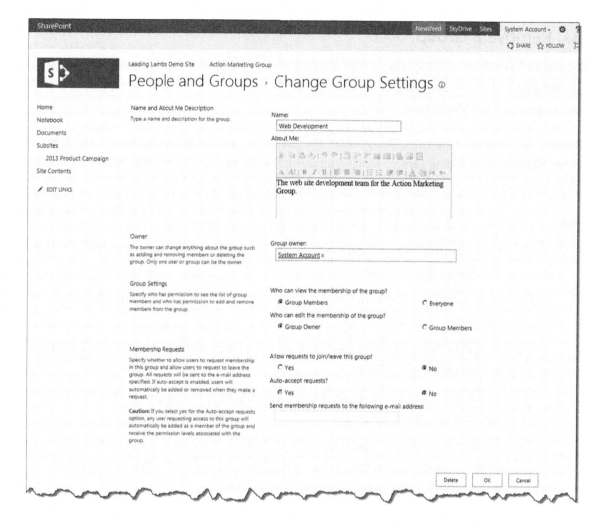

Figure 1: The Change Group Settings Page

7. On the bottom of the page, click **Delete**. A confirmation dialog box will open.

Figure 2: The Group Deletion Confirmation Dialog Box

8. Click **OK**. The Group page for the first Group appearing on the Quick Launch menu will open, with the previous group no longer appearing in the Groups list on the Quick Launch bar. Because only a few groups are listed on the Quick Launch menu, you may need to click the **More...** link in order to verify that the group has been removed.

Exception: If you can't delete the group, you do not have specific permissions to delete the group. Check the permissions settings to ensure you have the appropriate access rights.

Communicating Ideas

When group projects occur in the workplace, one of the old standbys for communication is the email discussion. Members of a team send emails back and forth, going over various approaches and ideas. But emails can be cumbersome. Which message had the file you needed for the annual statistics? Who was replying to whom about next week's meeting? Did you hit "reply" or "reply all"?

One good way to avoid these logistical problems is to use SharePoint's discussion board feature. In a discussion board, all the comments are in one place, for everyone to quickly see and read. Discussions are threaded, so their order and flow is easier to follow.

In this section, you will learn how to:

- **Create a Discussion Board**: By default, all new team sites created in SharePoint have a discussion board, but here's how to create one of your own.

- **Start a New Discussion:** Once a Discussion Board has been created, it is ready to be used by any member of the groups authorized to use the team site.

- **Reply to a Discussion:** After a discussion is started, you can add your own comments in much the same way you would create a regular email.

- **Edit Discussions:** From time to time, you may make a comment on a discussion board and then discover that you need to add something or change the original content of that comment.

- **Delete Discussions**: Once in a while, a comment might be completely in error, or applied to the wrong discussion.

- **Remove a Discussion Board**: Once the project is completed, you can remove the discussion board from the team site entirely.

Task: Create a Discussion Board

Purpose: When group projects occur in the workplace, one of the old standbys for communication is the e-mail discussion. Members of a team send e-mails back and forth, going over various approaches and ideas. But e-mails can be cumbersome. Which message had the file you needed for the annual statistics? Who was replying to whom about next week's meeting? Did you hit "reply" or "reply all"?

One good way to avoid these logistical problems is to use SharePoint's discussion board feature. In a discussion board, all the comments are in one place, for everyone to quickly see and read. Discussions are threaded so their order and flow is easier to follow. By default, all new team sites created in SharePoint have a discussion board, but here's how to create one of your own.

> **Caution:** SharePoint's discussion board feature isn't a replacement for a full-fledged forum management or bulletin board system. It's effective for a relatively small number (less than 100) of original threads. Plan to create many individual discussion boards if you need a large number of topics. You may also want to consider a new SharePoint 2013 and Exchange 2013 feature called Site Mailbox. This allows your site to have an email box just like a user.

Example: The Action Marketing Group would like to start a discussion board for issues concerning the team's goals. This discussion board should be viewable for all visitors to the Action Marketing Group site.

Steps:

1. Start Internet Explorer and type the URL for your organization's SharePoint server. The Start page will open.

2. Navigate to the site where you want to create a discussion board. The site's home page will open.

3. Click the **Settings** menu gear icon, then click the **Add an app** option. The Your Apps page will appear in the Newest view.

Figure 1: The Your Apps Page

4. Scroll down and click the **Discussion Board** icon. The Adding Discussion Board dialog box will appear.

Figure 2: Adding the Discussion Board Dialog Box

5. Click **Advanced Options**. The New Discussion Board page will appear.

The SharePoint Shepherd's Guide for End Users: 2013

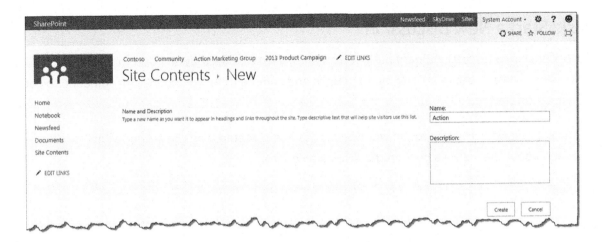

Figure 3: The New Discussion Board Page

6. In the Name field, type a name for the discussion board.

7. In the Description field, enter a description for the discussion board.

8. Click Create. The new discussion board will open.

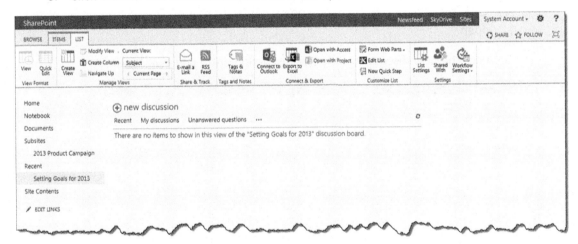

Figure 4: A New Discussion Board

Exception: If you cannot create a discussion board, there is an existing discussion board with the same name or URL or you do not have specific permissions to create a discussion board. Check the permissions settings to ensure you have the appropriate access rights.

Task: Start a New Discussion

Purpose: Once a Discussion Board has been created, it may be used by any user in the site. Discussions serve as topics for anyone to jump in and comment. All you need is for someone to get a conversation started.

Example: A new file relating to the yearly goals has been created, and the author wants to ask a question about the file via a post on the discussion board.

Steps:

1. Start Internet Explorer and type the URL for your organization's SharePoint server. The Start page will open.

2. Navigate to the site where you want to participate in a discussion. The site's home page will open.

3. Click the **Settings** menu gear icon, then the **Site Contents** option. The Site Contents page will open.

4. Click the icon for the discussion board you want to join. The board's home page will open.

5. Click the **new discussion** link. The Discussion entry page will open.

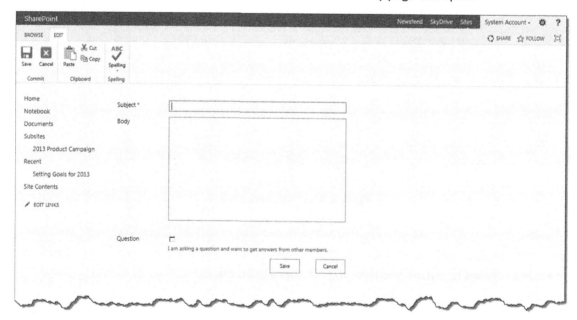

Figure 1: The Discussion Entry Page

6. In the Subject field, type a topic for the discussion. The subject field is the short description that will be displayed in the list.

The SharePoint Shepherd's Guide for End Users: 2013

7. In the Body field, add any message you want. The editing tools will appear. You can copy content in from a Word document, Web page, or any other source of content.

8. To attach a file, click the **Insert** tab, then **Upload File**. The Add a document dialog box will open. Each discussion item can have multiple files attached if necessary.

Figure 2: Add a New Document Dialog Box

9. Click **Browse**. The Choose File to Upload dialog box will open.

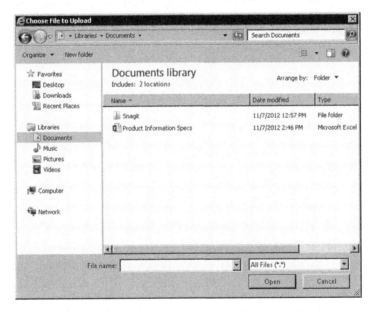

Figure 3: Choose File To Upload Dialog Box

10. Navigate to the file, click on it to select it, and click **Open**. The Choose File to Upload dialog box will close, and the file will appear in the Choose a File field on the Add a document dialog box.

Figure 4: An Attached File in Add a Document Dialog Box

11. Select the Destination Library for the new file. The library in which the attachment will be stored will be selected.

12. Click the **Overwrite existing files** checkbox if desired.

13. Click **OK**. The file will appear in the Body of the discussion.

14. Click **Save**. The new discussion will appear on the discussion board page.

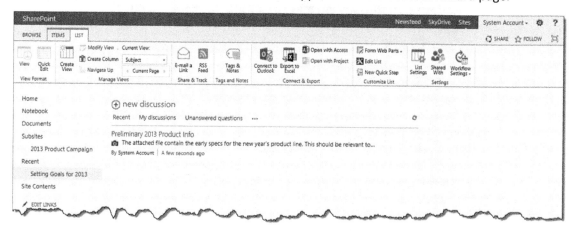

Figure 5: A New Discussion Listed on Discussion Board Page

Exception: If you cannot create a discussion, you do not have specific permissions to create discussions on a discussion list. Check the permissions settings to ensure you have the appropriate access rights.

Task: Reply to a Discussion

Purpose: After a discussion is started, you can add your own comments in much the same way you would create an email. Replying to a discussion keeps the responses threaded together so they're easy to see and read.

Example: As discussions begin, members of the Action Marketing Group will want to join in and deliver their own responses.

Steps:

1. Start Internet Explorer and type the URL for your organization's SharePoint server. The Start page will open.

2. Navigate to the site where you want to participate in a discussion. The site's home page will open.

3. Click the **Settings** menu gear icon, then the **Site Contents** option. The Site Contents page will open.

4. Click the icon for the discussion board you want to join. The board's home page will open.

5. Click the discussion topic to which you want to respond. The discussion page will open.

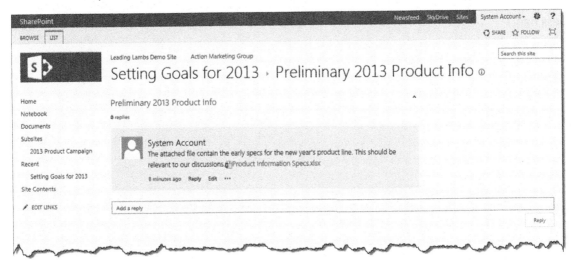

Figure 1: The Discussion Page

6. In the Add a Reply field, enter a reply.

7. Click **Reply**. The new comment will appear on the discussion page.

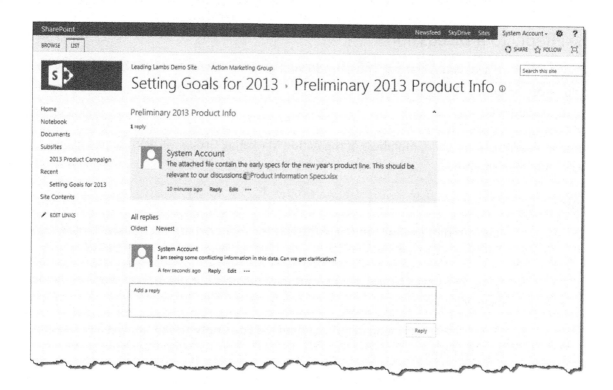

Figure 2: The Discussion Page with New Reply

Exception: If you can't reply to a discussion, you have read-only permissions and do not have specific permissions to create a reply. Check the permissions settings to ensure you have the appropriate access rights.

The SharePoint Shepherd's Guide for End Users: 2013

Task: Edit Discussions

Purpose: From time to time, you may make a comment on a discussion board and then discover that you need to add something or change the original content of that comment. SharePoint lets you, if need be, edit your own comments after they have been posted.

Example: The most recent comment in the discussion has an error, and the author would like to correct the mistake.

Steps:

1. Start Internet Explorer and type the URL for your organization's SharePoint server. The Start page will open.

2. Navigate to the site where you want to participate in a discussion board. The site's home page will open.

3. Click the **Settings** menu gear icon, then the **Site Contents** option. The Site Contents page will open.

4. Click the icon for the discussion board you want to join. The board's home page will open.

5. Click the discussion topic to join. The discussion page will open.

6. Find the comment you wish to edit and click **Edit** for that comment. The comment's text will be made available to edit.

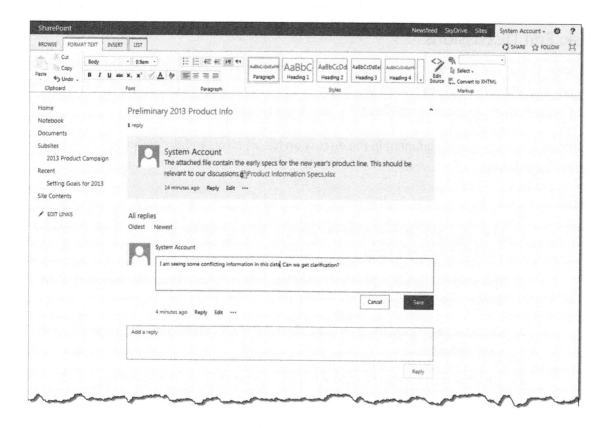

Figure 1: An Editable Comment

7. Edit the comment as needed and click **Save**. The edited comment will now appear in the discussion.

Note: If versioning is turned on for the list, prior versions of your comment will be available. Please see the task "Activate Version Control" for an example of how to access the version history of a SharePoint list item.

Exception: If you can't edit your response, you do not have specific permissions to edit discussions. Check the permissions settings to ensure you have the appropriate access rights.

Task: Delete Discussions

Purpose: Once in a while, a discussion board comment might be completely in error, or applied to the wrong conversation. In those cases, you may want to remove the comment altogether.

Example: After reviewing his comments, a user decides that he has replied to the wrong discussion topic, and just wants to remove his comment from the wrong thread altogether.

Steps:

1. Start Internet Explorer and type the URL for your organization's SharePoint server. The Start page will open.

2. Navigate to the site where you want to remove comments from a discussion board. The site's home page will open.

3. Click the **Settings** menu gear icon, then the **Site Contents** option. The Site Contents page will open.

4. Click the icon for the discussion board you want to join. The board's home page will open.

5. Click the conversation topic to join. The discussion page will open.

6. Find the comment you wish to remove and next to the **Edit** menu found below the reply for that comment, click **Open Menu**. The Open menu will open.

7. Click **Delete**. A confirmation dialog box will open.

Figure 1: Delete Item Confirmation Dialog Box

8. Click **OK**. The comment will be removed from the discussion board.

Exception: If you cannot delete a conversation, you do not have specific permissions to delete conversations. Check the permissions settings to ensure you have the appropriate access rights.

Task: Remove a Discussion Board

Purpose: Depending on the activity of a team, you may find that you have to set up specific discussion boards for things like special projects. Once the project is completed, you can remove the discussion board from the team site entirely.

Example: After the feedback for the Action Marketing Group's goals has been gathered and analyzed, the site administrator decides to delete the board to prevent confusion.

Steps:

1. Start Internet Explorer and type the URL for your organization's SharePoint server. The Start page will open.

2. Navigate to the site with the discussion board you want to remove. The site's home page will open.

3. Click the **Settings** menu gear icon, then the **Site Contents** option. The Site Contents page will open.

4. Click the icon for the discussion board you want to join. The board's home page will open.

5. In the ribbon click the **List** tab. The List ribbon will open.

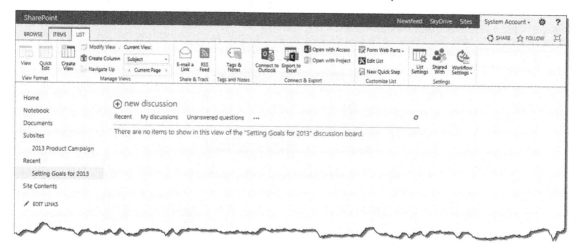

Figure 1: The List Tools Ribbon

6. Click the **List Settings** button. The Discussion Board Settings page will open.

The SharePoint Shepherd's Guide for End Users: 2013

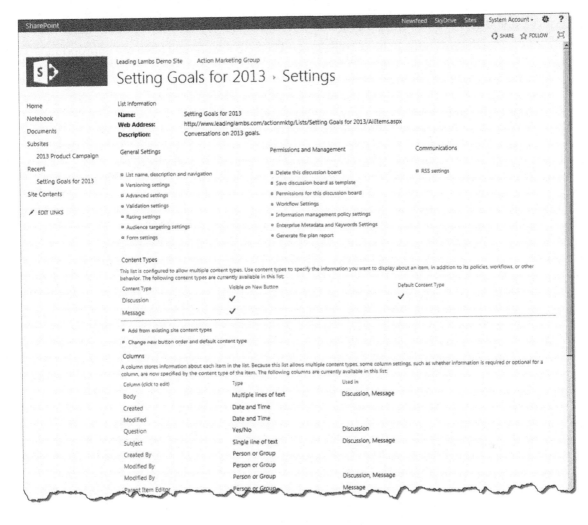

Figure 2: The Discussion Board Settings Page

7. In the **Permissions and Management** (center) column, click **Delete this discussion board**. A confirmation dialog box will open.

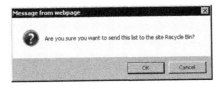

Figure 3: Delete Discussion Board Confirmation Dialog Box

8. Click **OK**. The discussion board will be removed from the site.

Exception: If you can't remove the discussion board, you do not have specific permissions to manage discussion boards. Check the permissions settings to ensure you have the appropriate access rights.

Conduct Effective Meetings

Collaboration comes in many forms. In the digital age, many people are encouraged to try online chats, shared document sessions, or email conversations to exchange ideas. Sometimes, though, a good old-fashioned face-to-face meeting is what's needed. SharePoint can create an online home for meetings, allowing attendees to be invited, agendas to be set, and tasks to be assigned.

Before all of this can happen, a new event must be created in the SharePoint calendar.

In this section, you will learn how to:

- **Create an Event**: The basics of creating an event are reviewed.

- **Create a Recurring Event**: Creating recurring events on your calendar is just a few steps more than creating a one-time event.

Task: Create an Event

Purpose: SharePoint can create an online home for meetings, allowing attendees to be invited, agendas to be set, and tasks to be assigned.

Before all of this can happen, a new event must be created in the SharePoint calendar.

This task will cover the creation of a one-time event; see the task "Create a Recurring Event" to make events that occur with regularity. Note, these events will be added to the SharePoint calendar, not the user's Outlook calendar.

Example: A client is planning to visit the Action Marketing Group offices, and the event needs to be posted on the team's calendar.

Steps:

1. Start Internet Explorer and type the URL for your organization's SharePoint server. The Start page will open.

2. Navigate to the site where you want to add the event. The site's home page will open.

3. In the Quick Launch for your site, click the appropriate **Calendar** link. The Calendar page will open. If the calendar you want to work with doesn't appear on the Quick Launch, you can click the **Settings** menu gear icon and the **Site Contents** link and select the Calendar from the list that appears.

Figure 1: The Calendar Page

4. Hover over the date on which you want add the event and click the **+Add** link when it appears. The Calendar - New Item dialog box will open.

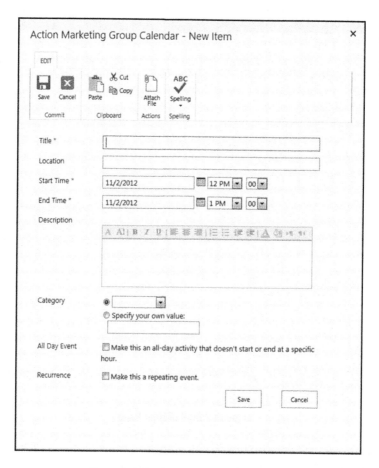

Figure 2: Calendar - New Item Dialog Box

5. In the Title field, enter the name of the event. This description is the one typically used when looking at a summary of events, or at the events in the calendar view.

6. In the Location field, enter a place for the event. This could be the room number for a meeting, or the city, state, and country for larger events.

7. Specify the Start and End Times. It is possible to customize the list such that events don't have times associated with them. If you want to create events without times, click the **Make this an all-day activity** checkbox.

8. In the Description field, enter a description of the event.

9. Select a classification for the event in the **Category** drop-down list, or select the **Specify Your Own Value** option and enter your own.

10. Click **Save**. The Calendar - New Item dialog box will close and the event will appear in the Calendar on the Calendar page.

Figure 3: The New Event on the Calendar Page

Exception: If you can't add an event to a calendar, you do not have specific permissions to change content within this calendar. Check the permissions settings to ensure you have the appropriate access rights.

Task: Create a Recurring Event

Purpose: Some events take place on a regular basis, such as the weekly staff meeting or the quarterly analysts briefing. Creating recurring events on your calendar requires just a few steps more than creating a one-time event.

Example: The Action Marketing Group works with several interns during the year, and as part of the program, a bi-weekly status meeting is needed to keep up-to-date on all interns' progress.

Steps:

1. Start Internet Explorer and type the URL for your organization's SharePoint server. The Start page will open.

2. Navigate to the site where you want to add the event. The site's home page will open.

3. In the Quick Launch for your site, click the **Calendar** link. The Calendar page will open. If the calendar you want to work with doesn't appear on the Quick Launch, you can click the **Settings** menu gear icon, the **Site Contents** link and select the Calendar from the list that appears.

4. Hover over the date on which you want to add the event and click the **+Add** link when it appears. The Calendar - New Item dialog box will open.

5. In the Title field, enter the name of the event. This description is the one typically used when looking at a summary of events, or at the events in the calendar view.

6. In the Location field, enter a place for the event. This could be the room number for a meeting, or the city, state, and country for larger events.

7. Specify the Start and End Times. It is possible to customize the list such that events don't have times associated with them. If you want to create events without times, click the **Make this an all-day activity** checkbox.

8. In the Description field, enter a description of the event.

9. Select a classification for the event in the **Category** drop-down list, or select the **Specify Your Own Value** option and enter your own.

10. Click the **Make this a repeating event** checkbox. The recurrence controls will appear.

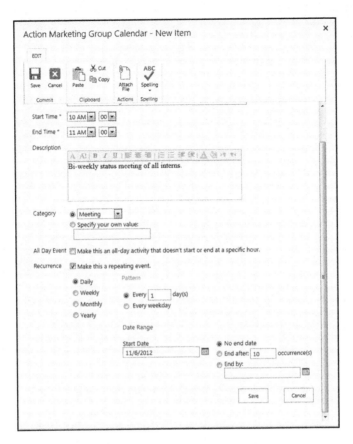

Figure 1: The Recurrence Controls for an Event

11. For a bi-weekly event, click the **Weekly** option. The Pattern section will change to accommodate a weekly recurrence. Each type of recurrence has its own pattern.

12. In the **Pattern** section, enter 2 in the Recur every __ week(s) field.

13. Select the **Start Date** for the recurring event. This is the first date when the event should appear.

14. Select an **End Date** option. In this case, enter a date near the end of summer.

15. Click **Save**. The new recurring events will appear on the calendar.

Figure 2: The New Recurring Events on the Calendar Page

Exception: If you can't add a recurring event to a calendar, you do not have specific permissions to change content within this calendar. Check the permissions settings to ensure you have the appropriate access rights.

Work Together on Content

One of the biggest advantages of using SharePoint is the ability to collaborate on documents using the cloud-based SkyDrive Pro tool. Using SkyDrive enables users to build an infrastructure on the team site where they can discuss, contribute, and edit any document. SharePoint is also tightly integrated with Microsoft Office – so much so, you can use any Office application to work with SharePoint.

In this section, you'll learn how to:

- **Open and Save Documents from Office 2013**: You can open a document in a SharePoint site and save it again directly from Office 2013.

- **Open and Save Documents from Office 2010**: You can open a document in a SharePoint site and save it again directly from Office 2010.

- **Open and Save Documents using Office Web Apps**: You can open a document from SharePoint, then save your changes back.

- **Share Documents in SkyDrive Pro**: Use cloud-based storage to quickly share documents with teammates.

- **Changing Document Permissions in SharePoint**: You can also grant more users access to a document in SharePoint itself.

- **Check Out a Document in Office 2013**: If many users are working on the same document, it is better to formally check the document out while making edits, to prevent other users from overwriting your changes.

- **Check Out a Document in Office 2010**: If many users are working on the same document, it is better to formally check the document out while making edits, to prevent other users from overwriting your changes.

- **Check Out Documents in SharePoint**: How to check out a document from within SharePoint.

- **Check Out Documents in SkyDrive Pro**: How to check out a document from the SkyDrive Pro cloud platform.

- **Check In a Document in Office 2013**: After you have completed your edits on a checked out document, you will need to check it back in to the document workspace so other users can see your changes.

- **Check In a Document in Office 2010**: After you have completed your edits on a checked out document, you will need to check it back in to the document workspace so other users can see your changes.

- **Check In Documents in SharePoint**: How to check in a document from within SharePoint.

- **Check In Documents in SkyDrive Pro**: How to check in a document from the SkyDrive Pro cloud platform.

- **Connect an Approval Workflow**: How a site administrator can tag a library, list, or workspace for improvement using the workflow process.

- **Follow a Document**: Use SharePoint's social tools to automatically track the status of a document.

- **Save a Site as a Template**: Learn how to create a template from any site, which can be reused to create other sites.

Task: Open and Save Documents from Office 2013

Purpose: When you are in Office and your system is connected to the Internet, you can open a document out on the SharePoint site, work with it on your local computer, then save your changes to SharePoint.

Example: Open the Action Marketing Group's Marketing Plan document from within Word 2013.

Steps:

1. Open an application in Microsoft Office. It can be Word, Excel, or PowerPoint.

2. Click the **File** tab and select **Open** from the menu. The Open screen will appear.

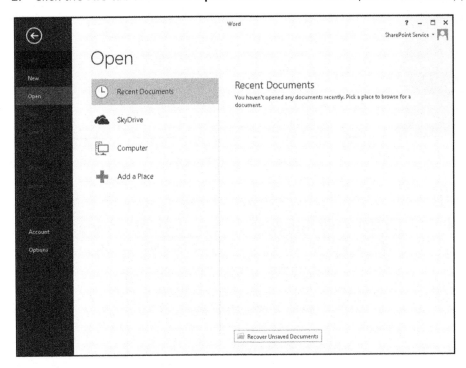

Figure 1: The Open Screen

3. Click the **Add a Place** link. The Add a Place pane will appear.

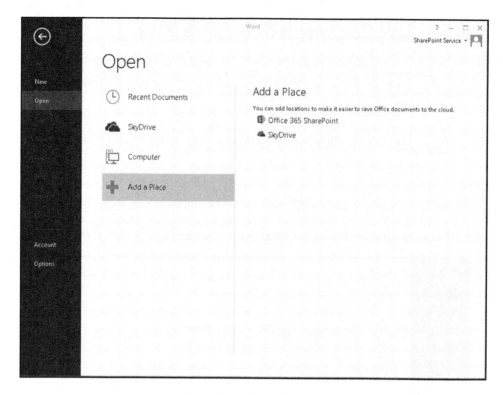

Figure 2: The Add a Place Pane

4. Click the **Office 365 SharePoint** link. If you have not connected to a SharePoint server before, Sign in to get started dialog box will appear.

Figure 3: The Sign In To Get Started Dialog Box

5. Enter the e-mail address for your company Office 365 account and click **Next**. The Sign In dialog box will appear.

Figure 4: The Sign In Dialog Box

6. In the Password field, type your login information, then click **Sign In**. Any SharePoint sites you have been connected to will be listed in the Open dialog box.

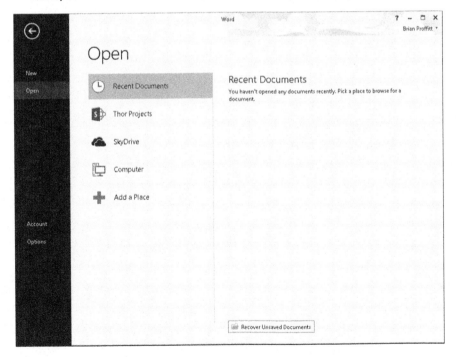

Figure 5: The Connected SharePoint Sites

7. Click the SharePoint site. Recent folders will appear in the right pane.

8. Click the Browse button. The Open dialog box will appear.

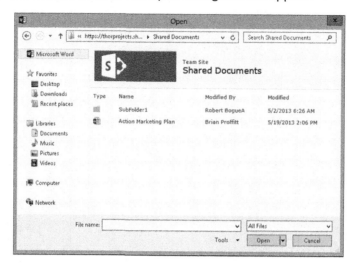

Figure 6: The Open Dialog Box

9. Click the desired document, then click **Open**. The document will open in the respective Office application.

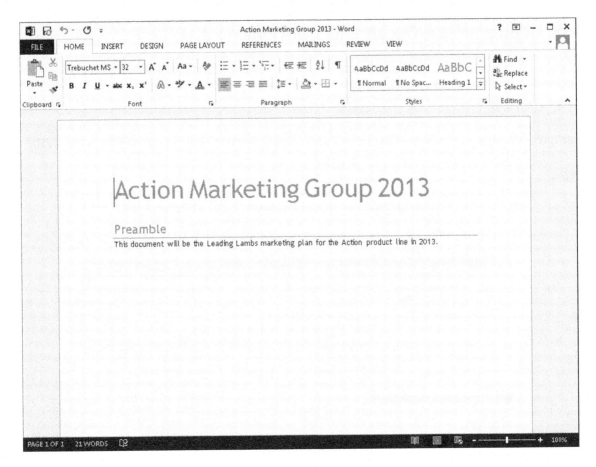

Figure 7: The Opened Document

10. Once the document editing is complete, click the **File** tab, then click **Save**. The new version of the document will be saved on the document workspace site, and the document will remain open in the Office application. If version control is activated for your workspace, you will be given a choice to save the document as a draft version or a published major version. For more information, see "Activate Version Control."

Note: If you try to save without checking in, you'll get a warning bar to indicate that the document is not checked in.

Task: Open and Save Documents from Office 2010

Purpose: When you are in Office and your system is connected to the Internet, you can open an existing document in a document library to work with it on your local computer, then save your changes in the library.

Example: Open the Action Marketing Group's Marketing Plan document from within Word 2010.

Steps:

1. Open an Office application. (It can be Word, Excel, or PowerPoint.)

2. Click the **File** tab and click **Open** from the menu. The Open window will appear.

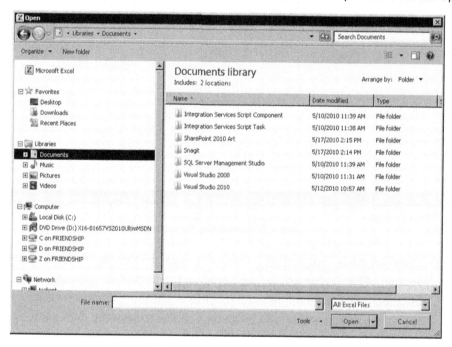

Figure 1: The Open Dialog Box

3. In either the File name or Location field, type the URL for the document library app you want to browse. The Site Contents page for your document library will open.**Error! Bookmark not defined.**

4. Click the document library that contains the document you would like to edit. The document library appears in the Open dialog box.

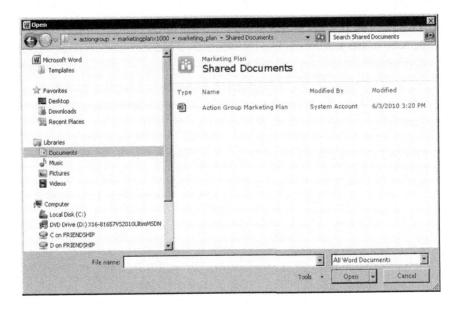

Figure 2: The Shared Documents Library Appears in the Open Dialog Box

5. Click the desired document, then click **Open**. The document will open.

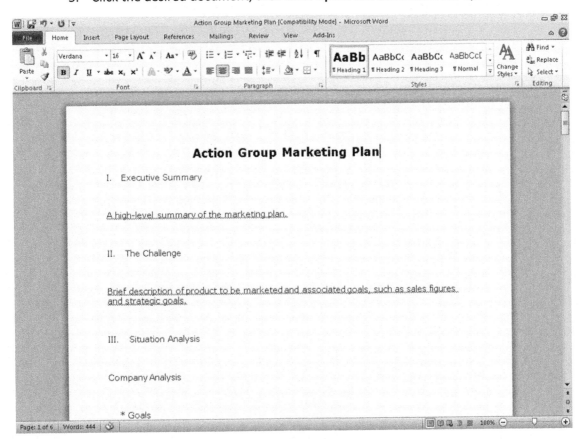

Figure 3: The Opened Document

6. Click the **File** tab, then click **Save,** once the document editing is complete. The new version of the document will be saved on the document workspace site, and the document will remain open in the Office application. If version control is activated for your workspace, you will be given a choice to save the document as a draft version or a published major version. For more information, see "Activate Version Control."

Note: If you try save without checking in, you'll get a warning bar to indicate that the document is not checked in.

Task: Open and Save Documents Using Office Web Apps

Purpose: If you are already working within a SharePoint site, you can open documents directly from SharePoint and view them right inside your browser.

Example: Open a spreadsheet from within SharePoint to view and edit it.

Steps:

1. Start Internet Explorer and type the URL for your organization's SharePoint server. The Start page will open.

2. Navigate to the document library where you want to edit a document. The document library page will open.

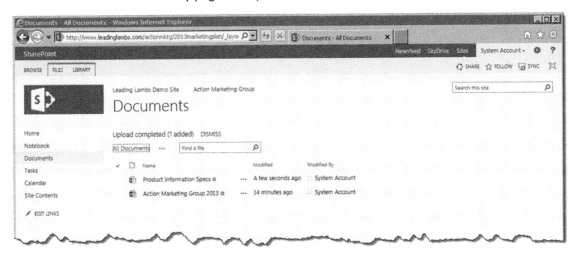

Figure 1: A Document Library

3. Click the link for the document. If the document library settings are set correctly, the document will open inside the Internet Explorer browser.

Figure 2: The Document Opened in Browser

4. To make changes, click the **Edit Workbook** menu and then click the **Edit in Excel Web App** option. The Excel Web App will open in Edit mode.

Figure 3: The Document Ready To Edit in the Browser

The SharePoint Shepherd's Guide for End Users: 2013

5. Once the document editing is complete, click the File tab and **Save As**. The Save As dialog box will open.

Figure 4: The Save As Dialog Box

6. Enter a new name for the document or click the Overwrite existing files check box.

7. Click Save. The new version of the document will be saved on the document workspace site.

8. Click the X closing icon to close the document. The most recent version of the document will be listed in the document library.

Task: Sync Documents in SkyDrive Pro

Purpose: SkyDrive Pro is a new feature in SharePoint 2013 that lets you synchronize the contents of a document library into a folder on your local machine. This is great for any user who needs to access documents while offline.

Example: One of the Action Marketing Group team members wants to synchronize shared documents in the Action Marketing Group library on their computer.

Steps:

1. Start Internet Explorer and type the URL for your organization's SharePoint server. The Start page will open.

2. Navigate to the document library that you want to synchronize to a local folder. The document library page will open.

3. In the Quick Access Toolbar, click the **Sync** link. The Microsoft SkyDrive Pro dialog box will open.

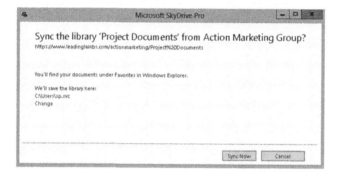

Figure 1: The SkyDrive Pro Dialog Box

4. To change the location of the shared folder on your local machine, click **Change**. The Browse for Folder dialog box will open.

Figure 2: The Browse for Folder Dialog Box

5. Navigate to the location you want the new folder to be, then click **OK**. The Browser for Folder dialog will close.

6. Click **Sync Now**. The contents of the library will be synced to your computer.

7. Click the **Show My Files** button. Windows Explorer will open to the folder in which the document library's files were synced.

Task: Changing Document Permissions in SharePoint

Purpose: When a document is assigned to a library, the collaborators of the document are typically the same users who were originally granted access to that library. You can, however, grant more users access to a document library within SharePoint itself.

Example: The marketing plan document is starting to be created, and at this time you only want to restrict access to a few people.

Steps:

1. Start Internet Explorer and type the URL for your organization's SharePoint server. The Start page will open.

2. Navigate to the document library site where the document you wish to modify is located. The document library page will open.

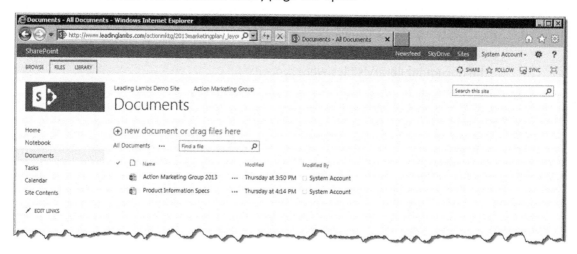

Figure 1: A Document Library

3. Click on the ellipsis control next to the name of the document you wish to edit. The document's menu will appear.

The SharePoint Shepherd's Guide for End Users: 2013

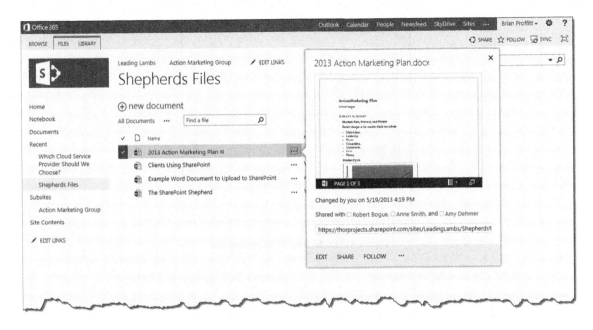

Figure 2: The Document Menu

4. At the bottom of the Document Menu, click the ellipsis control. The Properties Menu will open.

Figure 3: The Properties Menu

5. Click the **Shared With** option. The Shared With dialog box will open.

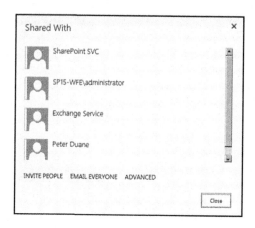

Figure 4: The Shared With Dialog Box

6. Click the **Advanced** option. The Permissions Tools page will open.

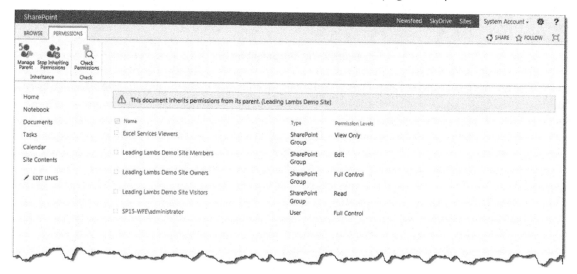

Figure 5: The Permissions Tools Page

7. Click the **Stop Inheriting Permissions** button. A confirmation dialog box will appear.

8. Click **OK**. The confirmation dialog box will close, the document will no longer have the same permissions set, and a new set of tools will appear on the page.

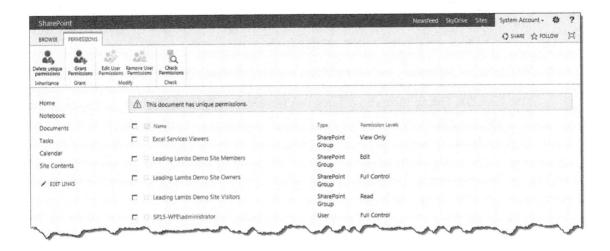

Figure 6: The Permissions Tools Page, Without Permission Inheritance

9. Click the **Grant Permissions** button. The Share dialog box will open.

10. In the Add People field, type in the name of the user. As the name is typed, a list of matching results will appear.

11. Click on the correct name when it appears in the list. The name will be added.

12. Add additional names as needed.

13. Click **Share**. The Share dialog box will close and the users will now appear on the Permission Tools page. Repeat Steps 9-12 to grant other users different permission levels.

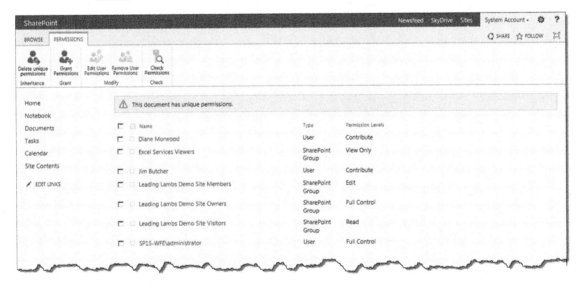

Figure 7: New Users Listed in the Permissions Tools Window

14. Click the checkboxes for all the users and groups you do not want to have access. The users and groups will be selected.

15. Click the **Remove User Permissions** icon. A confirmation dialog box will appear.

16. Click **OK**. The confirmation dialog box will close and the user(s) will be removed from the user list.

Task: Check Out a Document in Office 2013

Purpose: When a document is being edited from a document library, a user can quickly open the document, make changes, and then save the document back into the workspace. If there are many users who may be working on the same document at the same time and you intend to work on the document offline, it may be better to formally check the document out.

Example: When you have a document opened from a SharePoint document library, you can check it out from the Office application.

Steps:

1. Open an application in Office. (The application can be Word, Excel, or PowerPoint.)

2. Click the **File** tab and click **Open** from the menu. The Open window will appear.

3. Click the **Add a Place** link. The Add a Place pane will appear.

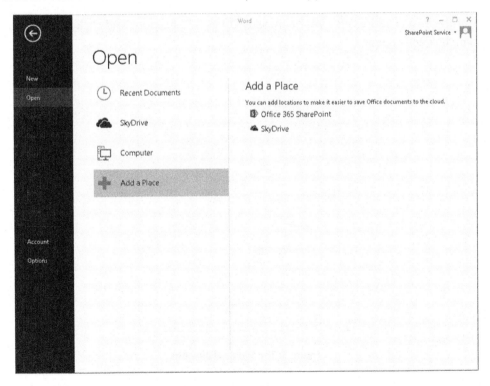

Figure 1: The Add a Place Pane

4. Click the **Office 365 SharePoint** link. If you have not connected to a SharePoint server before, Sign in to get started dialog box will appear.

Figure 2: The Sign In To Get Started Dialog Box

5. Enter the e-mail address for your company Office 365 account and click **Next**. The Sign In dialog box will appear.

Figure 3: The Sign In Dialog Box

6. In the Password field, type your login information, then click **Sign In**. Any SharePoint sites you have been connected to will be listed in the Open dialog box.

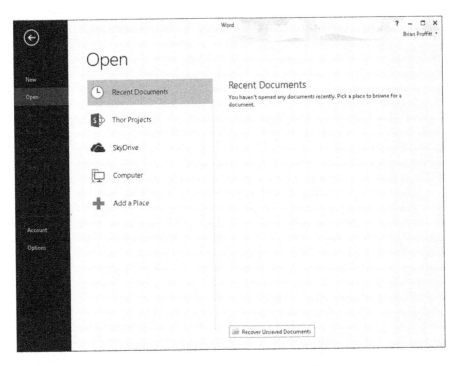

Figure 4: The Connected SharePoint Sites

7. Click the SharePoint site. Recent folders will appear in the right pane.

8. Click the Browse button. The Open dialog box will appear.

Figure 5: The Open Dialog Box

9. Click the desired document, then click **Open**. The document will open in the respective Office application.

---

10. Click the **File** tab and click **Info** from the menu. The Info window will appear.

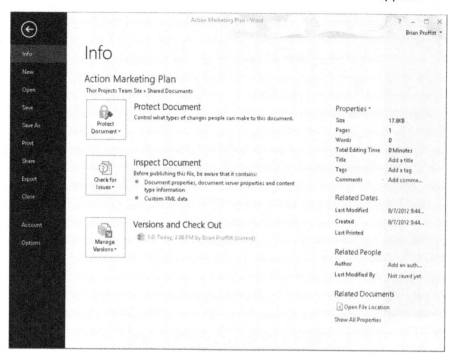

Figure 6: The Document Info Window

11. Click the **Manage Versions** button, then click the **Check Out** option. The document will be checked out to you, but will remain stored on the SharePoint system.

Task: Check Out a Document in Office 2010

Purpose: When a document is being edited from a document library, a user can quickly open the document, make changes, and then save the document back into the workspace. If many users are working on the same document, however, it is better to formally check the document out while making edits, to prevent other users from overwriting your changes. You also may be required to check out documents by a library's properties. Here's how to check out a document in Office 2010.

Example: When you have a document opened from a SharePoint document library, you can check it out from the Office application.

Steps:

1. Open an application in Office. (The application can be Word, Excel, or PowerPoint.)

2. Click the **File** tab and select **Open** from the menu. The Open window will appear.

3. In the Location field type the URL for the Document Workspace you want to browse and press Enter. The Site Contents page for the document workspace will open.

4. Click the desired document, then click **Open**. The document will open in the appropriate Office application.

Note: You may have to enter your login information when the file opens.

5. Click the **File** tab and select **Info** from the menu. The Info window will appear.

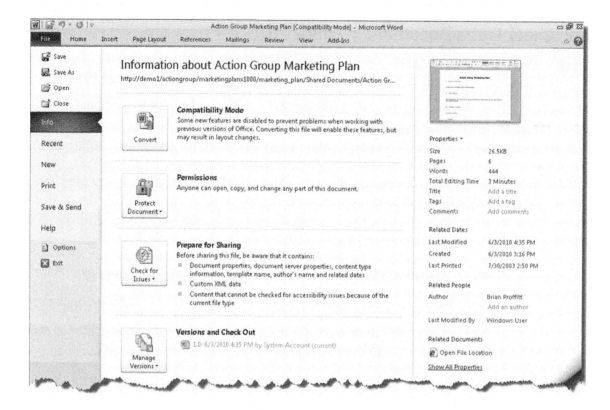

Figure 1: The Document Info Window

6. Click the **Manage Versions** button, then click the **Check Out** option. The document will be checked out to you, but will remain stored on the SharePoint system.

The SharePoint Shepherd's Guide for End Users: 2013

Task: Check Out Documents in SharePoint

Purpose: When a document is being edited from a document workspace, a user can quickly open the document, make changes, and then save the document back into the workspace. If many users are working on the same document, however, it is better to formally check the document out while making edits, to prevent other users from overwriting your changes.

Example: You need to check out a marketing plan document that you've already synchronized to your machine via SkyDrive Pro so that you can work on it during your commute home.

Steps:

1. Start Internet Explorer and type the URL for your organization's SharePoint server. The Start page will open.

2. Navigate to the document library site where the document you wish to check out is located. The document library page will open.

3. Find the document you wish to edit and next to the document title, click the ellipsis control to open the document's menu. The Document menu will appear.

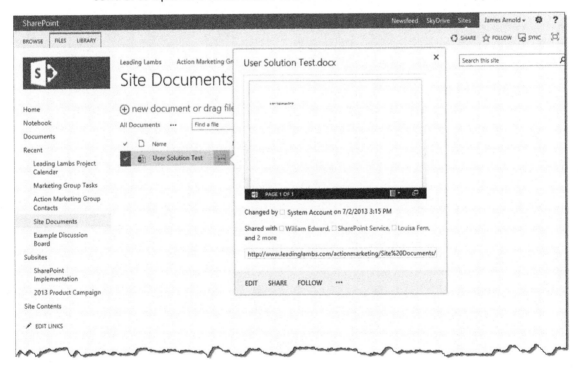

Figure 1: The Document Menu

4. Click the **ellipsis** control icon at the bottom of the Document Menu. The Properties Menu will open.

---

5. Click the **Check Out** option. The document will be checked out to you and can be edited by you alone until you check the document back in.

Note: If a confirmation dialog box appears, click **OK** to complete the process.

Task: Check Out Documents in SkyDrive Pro

Purpose: When a document is being edited from a document library, a user can quickly open the document, make changes, and then save the document back into the workspace. If many users are working on the same document, however, it is better to formally check the document out while making edits, to prevent other users from overwriting your changes.

Example: Here's how to check out the Action Marketing Group sales figures from SkyDrive Pro.

Steps:

1. Start Internet Explorer and type the URL for your organization's SharePoint server. The Start page will open.

2. Click the SkyDrive link at the top of the page. The SkyDrive Pro library page will open.

3. Next to the title of the document that you want to edit, click the ellipsis control, which will open the document's menu. The Document menu will appear.

4. Click the **ellipsis** control at the bottom of the Document Menu. The Properties Menu will open.

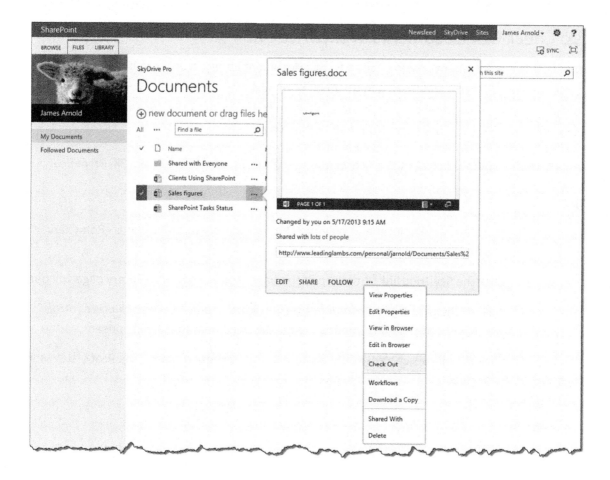

Figure 1: A Document's Properties Menu

5. Click the **Check Out** option. The document will be checked out to you and can be edited by you alone until you check the document back in.

Task: Check In a Document in Office 2013

Purpose: After you have completed your edits on a checked out document, you will need to check it back in to the document workspace so others can edit the document.

Example: After making changes to the marketing plan, you check the document back in so others can add their portions to the document.

Steps:

1. When your edits are complete in the checked out document, click the **File** tab and select **Info** from the menu. The Info pane will appear.

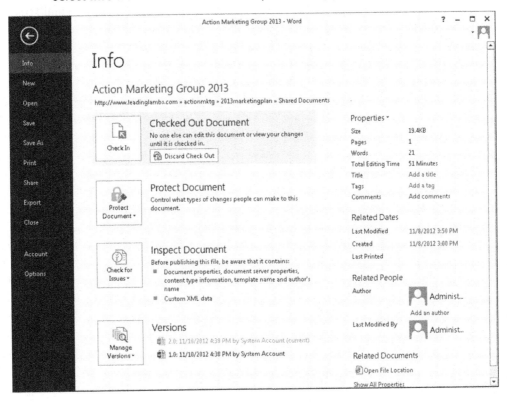

Figure 1: The Document Info Pane

2. Click the **Check In** button. The Check In dialog box will appear.

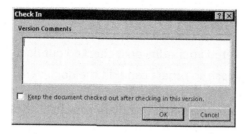

Figure 2: The Check In Dialog Box

3. In the Version Comments field, enter any notes.

4. Click **OK**. The document will be checked back in to the document workspace. Although the document has been checked in, the document will remain open, but read-only.

Task: Check In a Document in Office 2010

Purpose: After you have completed your edits on a checked out document, you will need to check it back in to the document workspace so others can edit the document

Example: After making changes to the marketing plan, you check the document back in so others can add their portions to the document.

Steps:

1. Open an application in Office. It can be Word, Excel, or PowerPoint.

2. Click the **File** tab and select **Open** from the menu. The Open window will appear.

3. In the Location field, type the URL for the Document Workspace you want to browse and press Enter. The Site Content page for your shared document site will open.

4. Click the desired document, then click **Open**. The document will open in your Office application.

5. When your edits are complete, click the **File** tab and select **Info** from the menu. The Info pane will appear.

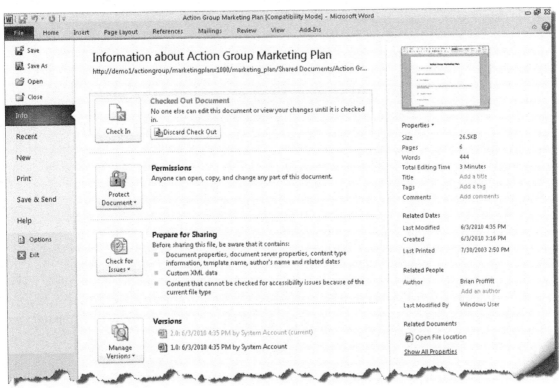

Figure 1: The Document Info Pane

6. Click the **Check In** icon. The Check In dialog box will appear.

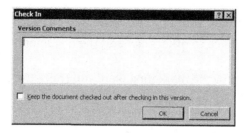

Figure 2: The Check In Dialog Box

7. In the Version Comments field, enter any notes.

8. Click **OK**. The document will be checked back in to the document workspace. Although the document has been checked in, the document will remain open, but read-only.

Task: Check In Documents in SharePoint

Purpose: After you have completed your edits on a checked out document, you will need to check it back in to the document workspace so others can see your changes and/or edit the document themselves.

Example: After making changes to the marketing plan, you check the document back in so others can add their portions to the document.

Steps:

1. Start Internet Explorer and type the URL for your organization's SharePoint server. The Start page will open.

2. Navigate to the document library site where the document you wish to modify is located. The document library page will open.

3. Find the document you wish to edit and next to the document title, click the ellipsis control to open the document's menu. The Document menu will appear.

4. Click the ellipsis control at the bottom of the Document Menu. The Properties Menu will open.

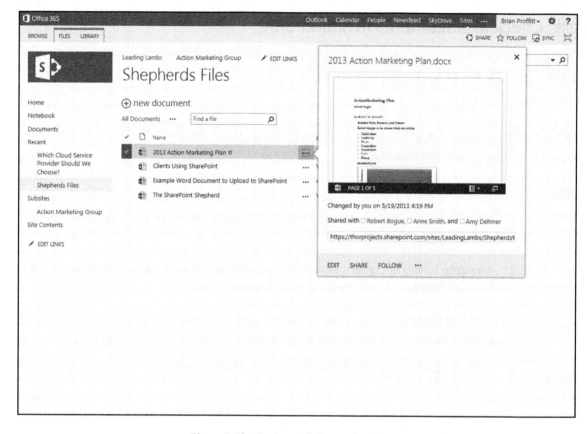

Figure 1: The Document's Properties Menu

5. Click **Check In**. The Check In dialog box will appear.

Figure 2: The Check In Dialog Box

6. In the Retain Check Out section, choose if you want to keep the document checked out after checking in this version.

7. In the Comments field, type any notes about this version of the document.

8. Click **OK**. The document will be checked in.

Task: Check In Documents in SkyDrive Pro

Purpose: After you have completed your edits on a checked out document, you will need to check it back in to the SkyDrive Pro library so others can see your changes, as well as edit the document themselves.

Example: Here's how to check in the Action Marketing Group sales figures into SkyDrive Pro.

Steps:

1. Start Internet Explorer and type the URL for your organization's SharePoint server. The Start page will open.

2. In the Suite bar click the SkyDrive link. The SkyDrive Pro library page will open.

3. Find the document you wish to check in and next to the title, click the ellipsis control to open the document's menu. The document's menu will appear.

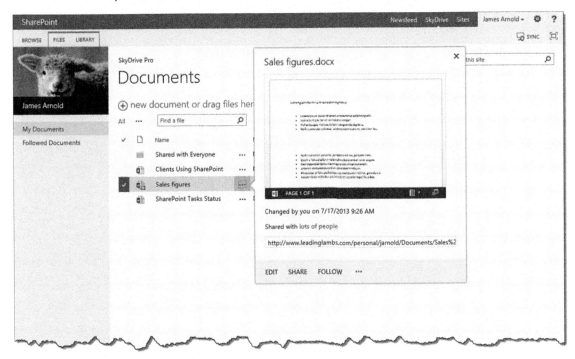

Figure 1: Checking In A Checked Out Document

4. Click the ellipsis control at the bottom of the Document Menu. The Properties Menu will open.

5. Click the **Check In** option. The Check In dialog box will appear.

6. In the Retain Check Out section, choose if you want to keep the document checked out after checking in this version. You would do this if you made a major change in

the document and wanted to be sure that others can see the change while you continue to work.

7. In the Comments field, type any notes about this version of the document.

8. Click **OK**. The document will be checked in.

Task: Connect an Approval Workflow

Purpose: Maintaining control of content is a problem for all web sites. By associating an approval workflow you can ensure that all of the content added to the library goes through an approval process.

Example: Action Marketing Group policies must be approved before being published to the employees. Associating an approval workflow ensures that every new piece of content is reviewed before being published.

Steps:

1. Start Internet Explorer and type the URL for your organization's SharePoint server. The Start page will open.

2. Navigate to the document library that needs a workflow started.

3. In the ribbon click the **Library** tab. The Library ribbon will open.

4. Click the **Library Settings** button. The Document Library Settings page will open.

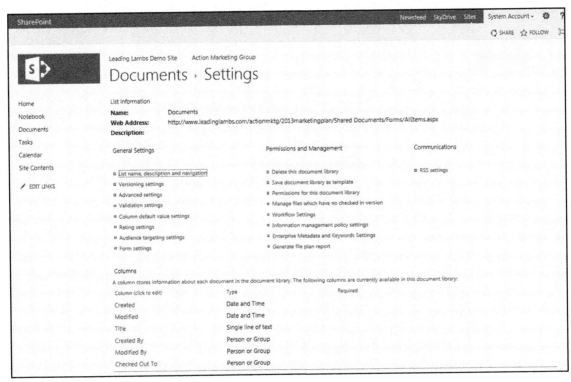

Figure 1: The Document Library Settings Page

5. In the Permissions and Management section, click the **Workflow Settings** link. The Workflow Settings page will open.

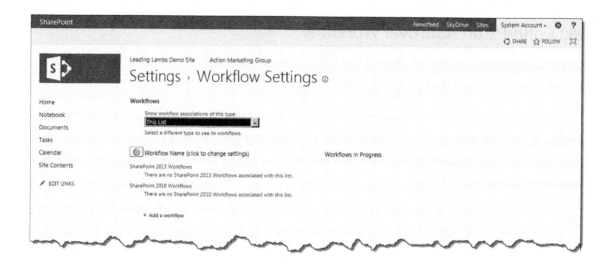

Figure 2: The Workflow Settings Page

6. Click the **Add a workflow** link. The Add a Workflow page will open.

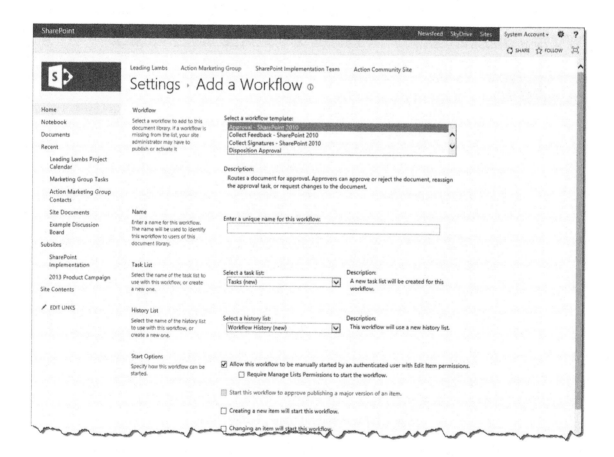

Figure 3: The Add a Workflow Page

7. In the Workflow section, click the **Publishing Approval** option.

    Note: Workflow templates for sites must be set up by the site administrator or created in SharePoint designer. If you do not have any workflows available, contact the site administrator.

8. In the Name section, enter a title for the workflow.

9. In the Task List section, select **Tasks (new)**.

10. In the Start Options section, click the **Creating a new item will start this workflow** checkbox.

11. Click **Next**. The Publishing Approval settings page will appear.

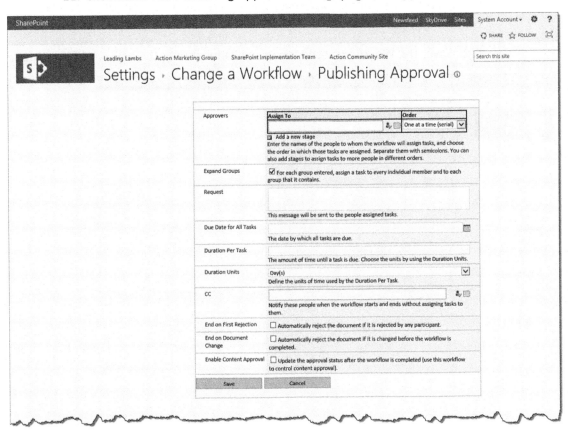

Figure 4: The Publishing Approval Settings Page

12. In the Approvers section's Assign To field, enter the user name of the people you want to approve documents, separating multiple names with semicolons.

13. Click the People Picker icon to validate the user name(s).

14. In the Order field, select the approval type: Serial or Parallel.

15. In the Request section, type in the message you want each approval recipient to receive.

16. Enter either a single due date or a length of time you want the approval to be completed.

17. Select the **End on First Rejection** check mark to stop the workflow if a rejection is made.

18. Select the **End on Document Change** check mark to stop the workflow if any changes to the document are made.

19. Select the **Enable Content Approval** check mark to ensure this workflow controls content approval.

20. Click Save. The Workflow Settings page will appear with the new workflow added.

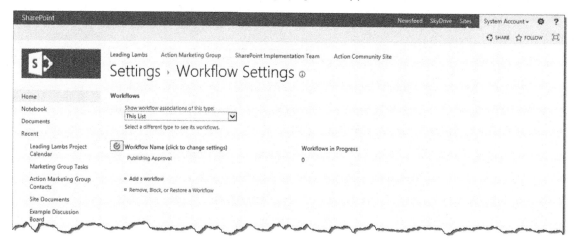

Figure 5: The Workflow Settings Page

The SharePoint Shepherd's Guide for End Users: 2013

Task: Follow a Document

Purpose: Keeping tabs on all of the documents in the organization that you're interested in isn't practical. SharePoint allows you to "follow" documents that are interesting to you so that you can be notified when they change. The changes appear in your newsfeed so you don't have to go looking for the documents that have changed.

Example: Action Marketing Group has a policy regarding vendor samples. As a purchasing manager you want to know when it changes so you can make sure you're following the right procedures.

Steps:

1. Start Internet Explorer and type the URL for your organization's SharePoint server. The Start page will open.

2. Navigate to the document library site where the document you wish to follow is located. The document library page will open.

3. Find the document you wish to edit and next to the document title, click the ellipsis control to open the document's menu. The Document menu will appear.

4. At the bottom of the Document menu, click the **Follow** command. The document will be followed.

5. To see documents that are followed or the changes to the documents, people, and sites you follow, in the Suite bar at the top of the page click the **Newsfeed** link. The Newsfeed page will open.

Figure 1: The Newsfeed Page

Task: Save a Site as a Template

Purpose: Once you have a site the way you want it, you can turn it into a template to create other sites by saving it as a template.

Example: The Action Marketing Group created a project template that includes the tasks that every project must do and the documents which must be filled out. They will save the template to be used for future projects.

Steps:

1. Start Internet Explorer and type the URL for your organization's SharePoint server. The Start page will open.

2. Navigate to the site to be templated. The site's home page will open.

3. Click the **Settings** menu gear icon and select **Site Settings**. The Site Settings page will open.

4. In the **Site Actions** section, click the **Save site as template** link . The Save as Template page will open.

Figure 1: The Save as Template Page

5. In the File Name, Template Name, and Template Description fields, enter the pertinent information.

The SharePoint Shepherd's Guide for End Users: 2013

6. To capture any items and files that have been added to the site, click the **Include Content** checkbox.

7. Click **OK**. The site will be saved as a template in the Solutions Gallery for later use in SharePoint.

In SharePoint 2013, information and files can be stored within apps. These collections combine the functionality and features of what were formerly known as libraries and lists.

A library app is simply a specialized app that contains, instead of just items of data, items with separate documents and files. These files can be photos, audio clips, Office documents...anything you can use on a PC, only better. That's because with a SharePoint server hosting your files, you get the added benefits of version control, having multiple views of your data, and the capability to add metadata to your content that will enable you and other users to quickly find the file you are seeking.

A list app in SharePoint is a valuable tool for organizing data. Many of the tools built into SharePoint are specialized lists: Contacts, Calendar, Tasks, and Surveys are just a few. But if none of the existing tools work for you, you can quickly build a new, custom list that collects exactly the kind of data you need.

In this section, you'll learn how to:

- **Create a Custom List App**: The basics of creating a custom list.

- **Create a Library App**: The basics of creating a library.

- **Create a File in a Library App**: Once you have a library app created, you can add items to that library fairly quickly.

- **Upload a Single File to a Library App**: Not only can you create a document and save it directly to a document library, you can also upload existing documents from your local PC to the SharePoint library.

- **Upload Multiple Files to a Library App**: If you have a lot of documents to upload, you don't have to upload them one at a time. You can simply upload them all at once.

- **Create a New Folder in a Library App**: Instead of just listing library items in a flat list, you can organize the library's contents by creating folders for the items.

- **Import a Spreadsheet to Create a List App**: Rather than retyping all of the data into SharePoint, you can quickly import an Excel spreadsheet and create a list or library.

- **Create a New Item for a List App**: Once you have an app created, you can add items to that app fairly quickly.

- **Add New List or Library App Columns**: When you add columns to the app, you are also providing additional fields to enter information.

- **Edit Existing List or Library App Columns**: Besides adding new columns to an app, you can also edit existing columns in case you need to make a correction or change.

- **Delete List or Library App Columns**: If a column in your app proves to be unnecessary, you can remove it from the app altogether.

- **Edit a List or Library App in Quick Edit View**: You can shift to Quick Edit view, which looks and functions very similarly to a spreadsheet, allowing you to edit a lot of app data at once.

- **View List or Library Item Properties**: You can easily see an app item's information on the item's properties page.

- **Edit List or Library Item Properties**: When you need to edit one item in an app, you don't have to use the datasheet view.

- **Manage List or Library App Item Permissions**: Occasionally, you may need to adjust an item's permissions to make sure only the right people are allowed to edit it.

- **Edit a Library App Item in a Preferred Application**: Learn how to edit compatible documents directly from SharePoint, just like opening a file from your local hard drive.

- **Download a Library App File**: Occasionally, you will have files in your library app that are important to the context of the library, but they may not be in a SharePoint-compatible format.

- **Move a File to Another Library App**: You can move files to another library app anywhere on your SharePoint site.

- **Email a Link to a Library App**: If you want to get many users involved in the editing/creation process for a document, an efficient way is to send a link to the document in an email.

- **Edit a List or Library App View**: By default, apps are displayed in a certain way within SharePoint. You can change these aspects of an app's view very easily.

- **Add a List or Library App View**: It is possible to create whole new app views, just the way you want them, rather than heavily modifying the All Items view.

- **Export a List or Library App to a Spreadsheet**: Rather than retyping all of the data from SharePoint into Excel, you can quickly export an app to an Excel spreadsheet.

- **Delete a Library App File**: If you need to remove an item from an app, it's a quick operation.

- **Recover a List or Library Item from the Recycle Bin**: How to retrieve deleted items from the app Recycle Bin.

- **Edit List or Library App Content Types**: You can customize the types of content to be stored in your app.

Task: Create a Custom List App

Purpose: A list in SharePoint is a valuable tool for organizing data. Many of the tools built into SharePoint are specialized lists; Announcements, Contacts, Calendar, Tasks, and Surveys are just a few examples of specially-formatted SharePoint lists. But if none of the existing tools work for you, you can quickly build a new, custom list that collects exactly the kind of data you need.

Example: The Action Marketing Group wants to create a collaborative list of trade shows that team members will be attending or participating in during the coming year.

Steps:

1. Start Internet Explorer and type the URL for your organization's SharePoint server. The Start page will open. If you want this custom list to appear in one of your subsites, navigate to that site.

2. Click the **Settings** menu gear icon. The Settings menu will appear.

3. Click **Add an App**. The Your Apps page will appear.

Figure 1: The Your Apps Page

4. Click the **Custom List** icon. The Adding Custom List dialog box will open.

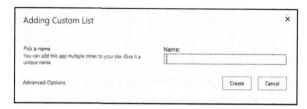

Figure 2: The Adding Custom List Dialog Box

5. Click **Advanced Options**. The Site Contents – New page will open.

6. In the Name field enter a title for the new list. This is used to identify the list throughout SharePoint.

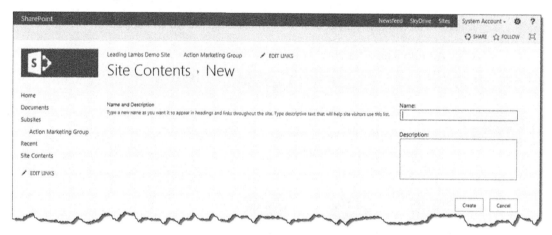

Figure 3: The Site Contents – New Page

7. In the Description field enter any notes about the new list. This appears as an information icon next to the list name when your list is open in SharePoint.

8. Click **Create**. The new list will be created.

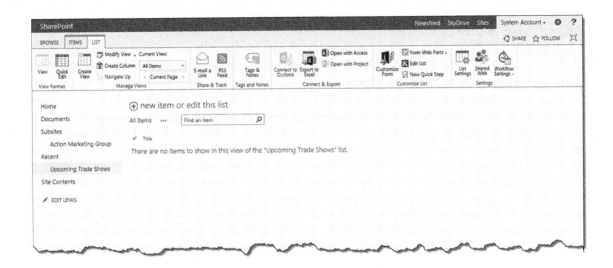

Figure 4: The New List

Note: When a custom list or library is created, it initially has just a few columns. For more information on adding columns to your list, see the task "Add New List or Library App Columns."

Exception: If you don't see the entry to create a custom list, you do not have specific permissions to view that app. Check the permissions settings to ensure you have the appropriate access rights.

Task: Create a Library App

Purpose: A library in SharePoint is very much like all the other list apps, though it has the specialized purpose of managing files. Creating a library allows you to have a place to store files.

Example: The Action Marketing Group wants set up a new document library for storing trade show documentation and marketing materials.

Steps:

1. Start Internet Explorer and type the URL for your organization's SharePoint server. The Start page will open. If you want your new site located as a sub-site of another site, navigate to that site.

2. Click the **Settings** menu gear icon. The Settings menu will appear.

3. Click **Add an App**. The Your Apps page will appear.

4. Click the **Document Library** icon. The Adding Document Library dialog box will open.

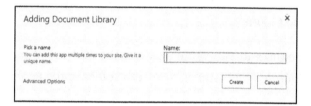

Figure 1: The Adding Document Library Dialog Box

5. Click **Advanced Options**. The Site Contents – New page will open.

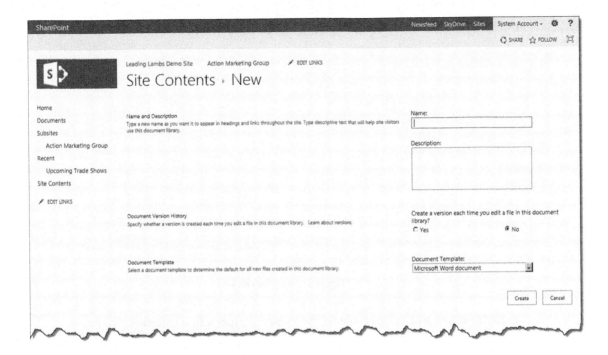

Figure 2: The Site Contents – New Page

6. In the Name field, enter a title for the new library. This is used to identify the library throughout SharePoint.

7. In the Description field enter any notes about the new library. This appears as a sub-heading when your library is open in SharePoint.

8. In the Document Version History section, click **Yes**.

9. Select the Document Template option you would like to use as the default file type for the library.

10. Click **Create**. The new library will be created.

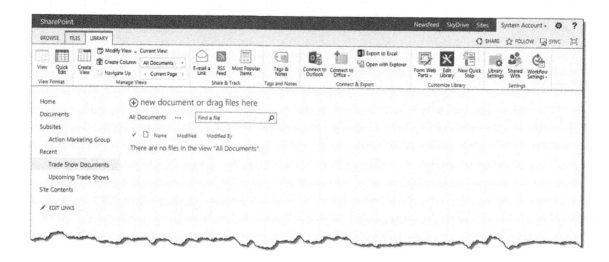

Figure 3: The New Library

Note: When a library is created, it initially has just a few columns. For more information on adding columns to your list, see the task "Create New List or Library App Columns."

Exception: If you don't see the app to create a library, you do not have specific permissions to view the app. Check the permissions settings to ensure you have the appropriate access rights.

Task: Create a File in a Library App

Purpose: Once you have a library app created, you can add items to that library fairly quickly. In this example, we will create a new document for a document library using the default document type defined for a library. You can directly upload documents to a library, which is covered in "Upload a Single File to a Library App."

Example: The first of many trade show documents needs to be uploaded to the new library.

Steps:

1. Start Internet Explorer and type the URL for your organization's SharePoint server. The Start page will open.

2. Click the **Settings** menu and select the Site Contents option. The Site Contents page will open.

3. Click the icon for the library where you want to add an item. The library page will open.

4. In the ribbon click the **Files** tab. The Files ribbon will appear.

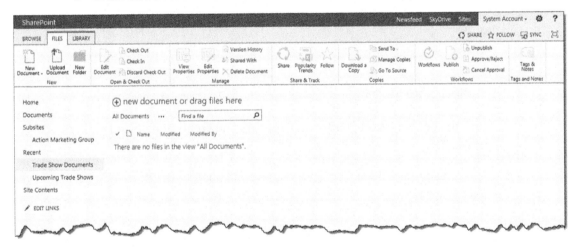

Figure 1: The Files Ribbon

5. Click the **New Document** button. A confirmation dialog box may open.

Note: The New Document button's drop-down list will reveal multiple content types if there are multiple content types associated with the library.

Figure 2: The Open Document Confirmation Dialog Box

6. Click **Yes**. The Office application will open with the basic document template or the library's default template in Protected Mode.

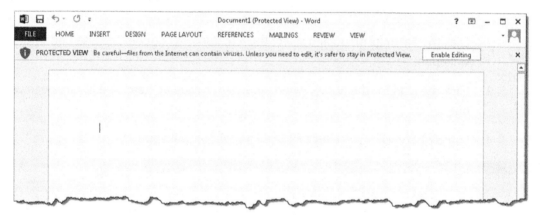

Figure 3: The New Document Opened using the Basic Document Template

7. Click the **Enable Editing** button if it appears and create the document in the Office application.

8. When ready, click **Save**. The Save As pane will open to the document library on your SharePoint server.

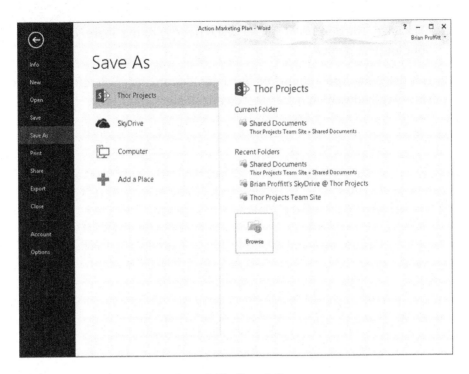

Figure 4: The Save As Pane

9. Click the folder icon representing the SharePoint library where the document was created. The Save As dialog box will open.

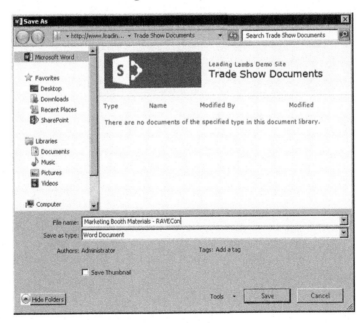

Figure 5: The Save As Dialog Box

10. In the File Name field, enter a file name.

11. Click **Save**. The document will be saved directly to the SharePoint library instead of your local hard drive.

12. Exit the Office application. The document library page will refresh and the document library will now contain the created document.

Task: Upload a Single File to a Library App

Purpose: Commonly you'll receive documents via email or create them while you're not online and need to upload them to SharePoint to maintain the file and collaborate with others.

Example: The Action Marketing Group needs to upload files to the Trade Show Materials library.

Steps:

1. Start Internet Explorer and type the URL for your organization's SharePoint server. The Start page will open.

2. Navigate to the library where you want to add an item. The document library page will open.

3. Click the **Files** tab. The Files ribbon will open.

4. Click **Upload Document**. The Add a document dialog box will open.

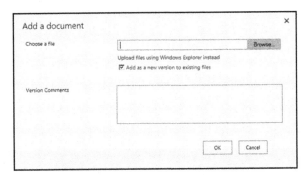

Figure 1: The Add a Document Dialog Box

5. Click the **Browse** button. The Choose File to Upload dialog box will appear.

Figure 2: The Choose File to Upload Dialog Box

6. Select a file and click **Open**. The file and its file path will appear in the Name field of the Upload Document dialog box.

7. In the Version Comments field, add any notes about the document if you have Versioning enabled on the library.

8. Click **OK**. The file will be uploaded and will appear on the document library page.

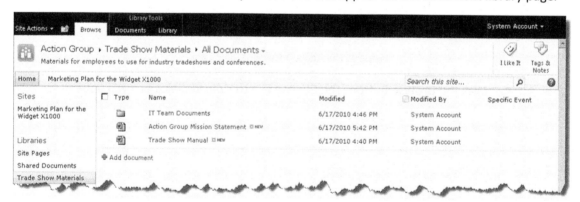

Figure 3: The New Uploaded Document on the Document Library Page

Task: Upload Multiple Files to a Library App

Purpose: While you can upload multiple files one-at-a-time it's more convenient to select a set of files and upload them all at once.

Example: The Action Marketing Group has multiple files from the recent tradeshow that the want to upload to SharePoint quickly.

Steps:

1. Start Internet Explorer and type the URL for your organization's SharePoint server. The Start page will open.

2. Navigate to the library where you want to upload documents. The document library page will open.

3. Open Windows Explorer and navigate to the files you want to upload.

4. Drag and drop the documents into the Drag Files Here section. The files will be uploaded and will appear on the document library page.

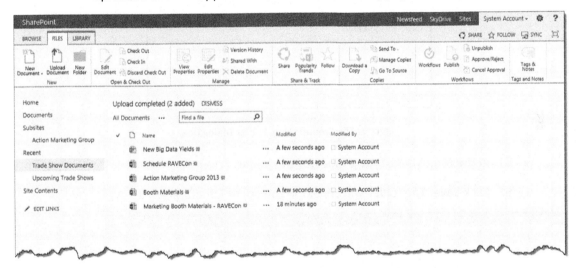

Figure 1: The New Uploaded Documents on the Document Library Page

Task: Create a New Folder in a Library App

Purpose: Nearly everyone is used to using folders on their computer to organize files. SharePoint document libraries allow you to use nested folders to organize files.

Example: The marketing team would like to have its documents organized separately from the general trade show documents. Creating a folder is the most familiar solution. For the best solution, see the decision tree for "folders or metadata".

Steps:

1. Start Internet Explorer and type the URL for your organization's SharePoint server. The Start page will open.

2. Navigate to the library where you want to add a folder. The document library page will open.

3. On the ribbon click the **Files** tab. The Files ribbon will appear.

4. Click the **New Folder** button. The Create a new folder dialog box will open.

Figure 1: The Create a New Folder Dialog Box

5. In the Name field, type a label for the folder.

6. Click **Save**. The folder will appear in the document library.

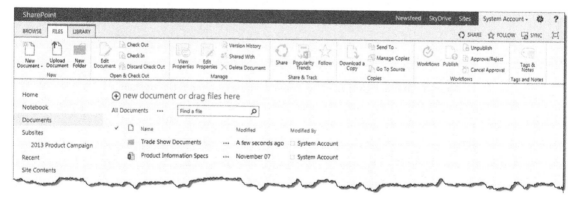

Figure 2: The New Folder on the Document Library Page

The SharePoint Shepherd's Guide for End Users: 2013

Task: Import a Spreadsheet to Create a List App

Purpose: List apps are essentially collections of data that SharePoint lets you publish for other users to see and change. In many organizations, such collections of data already exist in the form of Excel spreadsheets. Rather than retyping all of the data into SharePoint, you can quickly import an Excel spreadsheet and create a list from it.

Example: The Action Marketing Group has a list of VIP customers that they want to import into SharePoint.

Steps:

1. Start Internet Explorer and type the URL for your organization's SharePoint server. The Start page will open. If you want your new site located as a subsite of another site, navigate to that site.

2. Click the **Settings** menu gear icon. The Settings menu will appear.

3. Click **Add an App**. The Your Apps page will appear.

4. Scroll down and click the **Import Spreadsheet** app (you may have to click on the next app page to view this app). The Site Contents - New page will open.

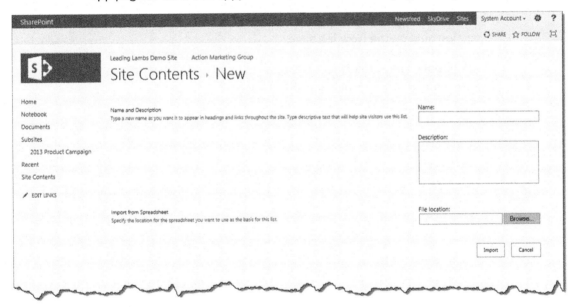

Figure 1: Site Contents - New Page for Importing Spreadsheets

5. In the Name field, enter a title for the new list. This will be the title of the list shown in any of the Site Content pages.

6. In the Description field, enter any notes about the new list. This should be a good description of what the list contains.

7. In the **Import from Spreadsheet** section, click **Browse**. The Choose File to Upload dialog box will appear.

Figure 2: The Choose File to Upload Dialog Box

8. Click the spreadsheet to import, then click **Open**. The Choose File to Upload dialog box will close and the file name and path for the spreadsheet will appear in the File Location field on the New list page.

9. Click **Import**. The spreadsheet will open in Excel and the Import to Windows SharePoint Services list dialog box will appear.

Figure 3: The Import to Windows SharePoint Services List Dialog Box

10. Excel spreadsheets can often contain specific table ranges or named ranges. If you have a table range or named range within Excel that you want to import, choose the appropriate option in the Range Type field and the desired range in the Select Range field.

11. If there is no range of cells within Excel that have been set as a named range or table that you want to import, select Range of Cells in the Range Type field and click the ⬛ control in the Select Range field. Use the mouse cursor to highlight the appropriate range on the spreadsheet and press Enter. Alternatively, enter the cell range in the Select Range field.

Figure 4: The Configured Range of Cells Range Type in the Import Dialog Box

12. Click **Import**. The Import to Windows SharePoint Services list dialog box will close and the new list with the imported data will appear.

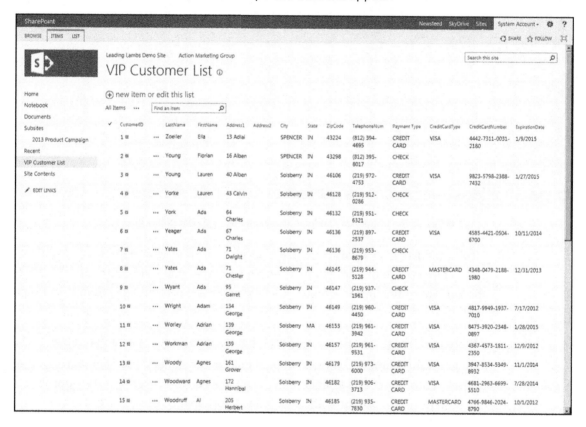

Figure 5: The New Imported List

The SharePoint Shepherd's Guide for End Users: 2013

Task: Create a New Item for a List App

Purpose: Data entry into SharePoint is quick and easy. SharePoint creates a dialog that matches the fields in your list. Entering data one item at a time can be a good way to process individual transactions.

Example: A few of the Action Marketing Group VIP customers were missed when the list was created, they need to add them to the VIP Customers List.

Steps:

1. Start Internet Explorer and type the URL for your organization's SharePoint server. The Start page will open.

2. Navigate to the list to which you want to add an item. The list page will open.

3. Click the **new item** link. The New Item page will open.

   Note: The New Item page is tailored automatically by SharePoint to match the list. Your view may be slightly different.

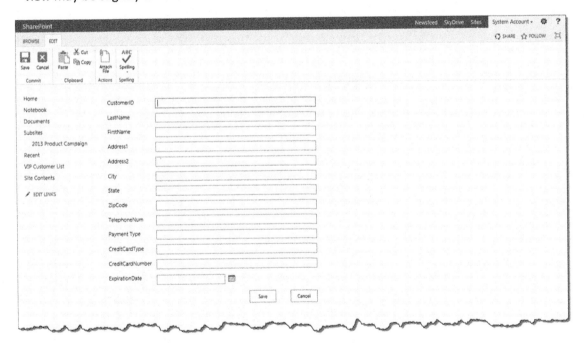

Figure 1: The New Item Page

4. Enter the information for the new item in the required fields (and enter information for any additional fields that may be listed).

5. Click **Save**. The item will be added to the list.

Task: Add New List or Library App Columns

Purpose: In any list or library app that you create, you can customize the columns that you want to use. This provides additional places to enter data about each item or file.

Example: The Action Marketing Group wants to capture the last contact date for their VIP customers in a new column.

Steps:

1. Start Internet Explorer and type the URL for your organization's SharePoint server. The Start page will open.

2. Navigate to the list you want to modify. The list page will open.

3. Click the **List** tab. The List ribbon will open.

Figure 1: The List Tools Ribbon

4. Click **Create Column**. The Create Column dialog box will open.

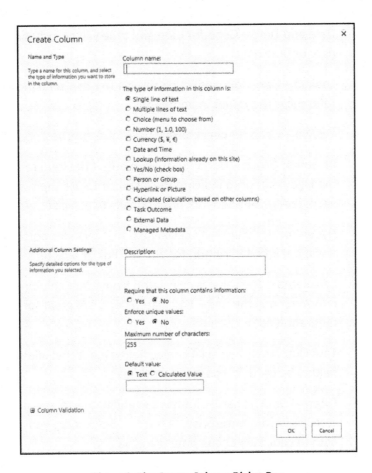

Figure 2: The Create Column Dialog Box

5. In the Column name field, enter a name for the new column.

6. Specify the type of information that will be contained in the list column. The options are:

  - Single Line of text – Good for short descriptions, titles, and information of less than 255 characters.

  - Multiple lines of text – Good for notes, comments, and other places where there may be a great deal of text to be entered.

  - Choice – Good for single-level predefined values including statuses, states, and conditions. Great for grouping.

  - Number – Good for numeric data including counts and values. Great when you'll need to sort the data numerically. Supports minimum and maximum values as well as integers and floating point numbers.

  - Currency – Good for currency values. Defaults the formatting to look good for your country's currency.

- Date and Time – Good for date and time values including values that are date or time only.

- Lookup – Good for connecting this list to other data in SharePoint. This references the values in another list.

- Yes/No – Good for checkboxes, true/false, and yes/no type data.

- Person or Group – Good for assignment of the item to a person or group for management, or to indicate the last user to use the system. Will be validated to your network or optionally to a specific group of people.

- Hyperlink or Picture – A special field that includes both the hyperlink (location) and description for either a link or a picture.

- Calculated – The value is calculated from other columns and static information in the item. Calculated fields are great for transforming different fields.

- Task Outcome – A special choice field variant that allows the results of the field to be used as a part of a workflow.

- External Data – SharePoint has the ability to access data stored in other systems in your enterprise. If this has been setup you can connect your list data to your master customer list, you

- Managed Metadata – A hierarchical collection

7. In the Description field, add notes for the column. This will appear in the New and Edit Item pages to tell users what information is needed.

8. Specify if the column is required to contain information. If it is required, the field will be denoted as such in the New and Edit Item pages.

9. Depending on the type of information selected in Step 6 above, additional settings may be needed. Set them as desired.

10. Click **OK**. The column will be added to the list.

Figure 3: The New Column Added to the List Page

Task: Edit Existing List or Library App Columns

Purpose: Sometimes when you setup a column in a list you don't get all the settings right. Perhaps it's needing to add an additional option to a choice field or editing the limits for a number. SharePoint allows you to adjust field settings after they have been created.

Example: When the Action Marketing Group imported the VIP Customer List some of the column names in the spreadsheet were cryptic. They need adjusted to be friendlier.

Steps:

1. Start Internet Explorer and type the URL for your organization's SharePoint server. The Start page will open.

2. Navigate to the list you want to edit. The list page will open.

3. In the ribbon, click the **List** tab. The List ribbon will open.

4. Click the **List Settings** button. The list's Settings page will open.

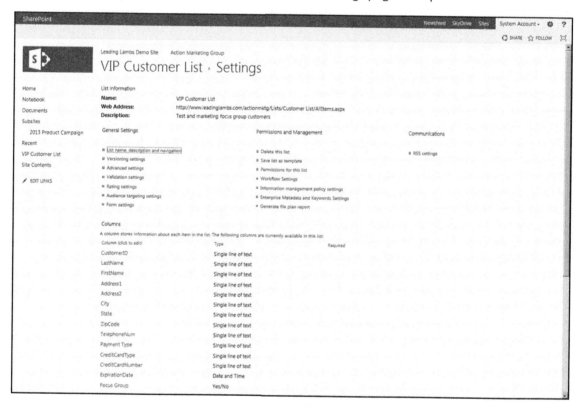

Figure 1: The List's Settings Page

5. In the **Columns** section, click on the name of the column you want to edit. The Change Column page will open.

The SharePoint Shepherd's Guide for End Users: 2013

Note: The Change Column page will vary, depending on what column/field you are trying to edit. You may also note that, depending on the column selected, your editing choices might be rather limited. Some columns cannot even be renamed.

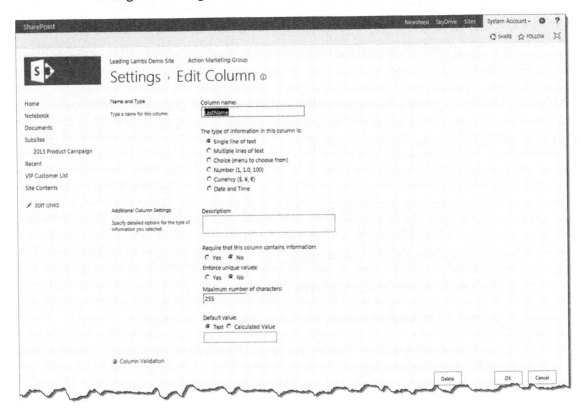

Figure 2: The Change Column Page

6. Enter or add the information you want to change about the column in the appropriate field.

7. Click **OK**. The List Settings page will open again, with the changes indicated in the **Columns** section.

Task: Delete List or Library App Columns

Purpose: If a column in your list proves to be unnecessary, you can remove it from the list altogether. An important thing to note, however, is that you can only remove certain columns. Some columns, including the default columns used by SharePoint, such as "Title," "Created By," "Modified By," and "Modified" are special fields that cannot be removed. Columns that users have added can always be removed.

Example: Initially the Action Marketing Group wanted to track product payment information for its VIP Customers, but after being warned of the potential for this information being misused, they have decided to remove the information from the VIP Customer list.

Steps:

1. Start Internet Explorer and type the URL for your organization's SharePoint server. The Start page will open.

2. Navigate to the list you want to edit. The List page will open.

3. In the ribbon click the **List** tab. The List ribbon will open.

4. Click the **List Settings** button. The List Settings page will open.

5. In the **Columns** section, click on the name of the column you want to remove. The Edit Column page will open.

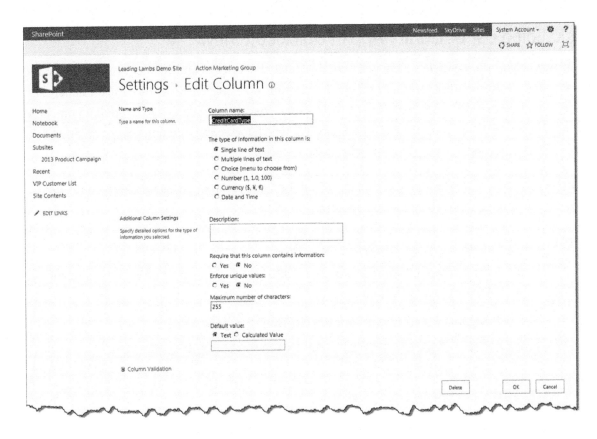

Figure 1: The Edit Column Page with Delete Button

6. Near the bottom of the page, click **Delete**. A confirmation dialog box will open.

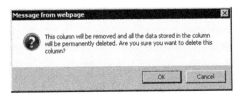

Figure 2: The Delete Column Confirmation Dialog Box

7. Click **OK**. The List Settings page will open again, with the column removed from the **Columns** section.

Task: Edit a List or Library App in Quick Edit View

Purpose: As you work with lists, you will note a distinct similarity to another collection of data: the spreadsheet. This is made even clearer if you have imported a spreadsheet from Excel to SharePoint. But editing information in a SharePoint list can be time consuming if you have to open up one item at a time. Fortunately, you can shift to Quick Edit view, which looks and functions very similarly to a spreadsheet, allowing you to edit a lot of list data at once.

Example: When Action Marketing Group imported the VIP Customer List, some of the data was not accurate. This data needs to be quickly updated.

Steps:

1. Start Internet Explorer and type the URL for your organization's SharePoint server. The Start page will open.

2. Navigate to the list you want to edit. The list page will open.

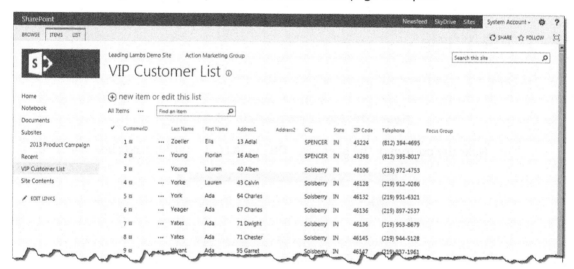

Figure 1: A List in Standard View

3. In the ribbon click the **List** tab. The List ribbon will open.

4. Click the **Quick Edit** button. The list will now appear in the Quick Edit view.

Note: Quick Edit View will work in any web browser that fully supports HTML5 including Internet Explorer 10 and current versions of Chrome and Firefox. Quick Edit will work in Internet Explorer 9 if Microsoft Office is installed.

The SharePoint Shepherd's Guide for End Users: 2013

Figure 2: A List in Quick Edit View

5. Click a cell you want to edit to select the cell and make any changes that are needed.

6. Repeat step 5 to edit other cells as needed.

7. Click the **Stop** editing this list link or click the **View** button. The list will change back to the Standard view.

Task: View List or Library Item Properties

Purpose: Views of a list or library are limited in how much information can be reasonably displayed for each item. It is sometimes necessary to be able to look in detail at all of the information for items. SharePoint allows you to quickly view all of the properties of an item.

Example: One of the Action Marketing Group's sales representatives is going to make a call to a VIP customer and needs to review the notes prior to speaking with them.

Steps:

1. Start Internet Explorer and type the URL for your organization's SharePoint server. The Start page will open.

2. Navigate to the list in which you are interested. The list page will open.

3. In the ribbon click the **Items** tab. The Items ribbon will open. (If you're working in a library this tab is named **Files**.)

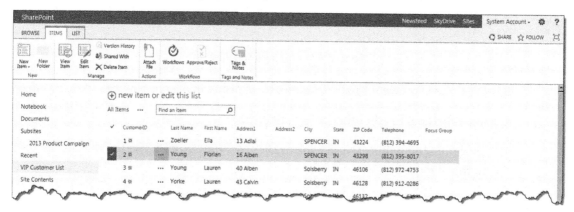

Figure 1: The Items Ribbon

4. Select a list item or file, then click the **View Item** button. The item's properties page will open if the list properties allow it. (In a library this button is called **View Properties**.)

The SharePoint Shepherd's Guide for End Users: 2013

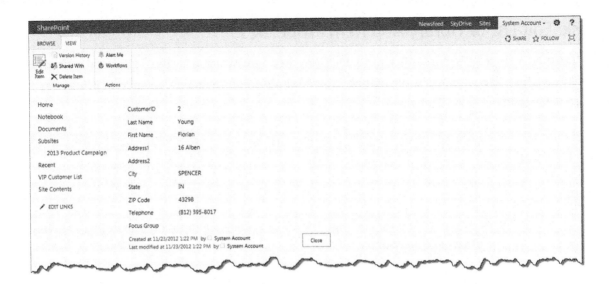

Figure 2: An Item's Properties Page

5. Click **Close** when finished. The list page will appear.

Task: Edit List or Library App Item Properties

Purpose: Sometimes it's more efficient to edit items in a view which provides better editing controls, descriptive text, and warnings while editing. SharePoint's edit form allows you to edit properties more richly than the Quick Edit view.

Example: The Action Marketing Group's VIP customer list has a customer with a bad address which needs corrected.

Steps:

1. Start Internet Explorer and type the URL for your organization's SharePoint server. The Start page will open.

2. Navigate to the list in which you are interested. The list page will open.

3. Click the **Items** tab. The Items ribbon will open.

4. Select a list item, then click the **Edit Item** button. The Edit Item page will open.

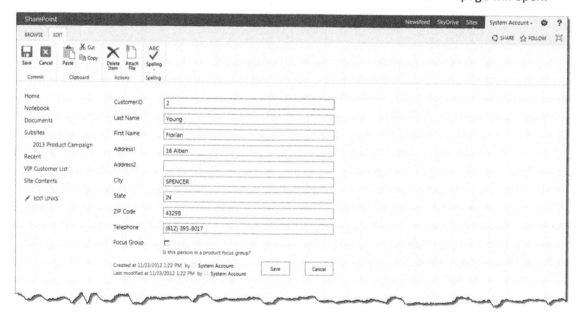

Figure 1: The Edit Item Page

Note: The Edit Item page may look different depending on the columns your list contains and the list settings.

5. Make the changes you want and click **Save**. The list page will appear with the updated item information.

The SharePoint Shepherd's Guide for End Users: 2013

Task: Manage List or Library App Item Permissions

Purpose: For the most part permissions are set at a site, library or folder level. However, some documents may need different permissions. SharePoint allows you to set the permissions of an item individually when necessary.

Example: The Action Marketing Group needs to limit the people who can modify the strategic plan.

Steps:

1. Start Internet Explorer and type the URL for your organization's SharePoint server. The Start page will open.

2. Navigate to the list in which you are interested. The list page will open.

3. Click the ellipsis control for the item you want to change permissions and click the Shared With option. The Shared With dialog box will open.

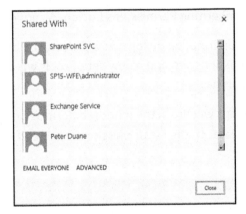

Figure 1: The Shared With Dialog Box

4. Click the **Advanced** button. The Permissions page will open.

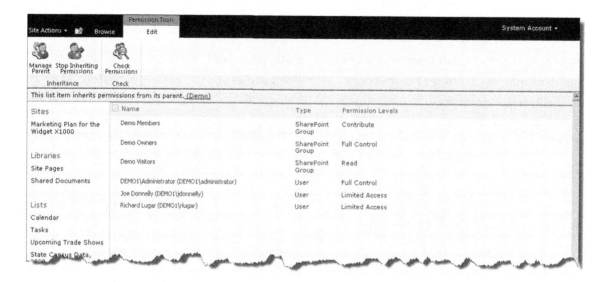

Figure 2: The Permissions Page

5. Click the **Stop Inheriting Permissions** button. A confirmation dialog box will appear.

6. Click **OK**. The confirmation dialog box will close, the document will no longer have the same permissions set, and a new set of tools will appear in the ribbon on the Permission Tools page.

    Note: These steps will break the inherited permissions from the parent list and any changes made later to the list permissions may need to be repeated for individual items.

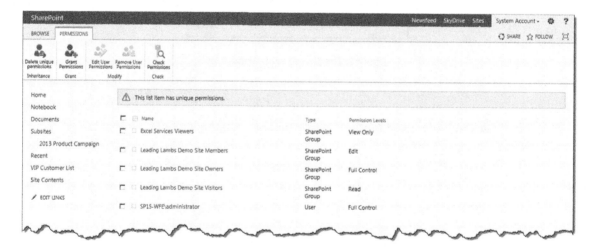

Figure 3: The Permissions Tools Page Without Permission Inheritance

7. Click the **Grant Permissions** button. The Share dialog box will open.

8. In the Invite people field, enter user names.

The SharePoint Shepherd's Guide for End Users: 2013

9. Click the **Show Options** link. The Select a permission level field will appear.

10. Select the permission level you wish to grant this set of users for this document.

11. Click **Share**. The Share dialog box will close and the users will now appear on the Permissions page. Repeat Steps 7-11 to grant different permission levels to additional users.

Task: Edit a Library App File

Purpose: Most Microsoft applications, and applications from many other vendors, can edit files directly from SharePoint. SharePoint launches the client application and the application saves the revised file back to SharePoint.

Example: The marketing manager needs to make a quick update to the Action Marketing Group plan in Word and save it back to the library.

Steps:

1. Start Internet Explorer and type the URL for your organization's SharePoint server. The Start page will open.

2. Navigate to the library app in which you are interested. The library page will open.

3. Click the ellipsis control for the item you want to view. The item's hover menu including a preview of the document will appear.

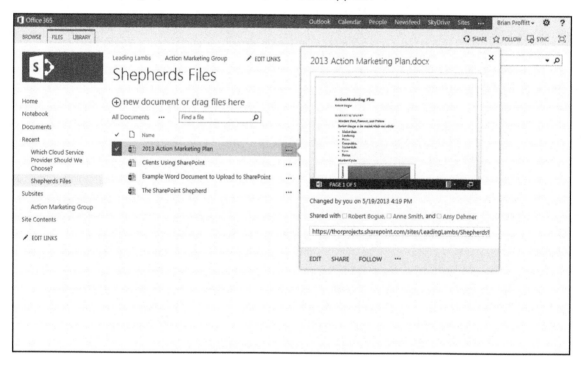

Figure 1: An Item's Open Menu

4. Click the **Edit** option. A login dialog box may appear.

    Note: You can also directly click the item to begin the editing process.

5. If prompted, login to the library item with the appropriate credentials. The document will be opened in the application.

Note: Some applications, particularly Office applications have a protected view that documents from untrusted sources open in. You may need to click the Enable Editing button.

6. When finished editing, click **Save** in the application and close it. All changes will be saved to the SharePoint document library.

Task: Download a Library App File

Purpose: Sometimes you will want to download a file rather than editing it directly from SharePoint. You might have an application that isn't directly compatible with SharePoint, you may want to bring a single file with you while you travel, or you may just need to grab a file to work on during the commute home. You may want to consider checking the file out if you suspect you and others may be modifying the file at the same time.

Example: The Action Marketing Group's trade show director is getting ready to get on a plane and needs to make sure that the Trade Show Manual document is correct.

Steps:

1. Start Internet Explorer and type the URL for your organization's SharePoint server. The Start page will open.

2. Navigate to the library in which you are interested. The library page will open.

3. Click the ellipsis control of the item you want to edit. The item's hover menu will appear.

4. At the bottom of the hover menu, click the ellipsis control and select the **Download a Copy** option. Your browser's download notification will appear.

5. Click the drop-down arrow next to the **Save** link and click **Save As**. The Save As dialog box will appear.

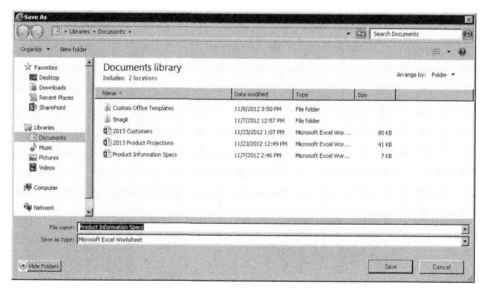

Figure 1: The Save As Dialog Box

6. Navigate to the location where you want to save the document and click **Save**. The file will be saved to the specified location. You've successfully downloaded the file.

7. When you're ready to work on the file, navigate to the specified location to edit and save changes to your copy of the file. When you have edited and saved the changes to your copy of the file, return to the document library in SharePoint.

8. In the ribbon click the **Files** tab. The Files ribbon will open.

9. Click the **Upload Document** button. The Add a Document dialog box will open.

Figure 2: The Add a Document Dialog Box

10. Click the **Browse** button. The Choose File to Upload dialog box will appear.

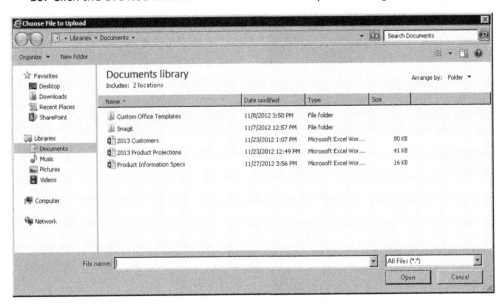

Figure 3: The Choose File to Upload Dialog Box

11. Select the local copy of the file and click **Open**. The file and its file path will appear in the Name field.

12. Verify that the Overwrite existing file checkbox is checked and click the OK button.

13. If a version dialog appears, add any notes about the document.

14. Click **OK**. The file will be uploaded and will appear in the library.

Task: Move a File to Another Library App

Purpose: Many times you will have a document that needs to be moved between library apps. You can use SharePoint 2013's drag-and-drop functionality to move a file to another library anywhere on your SharePoint site.

Example: The Action Marketing Group's trade show manager needs to move one of the trade show documents to the upcoming trade show documents because it was misfiled.

Steps:

1. Start Internet Explorer and type the URL for your organization's SharePoint server. The Start page will open.

2. Navigate to the target library where you want to move the document. The library page will open and the library will appear in the Quick Launch under the Recent section.

3. Click the **Settings** menu gear icon and click the **Site Contents** option. The Site Contents page will open.

4. Click the icon next to the library where the document you wish to move is located. The library page will open.

5. Click thecheck mark next to the item to select it.

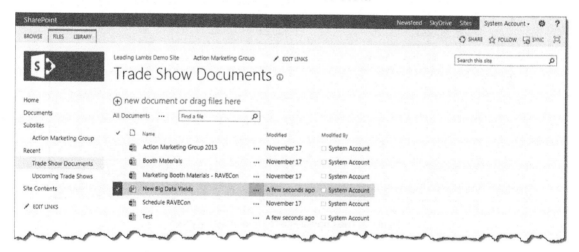

Figure 1: The Origin Library's Selected Item

6. Click and drag the item's link to the target library in the Quick Launch and release the mouse button. The file will appear in the destination library.

Note: If a circle with a slash appears, you will not be able to drag the file to the new library app. One of the most likely causes of this is that the site collection administrator has enabled the site collection feature Publishing Infrastructure which disables this functionality.

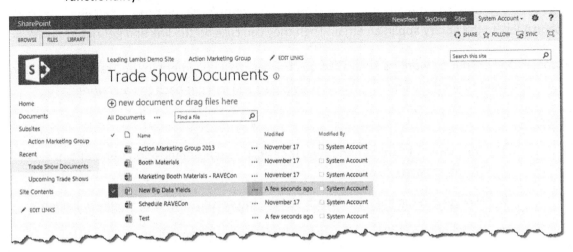

Figure 2: The Item in the Destination Library

Task: E-Mail a Link to a Library App

Purpose: If you want to get many users involved in the editing/creation process, an efficient way is to send a link to the library app in an email. Then they can click on the link and get right to work.

Example: One of your co-workers would like quick access to a document in the Trade Show Materials library. You want to send the link as quick as possible so you can get back to your work.

Steps:

1. Start Internet Explorer and type the URL for your organization's SharePoint server. The Start page will open.

2. Navigate to the library in which you are interested. The library page will open.

3. In the ribbon click the **Library** tab. The Library ribbon will open.

Figure 1: The Library Ribbon

4. Click the **Email a Link** button. An Outlook message window will appear.

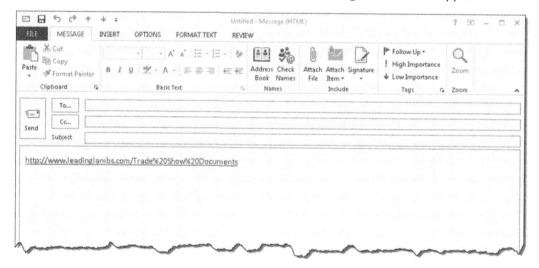

Figure 2: The Outlook Message Window with the Library Link

Note: If Microsoft Outlook is not your default email program, you will see a Compose Email window that contains a link to the document in the body of the email.

The SharePoint Shepherd's Guide for End Users: 2013

5. In the To field, type email address(es).

6. In the Subject field, enter a subject.

7. In the body of the email message, add a message.

8. Click **Send**. The message will be sent.

Task: Edit a List or Library App View

Purpose: Views are powerful in SharePoint. They allow you to have different ways to see the same information in a list or library differently. Editing views allows you to create views that match what you need to see and enables you to quickly find the right information.

Example: The Action Marketing Group's office manager does spot-checks for the number of files that have changed recently. The manager's existing view doesn't filter items that are more than a week old. She wants to modify the view to minimize the work she does checking files.

Steps:

1. Start Internet Explorer and type the URL for your organization's SharePoint server. The Start page will open.

2. Navigate to the library in which you are interested. The document library page will open.

3. In the ribbon click the **Library** tab. The Library ribbon will open.

4. Click the **Modify View** button. The Edit View page will open.

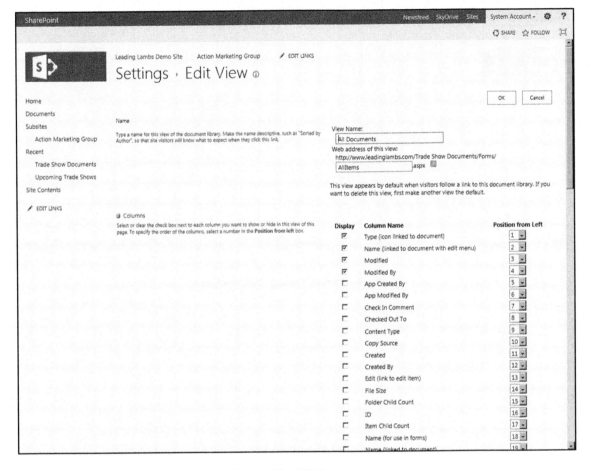

Figure 1: The Edit View Page

5. In the **Columns** section, click the Display checkbox for any fields you wish to be visible in the view.

6. To move a column's position, select a new **Position from Left** value for that column. The other values will adjust automatically.

7. In the **Sort** section, select the column by which you want to sort the items.

    Note: Some column names aren't really columns but are instead columns with additional formatting. This is important because you don't want Name of Event and Name of Event (Linked to Item) both to appear.

8. Click **OK**. The library app will open with the new view configuration.

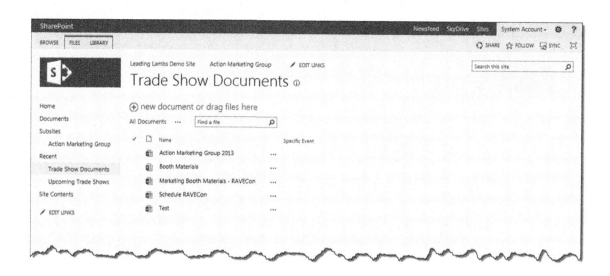

Figure 2: The New View of the Library App

Task: Add a List or Library App View

Purpose: SharePoint lists and document libraries start with an All Documents or All Items view. However, you can create many views allowing you to have different looks for the list or library based on the way that you need This task allows you to create your own custom views for the list or library.

Example: It is possible to create new list or library views, just the way you want them, rather than heavily modifying the default views.

Steps:

1. Start Internet Explorer and type the URL for your organization's SharePoint server. The Start page will open.

2. Click on the **Settings** menu gear icon and select the **Site Contents** option.

3. Click the library that you want to view. The document library page will open.

4. Click the **Library** tab. The Library ribbon will open.

5. Click the **Create View** button. The View Type page will open.

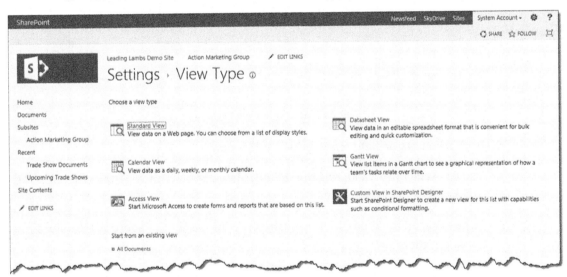

Figure 1: The View Type Page

Note: There are five view formats provided with SharePoint: the Standard, Calendar, Datasheet, Access database, and the Gantt project management view. A sixth option allows you to create a custom view in SharePoint Designer. For more information about views in SharePoint, see Appendix D, "Views."

6. Click a view format or existing view. The Create View page for that format will open.

Figure 2: The Create View Page

7. In the View Name field enter a title for the view.

8. You can select the **Make this the default view** option. This will make this view the opening view for this library.

9. Depending on the type of view you are creating, select the appropriate values to configure the view.

10. Click **OK**. The library or list will be displayed in the new view.

The SharePoint Shepherd's Guide for End Users: 2013

Task: Export a List or Library App to a Spreadsheet

Purpose: The columns that you enter data in for both lists and libraries resembles the information you would keep in a spreadsheet. While SharePoint views are powerful, they don't allow you the same level of flexibility that having an Excel Spreadsheet does. SharePoint allows you to export both list and library App views to an Excel Spreadsheet.

Example: The Action Marketing group wanted to review the documents in the library to evaluate when they were last updated for employee productivity. To do that exporting the library to Excel and working with the information in Excel seemed best.

Steps:

1. Start Internet Explorer and type the URL for your organization's SharePoint server. The Start page will open.

2. Navigate to the library you want to edit. The document library page will open.

3. In the ribbon click the **Library** tab. The Library ribbon will open.

4. Click the **Export to Excel** button. One or more security warnings may appear, depending on your personal computer's settings, as well as a login dialog box. If you accept these warnings, the file will be downloaded to your local machine and opened in an Excel workbook as a worksheet.

   Note: Changes made in the exported spreadsheet file will not be reflected in the library.

Figure 1: The Exported Spreadsheet

Task: Delete a Library App File

Purpose: If you need to remove an item from a library, it's a quick operation. And if you mistakenly delete a library item, it will be placed in the site's Recycle Bin, ready to be recovered. For more information, see the task "Recover Items from the Recycle Bin."

Example: The administrator for the Action Marketing Group accidentally uploaded a document which contained salary information to a publicly accessible library, it needs to be deleted.

Steps:

1. Start Internet Explorer and type the URL for your organization's SharePoint server. The Start page will open.

2. Navigate to the library in which you are interested. The library app will open.

3. In the ribbon click the **Files** tab. The Files ribbon will open.

4. Click an item's checkbox to select a library item, then click the **Delete Document** button. A confirmation dialog box will open.

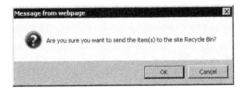

Figure 1: The Delete Document Confirmation Dialog Box

5. Click **OK**. The item will be removed from the library.

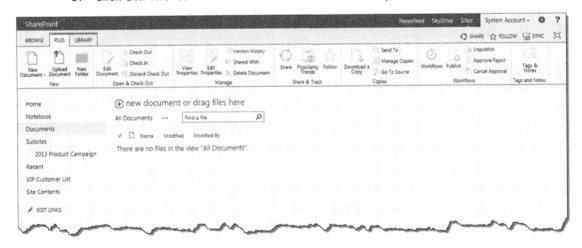

Figure 2: The Item is removed from the Document App

Task: Recover a List or Library Item from the Recycle Bin

Purpose: Sometimes files are accidentally deleted. On your computer you have a recycle bin so that you can recover an accidentally deleted file. SharePoint has a recycle bin as well to allow you to recover accidentally deleted files. Unlike your computer's recycle bin, the SharePoint recycle bin is automatically emptied of files and items. Typically this is every 30 days but the specific time can be changed by the administrator.

Example: The only copy of the trade show manual was mistakenly deleted from the library app, and must be recovered.

Steps:

1. Start Internet Explorer and type the URL for your organization's SharePoint server. The Start page will open.

2. Navigate to the site from which you want to recover an item from the Recycle Bin. The site's home page will open.

3. Click the **Settings** menu gear icon. The Settings menu will appear.

4. Click the **Site Contents** option. The Site Contents page will open.

5. Click the **Recycle Bin** link near the top right of the page. The Recycle Bin page will open.

   Note: The Recycle Bin only displays the removed content for the site where it's located. So, you need to navigate to that site first to see the correct set of removed files.

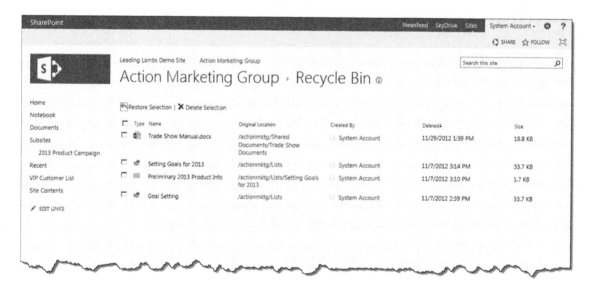

Figure 1 The Recycle Bin Page

The SharePoint Shepherd's Guide for End Users: 2013

6. Click the check boxes next to the items you want to restore to your site. The items are selected.

7. Click **Restore Selection**. A confirmation dialog box will open.

Figure 2: The Restore Selection Confirmation Dialog Box

8. Click **OK**. The selected items will be removed from the Recycle Bin and put back in their original location in the site.

Task: Edit List or Library App Content Types

Purpose: SharePoint allows you to have multiple content types in a single list or library app. A content type defines the columns that will be entered, templates, and rules for how the item will be processed. By adding multiple content types to a list or library you can encourage users to enter the right data for the right needs.

Example: The Action Marketing Group team wants to track contracts and proposals in the same library and will use content types to do this so that the right templates are used for each type of document.

Steps:

1. Start Internet Explorer and type the URL for your organization's SharePoint server. The Start page will open.

2. Navigate to the library in which you are interested. The library app will open.

3. In the ribbon click the **Library** tab. The Library ribbon will open. (For Lists this tab will be named **List**.)

4. In the ribbon click the **Library Settings** button. The Settings page will open. (For lists this button will be named **List Settings**.)

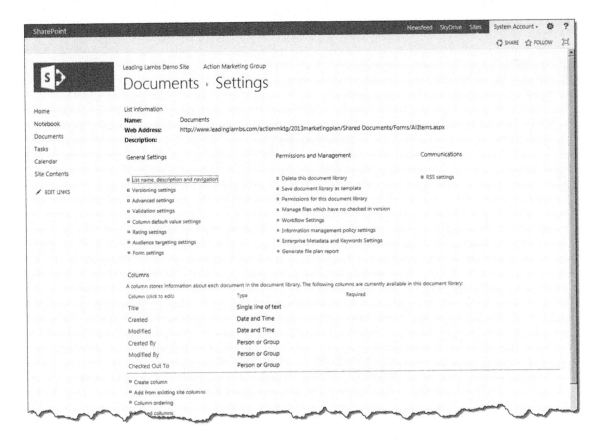

Figure 1: The Library Settings Page

5. In the General Settings section, click **Advanced Settings**. The Advanced Settings page will open.

6. In the Content Types section, click **Yes** to allow multiple content types.

7. Click **OK**. The Settings page will reopen.

8. In the **Content Types** section, click the **Add from Existing Content Types** link. The Select Content Types page will open.

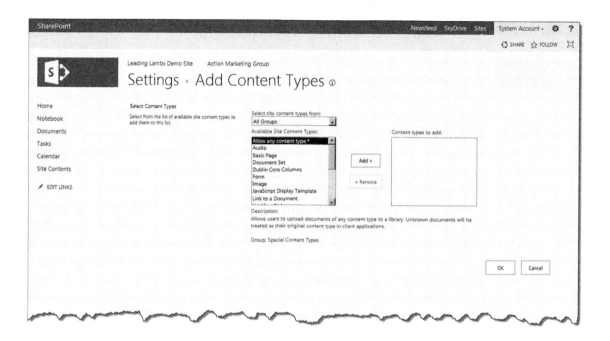

Figure 2: The Add Content Types Page

9. Select the content types you want to use, then click **Add**.

10. When complete, click **OK**. You will be returned to the settings page and the content types will be added to the **New** button for the list or library.

Use Outlook for Sharing

SharePoint is very tightly integrated to the Microsoft Office applications, including Microsoft Outlook, which allows for much more efficient communication of SharePoint-hosted information. SharePoint will allow you to connect its document libraries, tasks lists, and calendars directly to Outlook 2013 or 2010.

In this section, you'll learn how to:

- **Connect a SharePoint Library to Outlook**: The basics of connecting from SharePoint to Outlook.

- **Connect SharePoint Contacts to Outlook**: SharePoint allows you to connect contact list Apps to Outlook so you can view and modify SharePoint contacts via Outlook.

- **Share SharePoint Content with Outlook**: After an app is connected to Outlook, you can use Outlook to quickly share the contents of that resource with other users.

- **Edit a SharePoint Calendar in Outlook**: Editing SharePoint calendar entries in Outlook makes it easier to edit and consider team member schedules.

- **Connect a SharePoint Calendar with Outlook**: Shared calendars in SharePoint allow you to post dates, connect users to key information on a timeline, and allow them to work better together.

- **Connect to SharePoint from a Sharing Message in Outlook**: Once an app has been shared via an Outlook message, the recipients can quickly connect when they open that message.

- **Edit Library App Files in Outlook**: After you have connected to a document app in Outlook, you can access and edit the files in the library directly from Outlook, without connecting to the SharePoint server.

- **Remove a Connected Document from Outlook**: There may be instances where you won't need a copy of every document or file in the app. Here's how to remove offline copies of documents from Outlook 2010.

- **Remove a Library App from Outlook**: Once you no longer need a connection to a SharePoint resource, you can remove it from Outlook 2010 or 2007 with ease.

Task: Connect a SharePoint Library to Outlook

Purpose: Sometimes you travel and need to synchronize files that don't change very often or aren't a part of your core job. Other times you want to be able to see SharePoint files from inside Outlook. SharePoint allows you to connect libraries to Outlook and take files offline for editing.

Example: The Action Marketing Group's trade show team is going out to an offsite meeting in the woods where there will not be any Internet connectivity. They decide to bring a copy of the latest trade show manual with them via Outlook.

Steps:

1. Start Internet Explorer and type the URL for your organization's SharePoint server. The Start page will open.

2. Navigate to the resource you want to connect to Outlook. The resource's page (in this case, a document library) will open.

3. In the ribbon click the **Library** tab. The Library ribbon will appear.

4. Click the **Connect to Outlook** button. A confirmation dialog box will open.

   Note: In order to connect to Outlook, you may need to setup the web site in the Intranet zone within Internet Explorer.

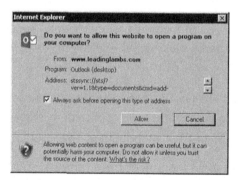

Figure 1: The Connect to Outlook Confirmation Dialog Box

5. Click **Allow**. Outlook will open and a Connect to Outlook dialog box will appear.

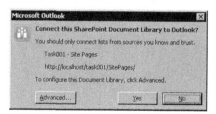

Figure 2: The Connect to Outlook Dialog Box

The SharePoint Shepherd's Guide for End Users: 2013

6. Click **Yes**. The library will appear in the SharePoint Lists section of the Outlook folder pane.

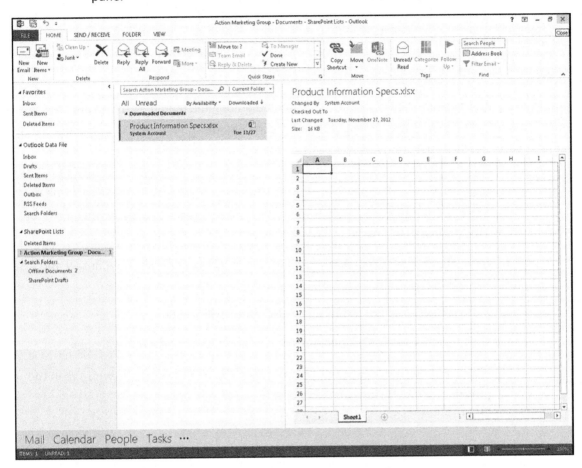

Figure 3: The Connected Document Library in Outlook

Task: Connect SharePoint Contacts to Outlook

Purpose: Keeping libraries of contacts makes them available for multiple users where having each user maintaining their own contacts would be inefficient. However, users are more comfortable using Outlook to manage contacts. SharePoint allows you to connect contact list Apps to Outlook so you can view and modify SharePoint contacts via Outlook.

Example: You want to share vendor contact information among the members of the purchasing team. The purchasing team spends most of their time in Outlook and wants to access those vendor contact records in SharePoint.

Steps:

1. Start Internet Explorer and type the URL for your organization's SharePoint server. The Start page will open.

2. Navigate to the Contact app you want to connect to Outlook. The Contact app's page will open.

3. In the ribbon click the **List** tab. The List ribbon will appear.

4. Click the **Connect to Outlook** button. A confirmation dialog box will open.

   Note: In order to connect to Outlook, you may need to setup the web site in the Intranet zone within Internet Explorer.

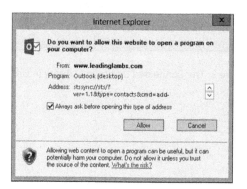

Figure 1: The Connect to Outlook Confirmation Dialog Box

5. Click **Allow**. Outlook will open (you may have to login first) and a Connect to Outlook dialog box will appear.

Figure 2: The Connect to Outlook Dialog Box

6. Click **Yes**. The list will appear in the Other Contacts section of the Outlook folder pane.

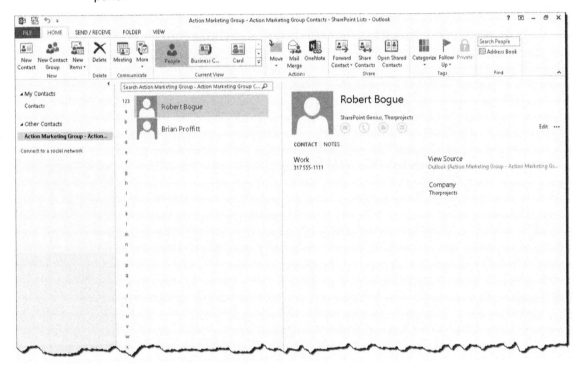

Figure 3: The Connected Contact List in Outlook

Task: Share Connected SharePoint Content with Outlook

Purpose: After a library or other SharePoint resource is connected to Outlook, you can use Outlook to quickly share the contents of that resource with other users. This is done by sending a message containing a special link that will automatically connect other users' Outlook installations to the SharePoint server.

Example: The Action Marketing Group wants to get the word out to employees about their Marketing library, and using Outlook to e-mail a link to the folder is the fastest way.

Steps:

1. In Outlook, navigate to the Mail screen.

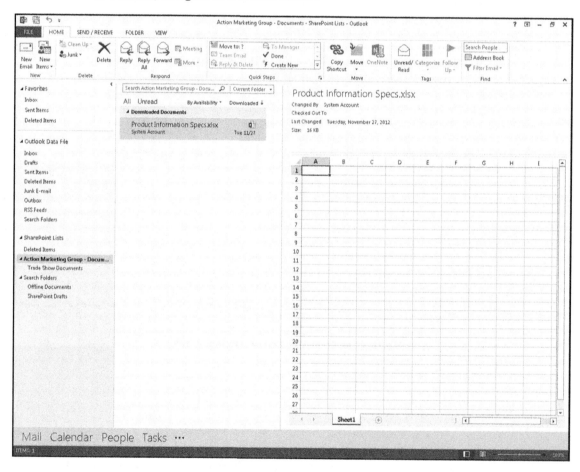

Figure 1: SharePoint Content in Outlook

2. Right-click the folder for the SharePoint resource you want to share. The context menu will appear.

The SharePoint Shepherd's Guide for End Users: 2013

3. Select the **Share** menu, then **Share this Folder**. A message window will open with a predetermined subject detailing the contents of the library.

4. In the To field, enter an email address.

5. Click **Send**. The message will be sent.

Task: Edit a SharePoint Calendar in Outlook

Purpose: SharePoint calendars are a great way to centralize events but often scheduling group events needs to take into account user's personal schedules. Editing SharePoint calendar entries in Outlook makes it easier to edit and consider team member schedules.

Example: Action Marketing Group wants to schedule a team recognition lunch and will review personal calendars before deciding on a time.

Steps:

1. Navigate to the Calendar pane in Outlook. The Calendar page will appear.

2. Click SharePoint Calendar check box to select it. The calendar will open.

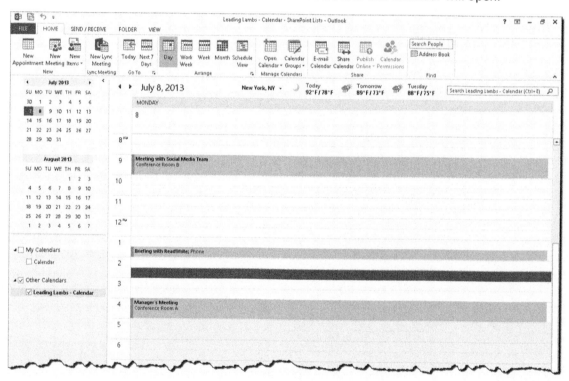

Figure 1: The Remote Calendar in Outlook

3. Click the **New Appointment** button. The Untitled Appointment dialog box will open.

Figure 2: The Appointment Dialog Box.

4. Fill in the fields and click **Save & Close**. The event changes will appear on the SharePoint calendar.

Task: Connect a SharePoint Calendar with Outlook

Purpose: Shared calendars in SharePoint allow you to post dates, connect users to key information on a timeline, and allow them to work better together. However, working with a calendar in SharePoint isn't as easy or as flexible as working on the calendar in Outlook. SharePoint allows you to connect a calendar so that you can view and edit it in Outlook.

Example: The Action Marketing Group manager wants to see the milestone calendar in Outlook so she can review it while approving vacation requests.

Steps:

1. Start Internet Explorer and type the URL for your organization's SharePoint server. The Start Page will open.

2. Navigate to the Calendar you want to connect to Outlook. The Calendar page will open.

3. In the ribbon click the **Calendar** tab. The Calendar ribbon will appear.

4. Click the **Connect to Outlook** button. A confirmation dialog box will open.

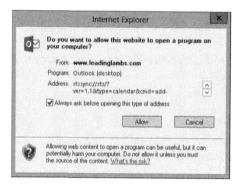

Figure 1: The Connection Confirmation Dialog Box

5. Click **Allow**. A confirmation dialog box will appear.

Figure 2: The Connect to Outlook Confirmation Dialog Box

Note: Clicking the Advanced button will display the SharePoint List Options dialog box, which will allow you to add more descriptive information, if needed.

6. Click **Yes**. The calendar will appear in the Calendar pane of Outlook.

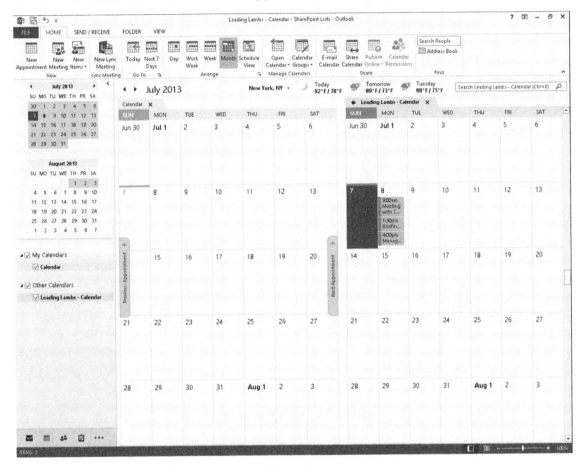

Figure 3: The Connected Calendar in Outlook

7. If you want to see both calendars at once to check for conflicts, right-click the SharePoint calendar's tab and select the **Overlay** option. The calendars will be merged.

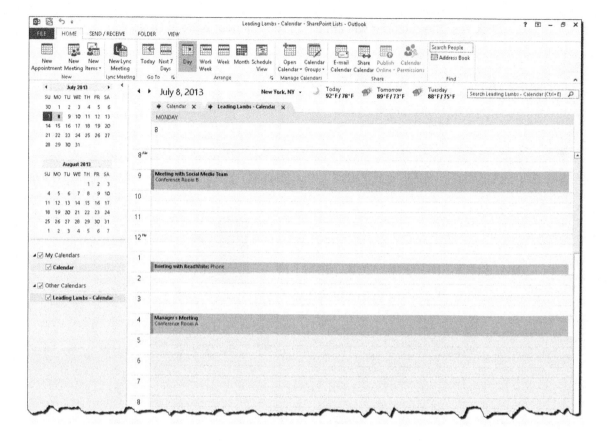

Figure 4: The View in Overlay Mode

8. To return to the default view, right-click either of calendar tabs and de-select the **Overlay** option. The calendars will be separated.

9. To view just the SharePoint calendar, under the My Calendars heading, click the **Calendars** check box. The local calendar will close.

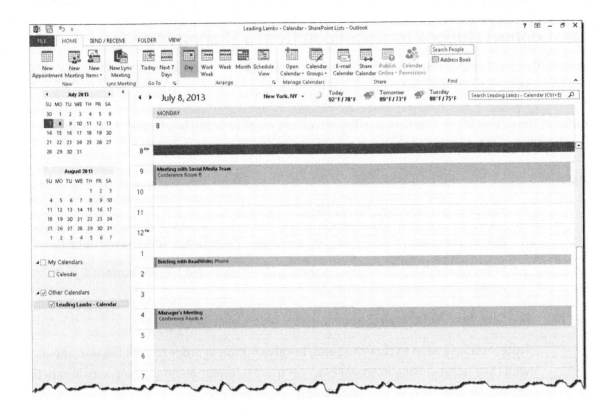

Figure 5: The Remote Calendar

Task: Connect Outlook to SharePoint from a Sharing Message

Purpose: Once a library or other SharePoint resource has been shared via an Outlook message, the recipients can quickly connect when they open that message.

Example: The Action Marketing Group has received the email with the link to the Trade Show Materials library and now need to open it.

Steps:

1. In Outlook, navigate to the Inbox.

2. In the Inbox pane, double-click the message. The message window will appear.

3. In the **Share** ribbon, click the **Connect to this Document Library** button. A confirmation dialog box will open.

4. Click **Yes**. The library will appear in the folders pane of Outlook.

Note: You may need to click the **Send/Receive** button in order to sync the documents with their latest version in SharePoint. For more information on working with library filed in Outlook, see the task"Edit Library App Files in Outlook."

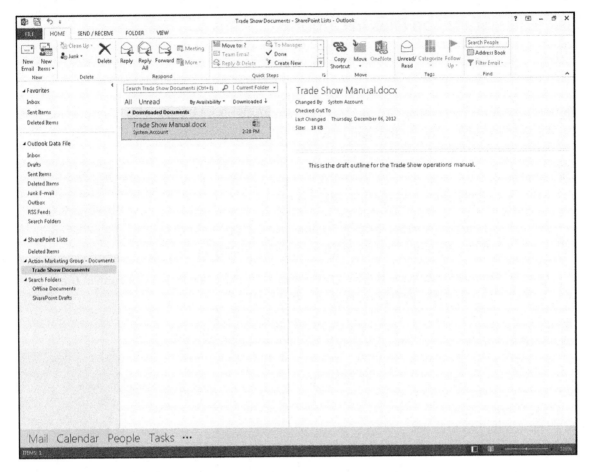

Figure 1: The Connected Library in Outlook

Task: Edit Library App Files in Outlook

Purpose: After you have connected to a document library in Outlook, you can access and edit the files in the library directly from Outlook, without connecting to the SharePoint server.

Example: The Action Marketing Groups' trade show manager is on the plane to the show and needs to add a few new procedures to the manual which she has synchronized to Outlook.

Steps:

1. In Outlook, navigate to the Mail column.

2. Under the SharePoint Lists heading, click the document library folder. The contents of the document library will appear in the library's pane.

3. In the library pane double-click a document. The document will open in the appropriate application in read-only form.

Figure 1: The Document is Still in Read-Only Form

4. Just above the document, click the **Edit Offline** button. The Edit Offline dialog box will open.

Figure 2: The Edit Offline Dialog Box

5. Click **OK**. The Edit Offline dialog box will close and the document will be stored in the SharePoint Drafts folder and can now be edited.

6. Edit and save the document.

7. Close the document. You will be required to log into the SharePoint library app and the Edit Offline dialog box will appear again if you are online.

Figure 3: The Edit Offline Dialog Box

8. Click **Update**. The Edit Offline dialog box will close and the changes will be saved to the SharePoint document and reflected in the Outlook connection. If Outlook is offline, then any changes made to the document will be communicated back to the SharePoint library when Outlook is online again or by clicking Send/Receive button.

Task: Remove a Connected Document from Outlook

Purpose: When you connect to a SharePoint library app, you get the whole contents of the library. There may be instances where you won't need a copy of every document or file in the library.

Example: Here's how to remove offline copies from Outlook. Note that this does not remove the original copy of the document from the SharePoint server.

Steps:

1. In Outlook, navigate to the Mail column.

2. Click the document library folder. The contents of the document library will appear in the library's pane.

3. In the library pane right click a document. The context menu will appear.

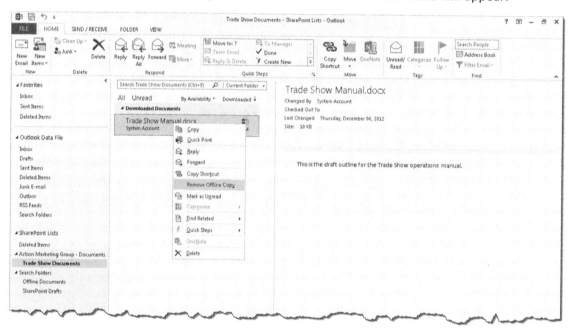

Figure 1: The Context Menu in the Library Pane

4. Select **Remove Offline Copy**. The document will now appear in the **Available for Download** section of the library pane.

   Note: There may be other additional documents in the Available for Download section since the last time you connected to the library.

The SharePoint Shepherd's Guide for End Users: 2013

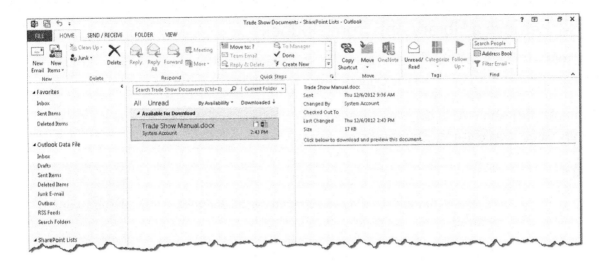

Figure 2: The Library Pane in Outlook

Task: Remove a Library App from Outlook

Purpose: Once you no longer need a connection to a SharePoint app, you can remove it from Outlook with ease. This disconnects Outlook from SharePoint for the specified app.

Example: The Action Marketing Group coordinator no longer needs a connection to the Trade Show library and will remove it.

Steps:

1. In Outlook, navigate to the pane containing the SharePoint resource you want to remove.

2. Right click the name of the resource. The context menu will appear.

Figure 1: The Context Menu in Outlook

3. Select the **Delete Folder** option. A confirmation dialog box will open.

Figure 2: The Delete Confirmation Dialog Box

4. Click **Yes**. The resource will be removed from Outlook. It will still exist on the SharePoint server, but as a user, you will not be able to connect to the resource through Outlook until you create the link again.

Conduct Surveys

When you need to quickly gather data or opinions from a group, a fast way to accomplish this is to use a SharePoint survey. Surveys, which are specialized SharePoint tracking lists, are easy to make, easy to distribute, and easy to read.

In this section, you'll learn how to:

- **Create a Survey**: The basics of creating a survey.

- **Preview Your Survey**: Once a survey is created, testing it is a good idea.

- **Enable Survey Branching**: Branching is used when a user's answer to a survey question will influence which questions are asked later in the survey. Branching is a vital component of effective survey design.

- **Send a Survey Link**: Like a document library or other SharePoint resource, it's often useful to send out a notice of a survey so users will be aware of it for participation.

- **View Survey Results**: Once a survey is completed, you can view the results in a comparative graphical form, or view the answers given by individual respondents.

- **Compile Survey Results**: When a survey with many questions and/or many respondents is completed, just viewing the results might not be enough. You may need to do some serious data tabulation and number crunching.

Task: Create a Survey

Purpose: When you need to quickly gather data or opinions from a group, a fast way to accomplish this is to use a SharePoint survey. Surveys, which are really specialized tracking lists, are easy to make, easy to distribute, and easy to read—complete with built-in analysis of the results.

Example: The Action Marketing Group human resource manager would like to survey employees about the new corporate leave policy.

Steps:

1. Start Internet Explorer and type the URL for your organization's SharePoint server. The Start page will open. If you want your new survey located as a subsite of another site, navigate to that site.

2. Click the **Settings** menu gear icon. The Site Actions menu will appear.

3. Click **Add an App**. The Your Apps page will appear.

4. Scroll down and click the **Survey** icon. The Adding Survey dialog box will appear.

5. Click **Advanced Options**. The new Survey page will appear.

6. In the Name field enter a title for the new survey. This will appear in any list of surveys in SharePoint.

7. In the Description field enter a summary of the survey.

8. In the **Survey Options** section, select the appropriate options. There are two options to select: you can choose whether you want user names to be displayed with each survey result, and if you want to allow users to submit multiple responses when filling out the survey.

9. Click **Next**. The New Question page will open.

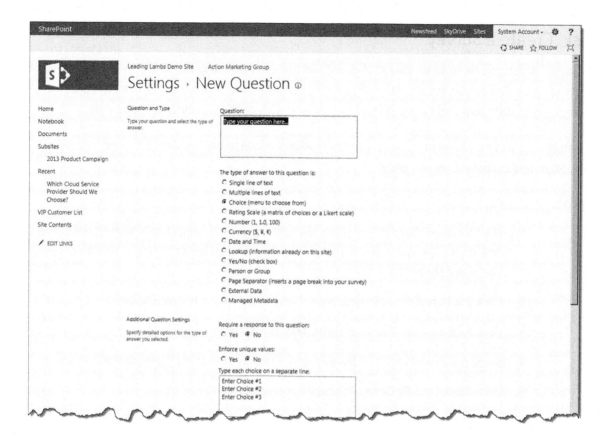

Figure 1: The New Question Page

10. In the Question field enter text for which you want to solicit user feedback.

11. Select a type of answer. Based on your selection, the fields in the **Additional Question Settings** section will change.

12. In the **Additional Question Settings** section, fill in the fields.

13. If there is another question in the survey, click **Next Question** and repeat Steps 10-12. Otherwise, click **Finish**. The Survey Settings page will appear.

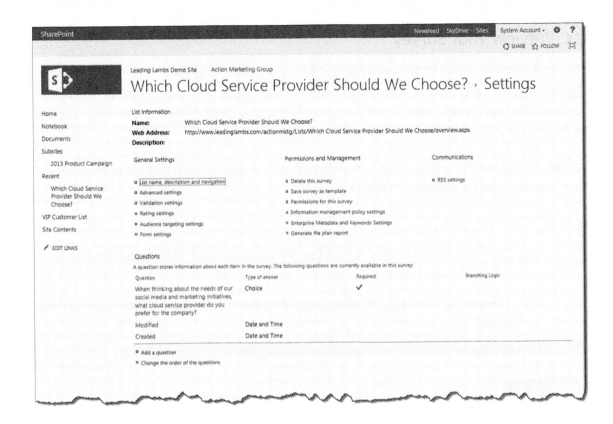

Figure 2: The Survey Settings Page

Task: Preview Your Survey

Purpose: SharePoint allows for the ability to test a survey before making it live. This allows you to make sure that the survey works as intended before asking a larger group of people to fill it out. This helps to ensure that it works as you intend it – particularly if you've implemented complex survey branching.

Example: The Action Marketing Group human resource manager wants to test the policy survey before sending it out for everyone to fill out.

Steps:

1. Start Internet Explorer and type the URL for your organization's SharePoint server. The Start Page will open.

2. Navigate to the survey in which you are interested. The Survey Overview page will open.

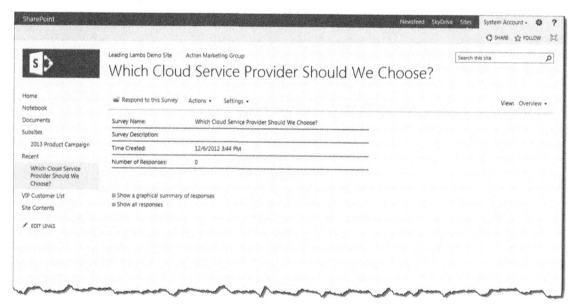

Figure 1: The Survey Overview Page

3. Click the **Respond to this Survey** link. The first survey question page will open.

Figure 2: The First Survey Question

4. Review the survey as a test to verify correctness. If all is in order, click the **Cancel** button on your browser so no results are actually saved.

5. To actually respond to the survey, answer all of the questions and click **Finish**. The answers will be recorded in the survey results.

Task: Enable Survey Branching

Purpose: When a survey is being created, not every question will be applicable to every respondent. For instance, if you want to poll users about their favorite candidate, and you've already asked their political party preference, you would want to narrow their choices to those candidates who are actually in that party. When a question asked depends on the answer of a previous question, this is known as branching.

Example: The survey for the copy vendors needs to be expanded, and the next question in the survey depends on the answer to the first.

Steps:

> **Note:** If you are creating a new survey, follow all of the steps listed below. To modify an existing survey, navigate to the survey, click on arrow next to the **Settings** link to open the Settings menu select the **Survey Settings** option and begin with Step 15.

1. Start Internet Explorer and type the URL for your organization's SharePoint server. The Start page will open. If you want your new site located as a sub-site of another site, navigate to that site.

2. Click the **Settings** menu gear icon. The Settings menu will appear.

3. Click **Add an App**. The Your Apps page will appear.

4. Scroll down and click the **Survey** icon. The Adding Survey dialog box will appear.

5. Click **Advanced Options**. The advanced create dialog box will appear.

6. In the Name field enter a title for the new survey. This will appear in any list of surveys in SharePoint.

7. In the Description field enter a summary of the survey.

8. In the **Survey Options** section select the appropriate options. There are two options to select: you can choose whether you want user names to be displayed with each survey result, and if you want to allow users to submit multiple responses when filling out the survey.

9. Click **Next**. The New Question page will open.

10. In the Question field enter text for which you want to solicit user feedback.

11. Select a type of answer. Based on your selection, the fields in the **Additional Question Settings** section will change.

12. In the **Additional Question Settings** section, fill in the fields.

13. If there is another question in the survey, click **Next Question** and repeat Steps 10-12. Otherwise, click **Finish**. The Survey Settings page will appear.

    Note: For survey branching to work, there must be more than two questions in the survey, or branching cannot be set up.

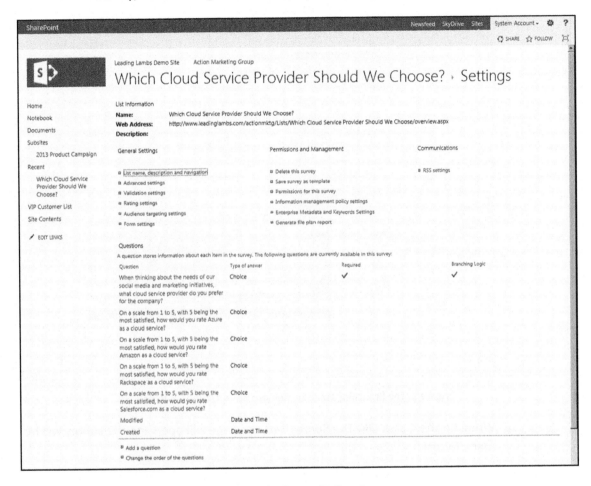

Figure 1: The Survey Settings Page

14. Click the link for the question with the answers that create a branch in the survey. The Edit Question page will open.

    Note: Selecting the last question will only allow branching to a Content Type.

15. In the **Branching Logic** section, select the question that will appear after each individual answer is selected.

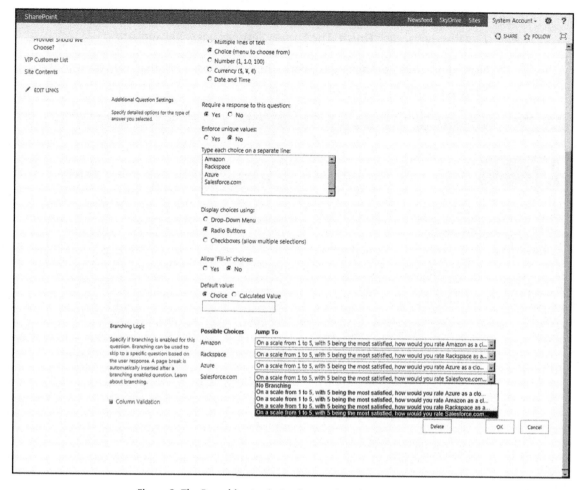

Figure 2: The Branching Logic Section on the Edit Question Page

16. When finished, click **OK**. The Survey Settings page will open and the survey will be ready for use.

Task: Send a Survey Link

Purpose: Once you've created a survey you need to let your users know where it is so they can respond to it. That requires sending out a link.

Example: Now that the survey is completed, the team members need to be notified of its existence and encouraged to participate.

Steps:

1. Start Internet Explorer and type the URL for your organization's SharePoint server. The Start Page will open.

2. Navigate to the survey in which you are interested. The Survey Overview page will open.

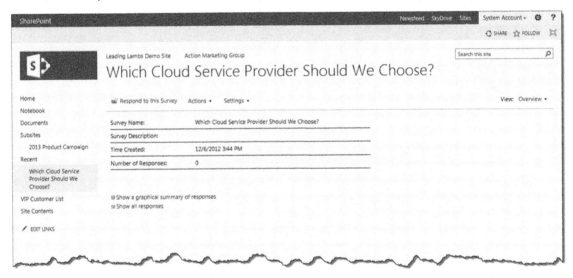

Figure 1: The Survey Overview Page

3. In the Address bar of your browser, select the entire address. Ctrl + A is useful for this.

4. Press Ctrl + C to copy the URL.

5. Open a new message window in Microsoft Outlook.

6. Press Ctrl + V to paste the URL into the body of the message.

7. Complete the message and press **Send**. The survey link will be distributed.

Task: View Survey Results

Purpose: SharePoint has the ability to graph the survey responses. Once a survey is completed by one or more respondents, you can view the results in a comparative graphical form, or view the answers given by individual respondents.

Steps:

1. Start Internet Explorer and type the URL for your organization's SharePoint server. The Start Page will open.

2. Navigate to the survey in which you are interested. The Survey Overview page will open.

3. Click the **Show a graphical summary of responses** link. The Graphical Summary page will open.

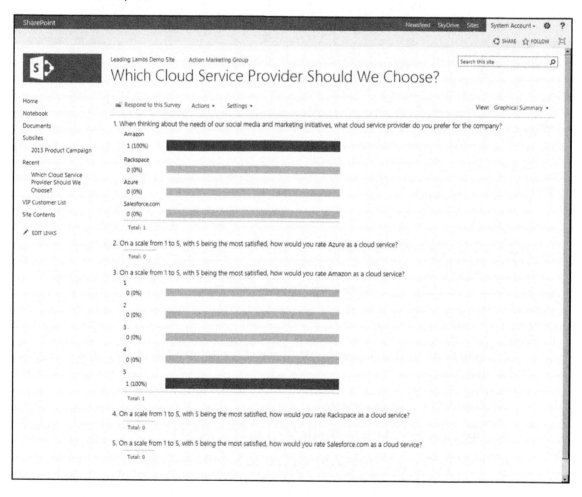

Figure 1: The Graphical Summary Page

4. On the upper right select the **View** menu and click the **Overview** option. The Survey Overview page will open again.

5. Click the **Show all responses** link. The All Responses page will open.

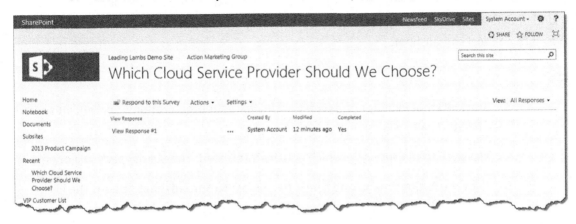

Figure 2: The All Responses Page

6. Click any **View Response** link. The View Response page will open.

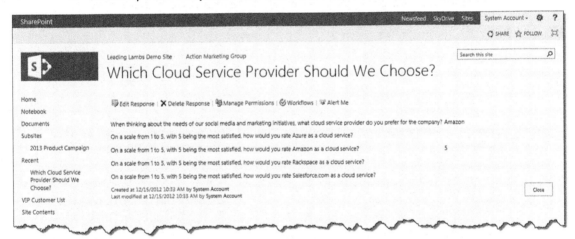

Figure 3: The View Response Page

7. When finished, click **Close**. You can now compile the survey, as demonstrated in the "Compile Survey Results" task.

Task: Compile Survey Results

Purpose: SharePoint surveys can capture a lot of information and viewing the results on the screen is great for a quick review, however, sometimes it will be necessary to look at the details and perform the kind of data analysis only available in Excel. Thankfully SharePoint can export the results of a survey into an Excel spreadsheet.

Steps:

1. Start Internet Explorer and type the URL for your organization's SharePoint server. The Start page will open.

2. Navigate to the survey in which you are interested. The Survey page will open.

3. Click the **Actions** menu and select the **Export to Spreadsheet** option. The File Download message box for your browser will appear.

4. Click **Open**. The file will download and Excel will open.

   Note: If a warning dialog box appears identifying a potential security concern, click **Enable** if you were the one who initiated the export from SharePoint.

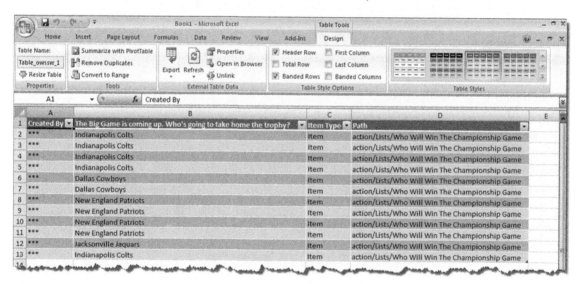

Figure 1: The Survey in Excel

5. Edit the spreadsheet as you normally would, using the table tools.

Getting Social with SharePoint

One of the more compelling features of SharePoint is its capability to create personal profiles for users. These profiles give users a place to express themselves more creatively, share interests and hobbies, and generally make the work environment a more pleasant place.

Other social tools within SharePoint include the capability to create and edit your own blog, as well as wiki pages. Content throughout a SharePoint site can be tagged so other users can find it faster.

In this section, you'll learn how to:

- **Configure a User Profile**: Create profiles for users to give users a place to express themselves.

- **Edit a Profile's Links**: The first thing a user should do is edit their profile with links to content.

- **Add a New Task to a Personal Site**: The Tasks page enables users to create their own task list so they can organize their work efforts.

- **Edit a Task in a Personal Site**: Once tasks are added to a user's personal task list, they can be edited if situations change.

- **Add an App to a Personal Site**: You can add new Apps (also known as Web Parts) to your profile and even position them where you want.

- **Edit an App in a Personal Site**: You can edit any app within a Profile page. Changing its name, moving it, or configuring its size – these are all options that are available.

- **Remove an App from a Personal Site**: You may not want to use all the Web Parts that are initially created for your Profile.

- **Create a Blog Entry in SharePoint**: How to create a blog site in SharePoint.

- **Register a Blog in Word**: Connecting a blog site to Word so blog entries can be published from Word.

- **Write a Blog Entry with Word**: How to post entries to a SharePoint blog from Word.

- **Post a Newsfeed Entry**: A new feature in SharePoint 2013 is the newsfeed, a component of a Profile page or other part of a site that acts as a microblogging tool.

- **Reply to a Newsfeed Entry**: Once newsfeed entries are posted, you can quickly reply to them, just as you would with any other microblogging tool.

- **Tag SharePoint Content**: One of the great new features of SharePoint is the capability to tag any SharePoint page you find as a favorite, thus allowing you to find it again.

- **Tag External Content**: Another nifty feature of SharePoint is the capability to tag any Internet page.

- **Edit a Wiki Page Page**: If you decide to use a wiki page in your SharePoint site, either as a home page or as some other utility, editing it will be a very straightforward process.

Task: Configure a User Profile

Purpose: One of the more compelling features of SharePoint is its capability to create profiles for users. These profiles give users a place to express themselves more creatively, share interests and hobbies, and generally make the work environment a more personal place.

Example: The human resources manager at the Action Marketing Group team members wants to enhance their user profile.

Steps:

1. Start Internet Explorer and type the URL for your organization's SharePoint server. The Start page will open.

2. In the upper-right corner of any SharePoint page click the menu with your user name and select the **About Me** option. The user's profile page will appear.

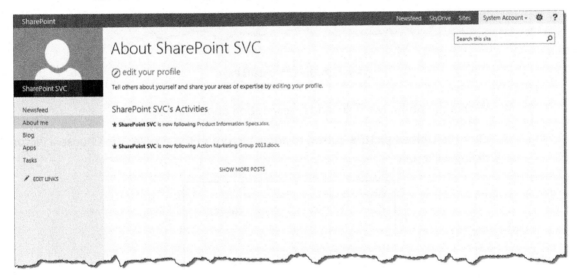

Figure 1: The User Profile Page

3. Click the **edit your profile** link. The Edit Details page for your user account will be displayed.

Figure 2: The Edit Details Page

4. Within the About Me field, add a description about yourself.

5. Click the **Upload picture** button to add a picture to the profile. The Choose a Picture dialog will open.

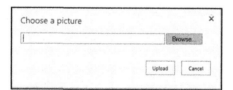

Figure 3: The Choose a Picture Dialog

6. Click the **Browse** button. The Choose File to Upload dialog will open.

7. Navigate to the image file you want to use and select it.

8. Click **Open**. The file path to the image will appear in the Choose a Picture dialog.

9. Click **Upload**. The image will appear in the Picture section.

The SharePoint Shepherd's Guide for End Users: 2013

Figure 4: The Updated Profile, In Progress

10. In the **Ask Me About** field, enter relevant information. This would be the topics that you're knowledgeable or an expert on.

11. At the top of the Edit Details page, click the **Contact Information** link. Enter relevant information on that page.

12. At the top of the Edit Details page, click the **Details** link. Enter relevant information on that page.

13. When complete, click the **Save all and close** button. A Profile Changes message box will appear.

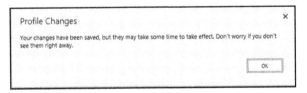

Figure 5: The Profile Changes Message Box

14. Click **OK**. The About Me page will appear, with new information.

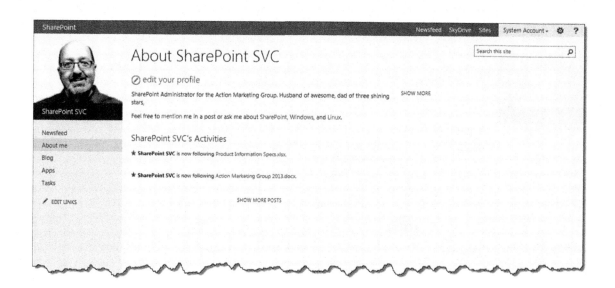

Figure 6: The Updated Profile Page

Task: Edit a Profile's Links

Purpose: A profile page is more than just a place where colleagues can find out more about you; it's also a place where you can start working, using apps and links to launch the tools you need throughout the day. SharePoint allows you to maintain links that are important to you.

Example: The Action Marketing Group human resources manager has a link to the Society of Human Resource Managers (SHRM) that she wants to keep handy for when she needs to learn more about human resources issues that may impact the organization.

Steps:

1. Start Internet Explorer and type the URL for your organization's SharePoint server. The Start page will open.

2. In the upper-right corner of any SharePoint page click the menu with your user name and select the **About Me** option. The user's profile page will appear.

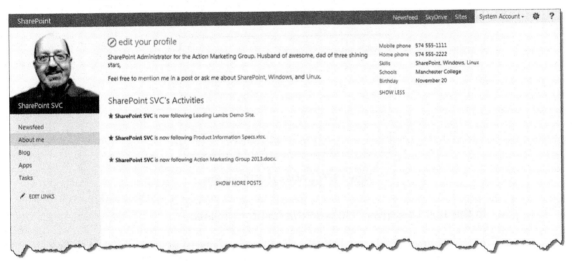

Figure 1: The User Profile Page

3. In the side navigation bar click the **Edit Links** link. The Edit Link tools will be displayed.

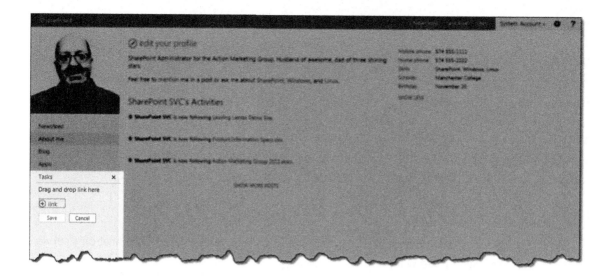

Figure 2: The Edit Link Tools

4. Click the **+ link** link. The Add a Link dialog box will open.

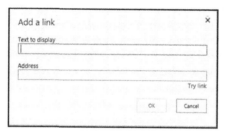

Figure 3: The Add a Link Dialog Box

5. In the Text to display field type the text for the link.

6. In the Address field type the URL for the page/site to which you want to link.

7. Click **OK**. The link will be added to the side navigation bar.

8. Click **Save**. The Edit Link tools will close and the new link will be added.

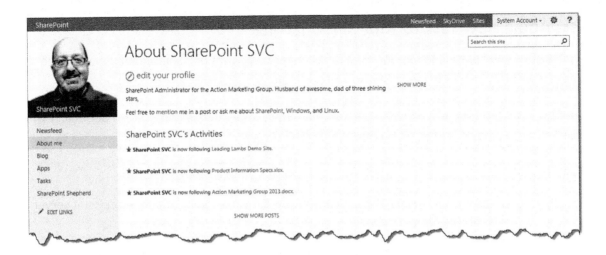

Figure 4: The Updated Links

9. In the side navigation bar click the **Edit Links** link to remove a link. The Edit Link tools will be displayed.

10. Next to the link you want to delete click the **Close** link. The link will be removed.

11. Click **Save**. The Edit Link tools will close.

Task: Add a New Task to Your Personal Site

Purpose: Tasks and getting things done is a part of every organization. SharePoint allows you to manage your tasks in your personal site so you can manage them from any computer.

Example: The operations officer for the Action Marketing Group needs to develop a periodic review procedure and wants to add a task so that she doesn't forget to do it.

Steps:

1. Start Internet Explorer and type the URL for your organization's SharePoint server. The Start page will open.

2. In the upper-right corner of any SharePoint page click the menu with the user name and select the **About Me** option. The user's profile page will appear.

3. Click the **Tasks** link in the side navigation bar. The My Tasks page will appear.

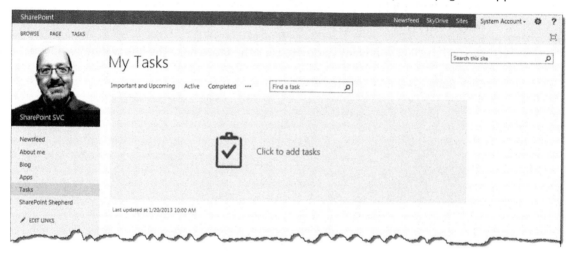

Figure 1: The My Tasks Page

Click the **Click to add tasks** link. A blank task template will appear.

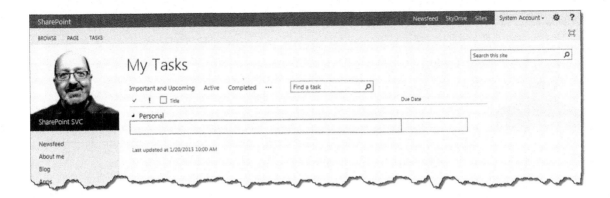

Figure 2: Adding a New Task

4. In the Title field type a description for the task.

5. In the Due Date field type a date the task needs to be completed.

6. Click anywhere on the page. The task will be added to the Personal task list.

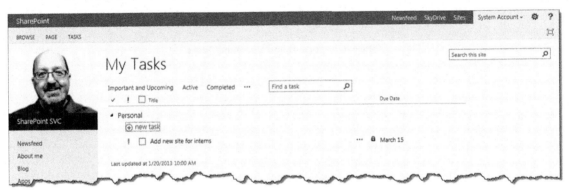

Figure 3: The New Task

7. To mark a task as Important, to the left of the task click the **Important** icon. The icon will display as a red exclamation point and the task will be classified as Important.

8. To view tasks coming up, click the **Important and Upcoming** link. The Important and Upcoming page will appear.

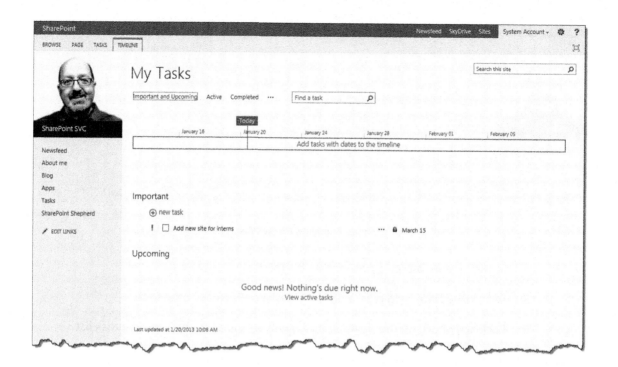

Figure 4: Important and Upcoming Tasks

Task: Edit a Task in Your Personal Site

Purpose: As time goes by, tasks change and grow. SharePoint allows you to modify your tasks to record additional information, or change them.

Example: The IT director for the Action Marketing Group has a new set of interns to be created – but the interns are coming later than expected. He'll change his task to reflect the updated timing of the interns.

Steps:

1. Start Internet Explorer and type the URL for your organization's SharePoint server. The Start page will open.

2. In the upper-right corner of any SharePoint page click the menu with the user name and select the **About Me** option. The user's profile page will appear.

3. In the side navigation bar click the **Tasks** link. The My Tasks page will appear.

4. Click the ellipsis control for the task to be changed. The task's menu will appear.

Figure 1: A Task's Menu

5. Click the **EDIT** link. The Edit Task page will appear.

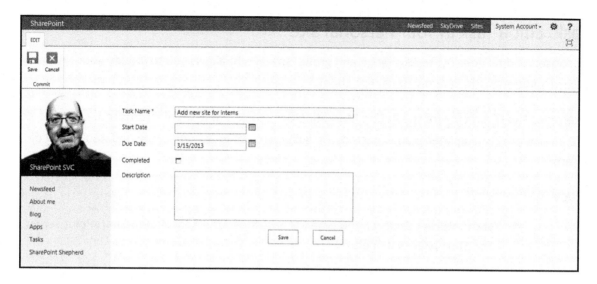

Figure 2: The Edit Task Page

6. Make any changes or additions to the appropriate fields.

7. Click **Save**. The edited task will appear with the new information in the Task list.

Task: Add an App to Your Personal Site

Purpose: Your personal space is a place where you can get work done much like a desk in the office. Also like a desk in the office you can add new things – like organizers – to make it quicker and more efficient to do your job. You can add new Apps in your Personal Site just like in other SharePoint sites.

Example: The Action Marketing Group receptionist would like to add a tag cloud to their Profile page.

Steps:

1. Start Internet Explorer and type the URL for your organization's SharePoint server. The Start page will open.

2. In the upper-right corner of any SharePoint page click the menu with your user name and select the **About Me** option. The user's profile page will appear.

3. In the left pane of the page, click the **Apps** link. The Site Contents page will open.

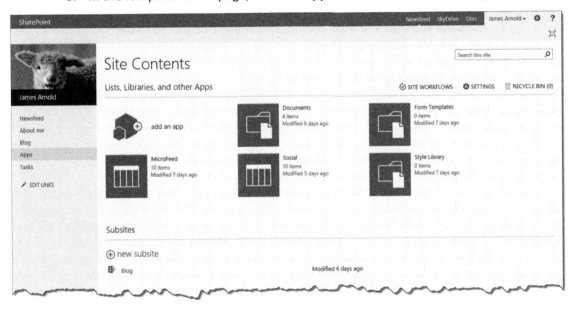

Figure 1: The User Site Contents Page

4. Click **add an app**. The Your Apps page will open.

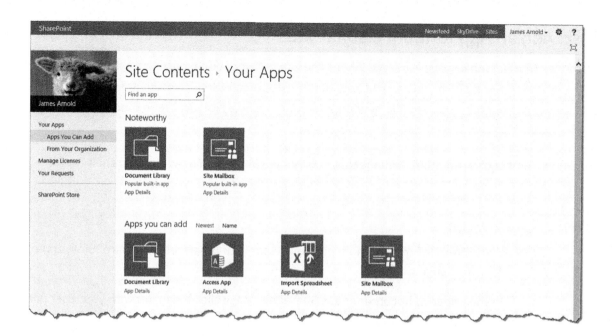

Figure 2: The Add Web Parts Header on the Profile Page in Edit Mode

5. Click the app that you want to add. The app will be added to the Site Contents page.

Task: Edit an App in a Personal Site

Purpose: The Apps in your Personal Site are like other applications anywhere in SharePoint. You can change the settings by going to the settings page.

Example: The Action Marketing Group team member would like to move an app to a new location on a page.

Steps:

1. Start Internet Explorer and type the URL for your organization's SharePoint server. The Start page will open.

2. In the upper-right corner of any SharePoint page click the menu with your user name and select the **About Me** option. The user's profile page will appear.

3. In the left pane of the page, click the **Apps** link. The Site Contents page will open.

4. Select an app's menu icon and click the ellipsis control. The app's menu will appear.

5. Click the **SETTINGS** option. The app's Settings page will open.

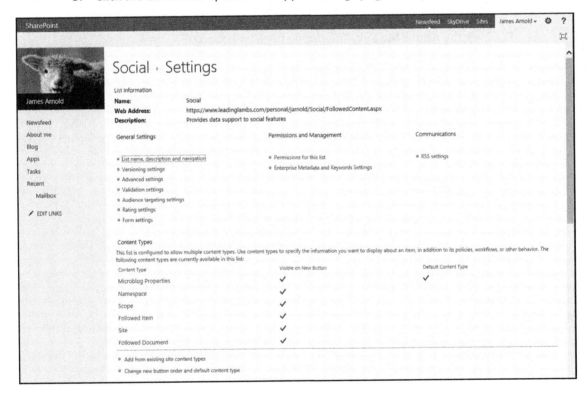

Figure 1: The App's Settings Page

6. Click the **List name, description and navigation** link. The General Settings page will open.

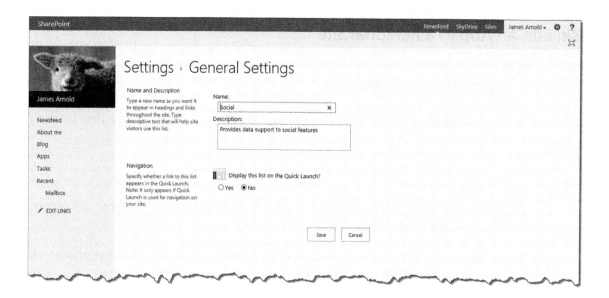

Figure 2: The General Settings Page

7. In the Name field, change the name of the app.

8. Click **Save**. The Settings page will appear.

9. Click the **About Me** link. The profile page will open.

Task: Remove an App from a Personal Site

Purpose: Like any site you may add an App to your Personal Site only to realize later that you no longer need it. Safely deleting an application is quick and easy.

Example: The operations manager at the Action Marketing Group was using a list to track the effectiveness of a new training program that has now been discontinued. She wants to remove the application to prevent cluttering her Personal Site.

Steps:

1. Start Internet Explorer and type the URL for your organization's SharePoint server. The Start page will open.

2. In the upper-right corner of any SharePoint page click the menu with your user name and select the **About Me** option. Your user profile page will appear.

3. In the left pane of the page, click the **Apps** link. The Site Contents page will open.

4. Select an app's menu icon and click the ellipsis control. The app's menu will appear.

   Note: You can only remove apps that you added to your Personal Site, as some apps are required.

5. If available, click the **REMOVE** option. The Message from webpage dialog box will appear.

Figure 1: The Message from Webpage Dialog Box

6. Click **OK**. The app will be removed from your Personal Site.

Task: Create a Blog Entry in SharePoint

Purpose: One of the fastest growing aspects of the Internet is the web log, or blog. Blogs serve as a daily (or other interval) diary of your activities, whether business or personal. SharePoint includes a blog management system to get you started on a blog right away.

Example: The Action Marketing Group office manager wants to add blog entries to her blog.

Steps:

1. Start Internet Explorer and type the URL for your organization's SharePoint server. The Start page will open.

2. Click the menu with the user's name in the upper-right corner of any SharePoint page and select the **About Me** option. The user's profile page will appear.

   Note: Not all blogs are in your personal site, if the blog you want to post to isn't in a personal site navigate to it and resume at step 4.

3. In the side navigation bar, click the **Blog** link. The Blog page will open.

Figure 1: The Blog Page

4. In the Blog tools section click the **Create a post** link. The new Blog entry page will open.

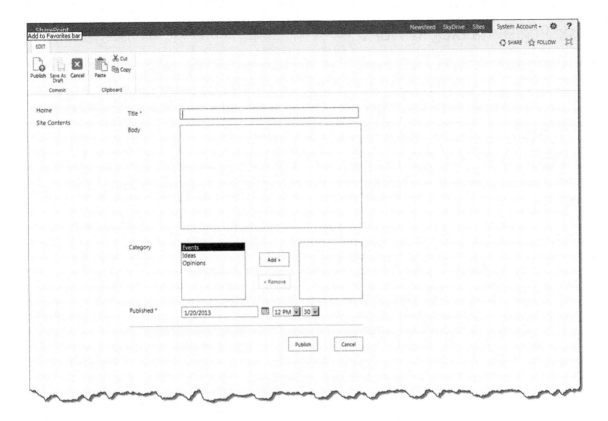

Figure 2: The New Blog Entry Page

5. Enter information and content into the appropriate fields.

6. Click **Publish**. The new blog entry will appear on the Blog home page.

Task: Register a Blog in Word

Purpose: SharePoint allows you to create blog entries directly from the web interface, however, most office workers are more comfortable writing in Word than they are writing long works in a web page. Word can be connected to SharePoint so that you can author your blog posts in Word and directly post them.

Example: The Action Marketing Group human resources clerk will be posting to the corporate blog and wants to route content to others for comment before posting and so will be using Word to post to the blog.

Steps:

1. In Word, click the File tab. The File screen will appear.

2. Click the New option. The templates screen will appear.

3. Click the Blog post template. The Blog Post dialog box will open.

Figure 1: The Blog Post Dialog

4. Click Create. If you have never used the template before, it will be downloaded. Then the Register a Blog Account dialog box will open

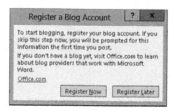

Figure 2: The Register a Blog Account Dialog

5. Click **Register Now**. A New Blog Account dialog box will appear.

   Note: If you've already registered a blog and need to register another you can look in the ribbon for a **Manage Accounts** button and click it. Once the Blog Accounts dialog box comes up you can click the New button and follow the rest of the steps here.

Figure 3: The New Blog Account Dialog

6. In the Blog drop-down control, select the **SharePoint blog** option, then click **Next**. The New SharePoint Blog Account dialog box will appear.

Figure 4: The New SharePoint Blog Account Dialog

7. In the Blog URL field, enter the URL for your SharePoint blog and click OK. A confirmation dialog box will open.

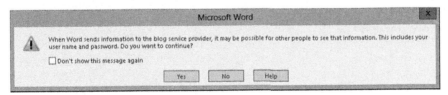

Figure 5: Confirm You Want to Share Account Information

8. Click **Yes**. A notification dialog box will open.

9. Click **OK**. The New SharePoint Blog Account dialog box will close and Word will be ready to create a new blog post.

Task: Write a Blog Entry with Word

Purpose: One of the standard templates in Word is a blog post template which can be used to create blog posts in SharePoint – once SharePoint has been registered as a blog provider.

Example: The Action Marketing Group human resource clerk wants to post a new blog post about the company picnic using Word

Steps:

1. In Word, click the **File** tab. The File window will open.

   Note: You can also just start Word, word will open with a page to select the right template in step 3.

2. Click **New**. The Available Templates pane will appear.

3. Click **Blog Post**, then click **Create**. A Blog Post tab will open and Word will be ready to create a new blog post.

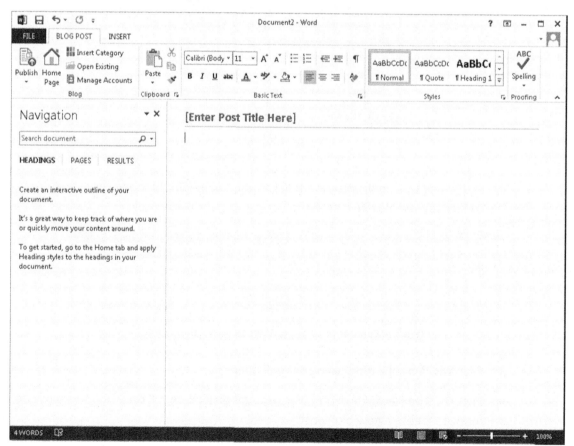

Figure 1: The Blog Post Page in Word

The SharePoint Shepherd's Guide for End Users: 2013

4. Create a blog entry including a title and content.

5. Click **Publish**. The entry will be posted to your blog.

Task: Post a Newsfeed Entry

Purpose: SharePoint includes a newsfeed feature that allows you to publish short messages about what you're thinking or doing. This microblogging approach has been popularized by Twitter. It's a way that your colleagues can see what's going on in your world and in your head.

Example: Action Marketing Group's IT team had some leftover pizza from a lunch and learn. The IT manager wants to let everyone know that they can have the remaining pizza in the break room.

Steps:

1. Start Internet Explorer and type the URL for your organization's SharePoint server. The Start page will open.

2. Click the Newsfeed link in the suite bar. The Newsfeed page will open.

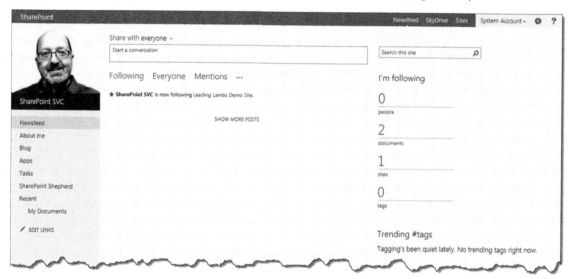

Figure 1: The Newsfeed Page

3. Click the Start a conversation field. The field will appear in Edit mode.

4. Type a brief message and click the **Post** button. The entry will appear in the newsfeed.

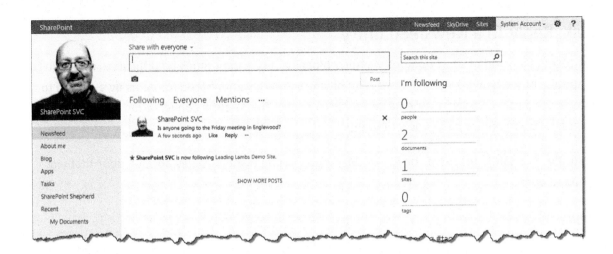

Figure 2: The New Newsfeed Entry

Task: Reply To a Newsfeed Entry

Purpose: In a world of short updates via microblogging it can sometimes be difficult to maintain the continuity of the conversation. Rather than having to search a newsfeed for posts by a person to regenerate a conversation, everyone can reply to posts. This keeps a conversation together and makes it easy to review everyone's thoughts.

Example: The safety officer at the Action Marketing Group wants to reply about a door that was propped open.

Steps:

1. Start Internet Explorer and type the URL for your organization's SharePoint server. The Start page will open.

2. Click the Newsfeed link in the top suite bar. The Newsfeed page will open.

3. Click the Reply link for the newsfeed entry to which you want to reply. An entry field will appear in Edit mode.

4. Type a brief message and click the Post button. The reply will appear in the newsfeed.

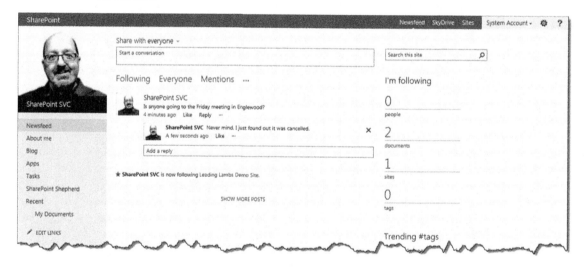

Figure 1: The Newsfeed Entry With Reply

Task: Tag SharePoint Content

Purpose: Finding content across the information resources of the organization can be difficult. Refinding content that you once found can be even harder. SharePoint allows you to tag content so that you can browse through your tags later and refind the information you're looking for.

Example: The Action Marketing Group's new manufacturing intern wants to tag interesting company history information for him to read on break.

Steps:

1. Start Internet Explorer and type the URL for your organization's SharePoint server. Visit any page on the SharePoint site.

2. When you find a page that interests you, in the Sites submenu top navigation bar click the **Follow** link. The page will be tagged.

3. To manage tags for a page, click the Page, Library, or List tab to open the page's toolbar.

4. Click the **Tags & Notes** icon for a tagged page. The Tag dialog box will open.

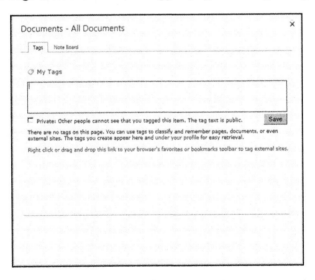

Figure 1: The Tag Dialog Box

5. In the My Tags field, add tags, separated by commas or semicolons. As you type, suggested keywords may appear that you can click if appropriate.

6. Click **Save**. The page will be tagged with the new tags.

7. Click the **Note Board** tab. The Note Board page will appear.

8. In the main field, add notes about the page.

---

9. Click **Post**. The notes will be assigned to this page.

10. Click the **Close** control in the top right corner. The Tag dialog box will close.

Task: Tag External Content

Purpose: Tagging content in SharePoint is an important start to allowing you to organize information that you want to find again, however, not everything that you care about will be on SharePoint. SharePoint allows you to tag content which isn't on your server.

Example: The Action Group team production intern has found an important regulatory guideline that he wants to tag for finding later.

Steps:

1. Start Internet Explorer and type the URL for your organization's SharePoint server. The Start page will open.

2. Click the **Page** link to open the page's toolbar.

3. Click the **Tags & Notes** icon. The Tag dialog box will open.

4. Right-click the **Right click or drag and drop this link to your browser's favorites or bookmarks toolbar to tag external sites** link. The context menu will appear.

5. Select the **Add to favorites** option. The Add a Favorite dialog box will open.

Figure 1: The Add a Favorite Dialog Box

6. In the Create in field select the **Favorites Bar** option, then click **Add**. The favorite will appear in the browser's Favorites Bar.

   Note: You may receive an Overwrite dialog box if the favorite already exists.

7. Navigate to any page of interest. This can be any Internet page.

8. Click the **Tags & Note Board** favorite. The Tags & Note Board page will appear in a separate window.

9. Add tags, separated by commas or semicolons, to the My Tags field. As you type, suggested keywords may appear that you can click if appropriate.

   Note: Click in the extreme upper left corner of the box for tags to get started and expect a slight delay before you'll see typing or suggestions.

---

10. Click **Save**. The page will be tagged with the new tags.

11. If you would like to add a note, click the **Note Board** tab. The Note Board page will appear.

12. Add notes about the page in the main field.

13. Click **Post**. The notes will be assigned to this page.

14. Close the window displaying the Tags and Note Board page and navigate to another page and continue your Internet session.

Task: Edit a Wiki Page

Purpose: Editing a page in SharePoint is a simple process whether you want to add apps or simply modify the text.

Example: The Action Marketing Group's research team wants to record some best practices for research in the Wiki.

Steps:

1. Start Internet Explorer and navigate to the page you want to edit. The page will open, though it may take some time.

2. Click the Page link at the top of the page. The Page ribbon will appear.

3. Click the **Edit** button. The Format Text ribbon will be displayed.

Figure 1: The Format Text Ribbon on the Wiki Home Page in Edit Mode

> **Note:** If your page looks different, you may not be trying to edit a Wiki page. It may be a web part page or a publishing page.

4. Edit the page as needed.

5. When finished, click the **Save** button. The changes will immediately be saved and published, without the need for a formal approval process.

SharePoint primarily deals with two kinds of sites. The first type is the collaborative site, which has been discussed through much of this manual. The second type, which will be addressed in this section, is the publishing site. A publishing site contains content intended not to be created but rather shared as is. It can be your team's web presence, or a collection of documents and tools for fellow users to read and use.

In this section, you'll learn how to:

- **Create a Site for Published Content**: The basics of creating a publishing site.

- **Create a Content Page**: Once a publishing site is created, users can start creating the content for the site.

- **Edit Page Content**: Any time you need to make changes on your pages, you can quickly enter edit mode to implement the changes with ease.

- **Spell Check Page Content**: One of the handier tools in the page content editor is the spell checker. It might seem obvious, but web editor spell checkers are not as robust as one would think...until now.

- **Add an Image to a Content Page**: Images are sometimes the best thing about a web page. Add your images easily in SharePoint.

- **Add Publishing Approvers**: Within a publishing Web site, all pages must be approved for publication every time they are changed or added to the site. This is known as a workflow.

- **Submit Page for Publishing Approval**: Since publishing sites are more static and represent you or your business, you should not just create the site on your own and publish it as is.

- **Approve Content for Publication**: If you are designated as a content approver, here's how to edit and formally approve the document.

- **Change Page Schedule Expiration Date**: Sometimes, you will have a page that only needs to be up for a limited amount of time. Perhaps for a sale, or a contest.

- **Manually Start a Workflow for Publication**: At any time, a site administrator can tag a page for improvement using the workflow process.

- **Create a Custom Permission Level**: Whenever you create a site, you may need to grant permission levels for users that don't match existing types of permissions. In SharePoint, you can create a brand-new permission level to meet your needs

Task: Create a Site for Published Content

Purpose: SharePoint primarily deals with two kinds of sites. The first type is the collaborative site, which has been discussed through much of this book. Collaborative sites are many-to-many conversations which evolve content. The second type, which has not been as fully addressed, is the publishing site. A publishing site contains content to be shared "as is," and not worked on collaboratively. Publishing sites are also structured in that every piece of data has a place. Finally, publishing sites are one-to-many in that few people write content and many consume it.

Example: The Action Marketing Group Intranet administrator needs to create a new department site.

Steps:

1. Start Internet Explorer and type the URL for your organization's SharePoint server. The Start page will open. If you want your Publishing Site located as a subsite to another site, navigate to that site.

2. Click the **Settings** menu and click the **Site Contents** option. The Site Contents page will appear.

3. In the Subsites section, click the **new subsite** link. The New SharePoint Site page will open.

4. In the Title field, type a title for the Publishing Site. The title of your site should be descriptive and can be up to about 50 letters before becoming intrusive.

5. In the Description field, type a description for your site. The description is like a subtitle that will be displayed on some of the pages. It should further clarify the title so that anyone can understand the site's purpose.

6. In the URL Name field, type a short, descriptive name for your group. This will become part of the full Web Site Address for your new Project Site. Some features don't work with long URLs, so keeping the name in the URL short but descriptive is recommended.

7. In the select a template section, click the **Publishing** tab. The Publishing templates will appear.

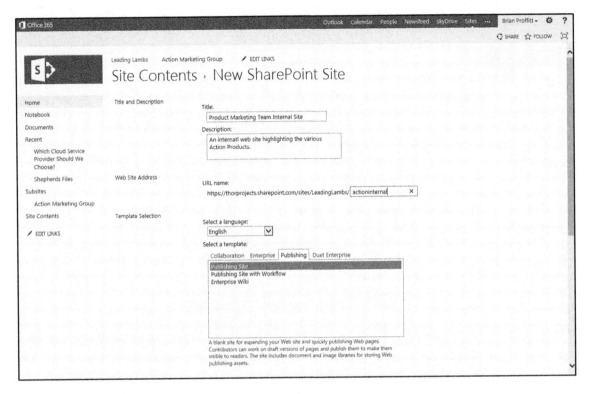

Figure 1: The New SharePoint Site Page

8. In the Select a template field, select **Publishing Site** as the template.

    Note: If a Publishing site option is not available, a SharePoint administrator may need to activate the SharePoint Server Publishing Infrastructure site collection features.

9. In the User Permissions field, select the **Use same permissions as parent site** option. You can change to unique permissions later as shown in "Assign Users to a Group."

10. In the Use the top link bar from the parent site field, select the **Yes** option.

11. Click **Create**. The "Working on it..." screen will briefly appear, followed by the new Publishing Site page.

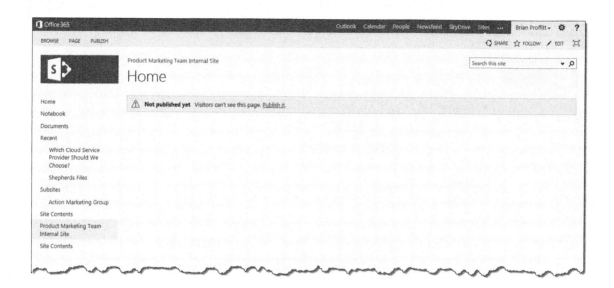

Figure 2: The New Publishing Site Home Page

Exception: If the desired publishing site template is not listed, you do not have specific permission to access the correct site templates or the site collection's publishing features have not been activated. Check the permissions settings to ensure you have the appropriate access rights for creating publishing sites, and it that is the case, contact your SharePoint administrator to inquire about the site collection publishing features.

Task: Create a Content Page

Purpose: At the core SharePoint is a web platform and content management system. Creating content, whether you're in a Wiki site or a Publishing site is easy. You can create additional content pages and then add the content and apply metadata to the page.

Example: The new Action Marketing Group's Internet manage needs to create a new page for an upcoming promotion.

Steps:

1. Start Internet Explorer and type the URL for your organization's SharePoint server. The Start page will open.

2. Navigate to the publishing site. The publishing site's home page will open.

3. Click the **Settings** menu and select **Add a Page**. The Add a Page dialog box will open.

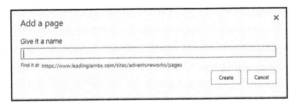

Figure 1: The Add a Page Dialog Box

4. In the Give it a name field, enter a name for the new page. This is used as the listing for this page throughout SharePoint.

5. Click **Create**. The new page with the Format Text ribbon will appear.

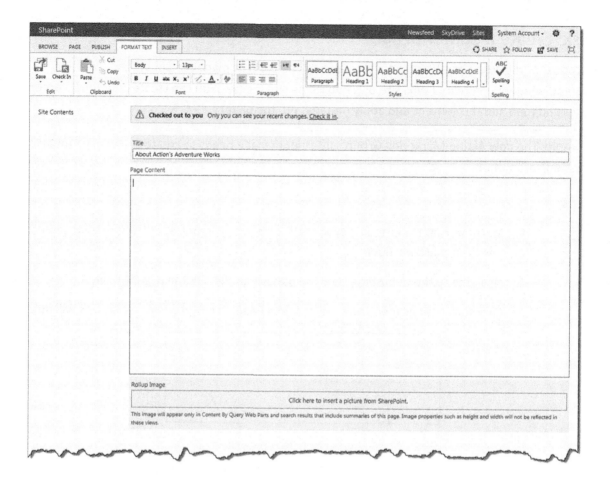

Figure 2: The New Page with the Editing Tools Ribbon

6. Click the **Page** tab. The Page ribbon will appear.

7. Click the **Page Layout** button. A list of possible layouts for the page will appear.

8. Select the layout option you want to use. The layout of the page will be adjusted.

9. Enter the content on the page, using the available tools to format the text.

10. Click the **Check In** button. The Check In dialog box will appear.

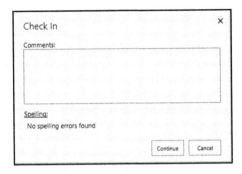

Figure 3: The Check In Dialog Box

11. Enter any comments you might have for this version of the page and click **Continue**. The page will be checked in and viewable to just the users with the appropriate permission.

12. Click the **Publish** tab. The Publish ribbon will appear.

13. Click **Publish**. The page will now be viewable to all users.

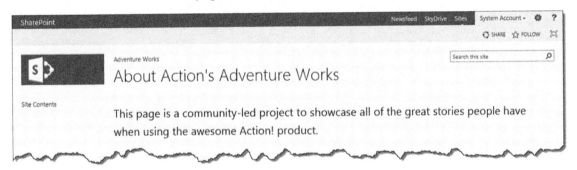

Figure 4: The New Page

Task: Edit Page Content

Purpose: The authoring experience in SharePoint extends to editing content. You can quickly edit a page from the browser.

Example: The human resource manager at the Action Marketing Group needs to update the recognized holidays for the new year.

Steps:

1. Start Internet Explorer and navigate to the page you want to edit. The page will open.

2. Click the **Settings** menu gear icon, and then the **Edit Page** option. The Format Text ribbon will appear.

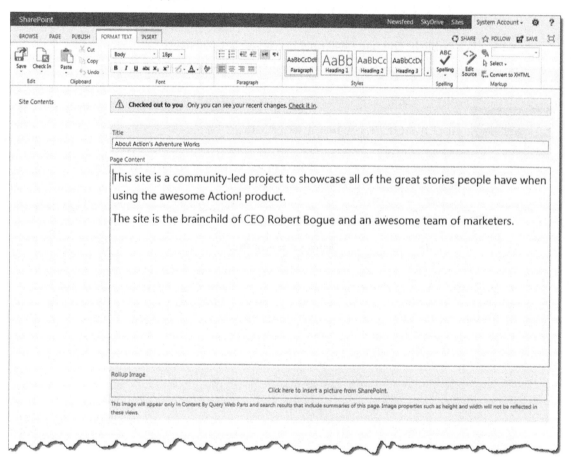

Figure 1: The Format Text Ribbon

3. Edit the document as needed.

4. When finished, click the **Check In** button. The Check In dialog box will appear.

The SharePoint Shepherd's Guide for End Users: 2013

5. Enter any comments you might have for this version of the page and click **Continue**. The page will be checked in and viewable to just the users with the appropriate permission.

6. Click the **Publish** tab. The Publish ribbon will appear.

7. Click **Publish**. The page will be now viewable to all users.

Task: Spell Check Page Content

Purpose: SharePoint has integrated spell checking. Like the spell checking in Microsoft Word, it helps to ensure that the words are all spelled correctly, even if they may occasionally not be the right meaning.

Example: The Action Marketing Group intranet manager checks the spelling of the About us page before publishing.

Steps:

1. Start Internet Explorer and navigate to the page you want to edit. The page will open.

2. Click the **Settings** menu, and then the **Edit Page** option. The Format Text ribbon will appear.

3. Edit the document as needed.

4. In the Format Text ribbon, click the **Spelling** icon. The Spell Check message box will appear, notifying you of any spelling errors.

Figure 1: The Spell Check Message Box

5. Click OK. The Spell Check dialog box will close, and the spelling errors will be highlighted on the page.

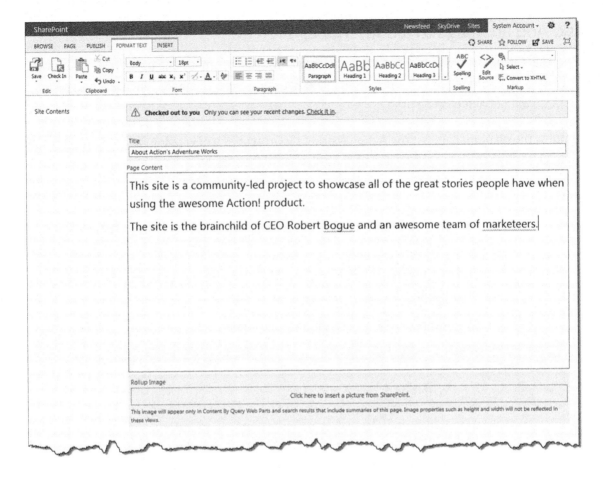

Figure 2: The Highlighted Spelling Errors on the Page.

6. Click on each error to see potential suggestions. You can select a suggested spelling or choose to ignore the word.

7. When the errors are corrected, click the **Check In** button. The Check In dialog box will appear.

8. Enter any comments you might have for this version of the page and click **Continue**. The page will be checked in and viewable to all users with the appropriate permission.

9. Click the **Publish** tab. The Publish ribbon will appear.

10. Click **Publish**. The page will be now viewable to all users.

Task: Add an Image to a Content Page

Purpose: Reading large blocks of text can be exhausting. Adding images helps to make your pages more interesting. SharePoint supports both inline images as well as images that are a part of the structured data of a publishing page.

Example: The plant manager at the Action Marketing Group has a new plant photo showing the new line that he wants to add to the facility page to showcase the new line.

Steps:

1. Start Internet Explorer and navigate to the page you want to edit. The page will open.

2. Click the **Settings** menu gear icon, and then the **Edit Page** option. The Format Text ribbon will appear.

3. Click the **Insert** tab. The Insert ribbon will appear.

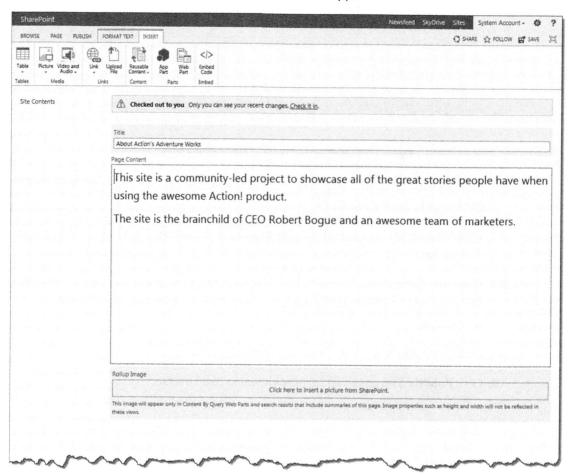

Figure 1: The Insert Ribbon

4. Click the **Picture** button. The Picture menu will appear.

5. Click the **From Computer** button. The Upload Image dialog box will appear.

6. Click **Browse**. The Choose File to Upload dialog box will appear.

7. Select a file and click **Open**. The file and its file path will appear in the Choose a file field.

8. In the Destination Library field, select the **Site Collection Images** option.

9. Click **OK**. The Site Collection Images dialog box will appear.

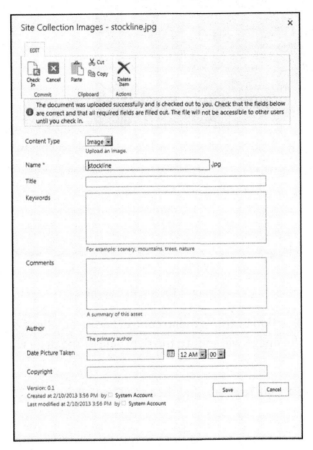

Figure 2: The Site Collection Images Dialog Box

10. Add any pertinent information and click **Save**. The Site Collection Images dialog box will close and the image will appear in the Page Content field at the insertion point.

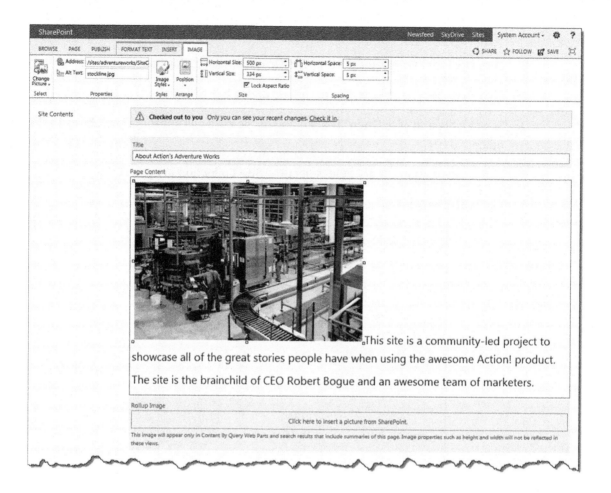

Figure 3: The Inserted Image

11. Click the **Position** button's menu control and select **Right** option in the menu's Float section. The image will shift to the right side of the page with the text wrapping around it.

12. Click the **Format Text** tab, and then the **Check In** button. The Check In dialog box will appear.

13. Enter any comments you might have for this version of the page and click **Continue**. The page will be checked in and viewable to all users with the appropriate permission.

14. Click the **Publish** tab. The Publish ribbon will appear.

15. Click **Publish**. The page will be now viewable to all users.

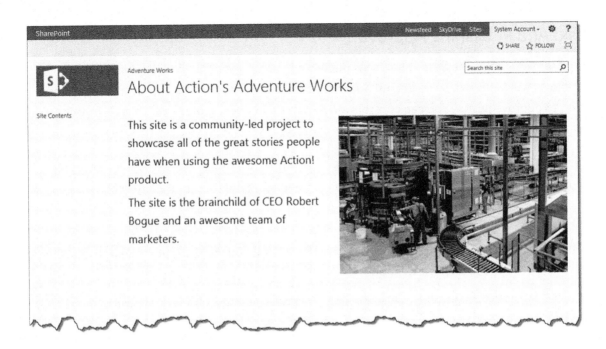

Figure 4: The Updated Page with Inserted Image

Task: Add Publishing Approvers

Purpose: SharePoint allows for numerous publishing models including direct publishing and workflow based approval. The default approval workflow will ask for the approvers SharePoint group to approve pages. You can control who is in this approvers group. Alternatively, you can create a custom workflow with SharePoint Designer.

Example: The Action Marketing Group has hired a compliance officer responsible for ensuring regulatory compliance that needs to review all of the pages published to the Internet web site.

Steps:

1. Start Internet Explorer and type the URL for your organization's SharePoint server. The Start page will open.

2. Navigate to the publishing site. The publishing site's home page will open.

3. Click the **Settings** menu gear icon and select **Site settings**. The Site Settings page will open.

Figure 1: The Site Settings Page

4. In the Users and Permissions section click the **Site permissions** link. The Permissions ribbon will open on the Permissions page.

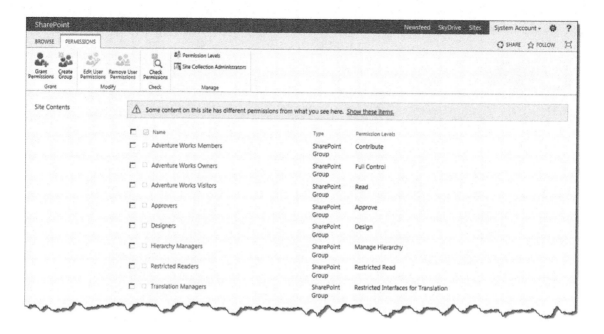

Figure 2: The Permissions Ribbon on the Permissions Page

5. Click the **Approvers** group link. The page for the approvers group will appear.

6. Click the **New** link. The Share '*Site Name*' dialog box will open.

7. In the Add people to the Approvers group field, type in the name of a user. If the user is part of the authenticated network, their name will be underlined, which means they are authorized. If a user is not recognized, a red squiggly line will appear. You will need to correct the user name.

8. Add additional names, separating the names with semicolons.

9. Click **Share**. The Grant Permissions dialog box will close and the user will appear in the group list on the People and Groups – Approvers page.

Task: Submit Page for Publishing Approval

Purpose: SharePoint's models for publishing allows the site administrator to decide that pages must run through an approval workflow. If your administrator requires an approval workflow, here's how you start that process.

Example: The Action Product Line home page is ready to be formally published, but must first be submitted for approval.

Steps:

1. Start Internet Explorer and navigate to the page you want to edit. The page will open.

2. Click the **Settings** menu gear icon, then the **Edit page** option. The Format Text ribbon will appear.

3. Edit the document as needed.

4. When finished, click the **Check In** button. The Check In dialog box will appear.

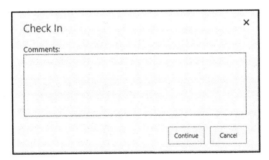

Figure 1: The Check In Dialog Box

5. Enter any comments you might have for this version of the page and click **Continue**. The page will be checked in.

6. Click the **Submit** button. The Start "Page Approval" default page will open.

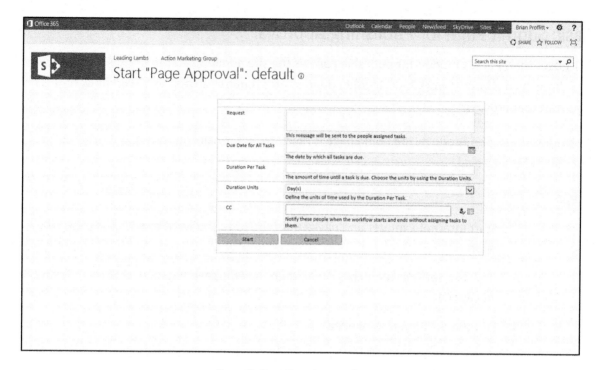

Figure 2: Start Page Approval Page

7. Fill in the necessary information in the fields and click **Start**. After a brief processing time, the page will be ready submitted to the approval workflow.

Figure 3: A Page to be Approved

The SharePoint Shepherd's Guide for End Users: 2013

Task: Approve Content for Publication

Purpose: When publishing approval workflows are enabled and you are in the approvers group you'll receive emails to indicate that your approval is necessary on a page. Once you have reviewed the content on the page, you need to complete your approval of the content for publishing.

Example: The Action Product Line home page has been submitted for approval and will need to be approved for publication.

Steps:

1. Start Internet Explorer and type the URL for your organization's SharePoint server. The Start page will open.

2. Navigate to the page to be approved. The page will open.

3. Click the **Publish** tab. The Publish ribbon will appear.

4. Click the **Approve** button. The Approve dialog box will appear, with a place to comment on the approval.

Figure 1: The Approve Dialog Box

5. Enter any comments about the approval and click Continue. The approval task page will appear.

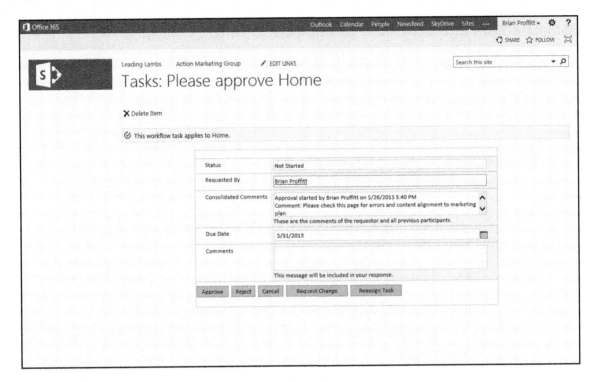

Figure 2: The Approval Task

6. If the page is satisfactory, enter any pertinent information in the fields and click the **Approve** button. After a brief period of processing, the task will be approved and the page published.

Exception: If the **Approve** button is disabled, you may be trying to approve your own changes or you do not have specific permission to change content within this particular workflow. Or the Publishing features for the site may not be activated. Have another authorized user approve your changes, or check the permissions settings to ensure you have the appropriate access rights. Contact the SharePoint administrator to make sure the Publishing features for the site are activated, as well.

Task: Change Page Schedule or Expiration Date

Purpose: SharePoint allows you to define the date and time that pages become available and when they become unavailable. This is useful when you need to have a page for a promotion disappear – or when you need to have a special offer show up at some point in the future.

Example: The Action Marketing Group has a contest page that only needs to run for three months, so it will be scheduled to expire.

Steps:

1. Start Internet Explorer and type the URL for your organization's SharePoint server. The Start page will open.

2. Navigate to the publishing site. The publishing site's home page will open.

3. Navigate to the page you want to schedule. The page will open.

4. Click the **Settings** menu gear icon and then the **Edit page** option. The Format Text ribbon will appear.

5. In the ribbon click the **Publish** tab. The Publish ribbon will appear.

6. Click the **Schedule** button. The Schedule Page dialog box will appear.

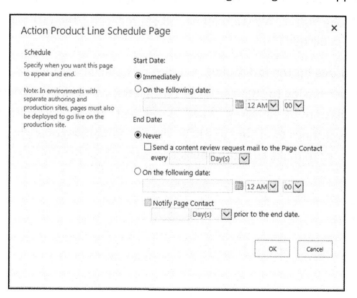

Figure 1: The Schedule Page Dialog Box

7. Set the Start and End Dates for the page.

8. Click **OK**. Schedule Page dialog box will close and the page will need to be submitted for approval and approved.

Note: Upon approval by the designated person, the page will sit in a Scheduled status (i.e., the Content Approval field will indicate Scheduled), rather than Approved, until the scheduled start date. This is to ensure only Approved pages are visible to readers. Once the expiration date occurs, the page is put back in Draft status for the same reason.

Exception: If the **Schedule** button is disabled, you may be trying to approve your own changes or you do not have specific permission to change content within this particular workflow or the manage item scheduling is not enabled in this library. Have another authorized user approve your changes, or check the permissions settings to ensure you have the appropriate access rights. If permissions are not the issue, contact the SharePoint administrator to have item scheduling enabled for the library.

Task: Manually Start a Workflow for Publication

Purpose: Even in scenarios where a content author would normally be able to approve content, there may be times when they want to get approval from others. SharePoint allows content creators to manually start an approval workflow.

Example: The Action Product Line page is being updated to make some product claims that should be validated by the legal department. The content manager wants to send the page for legal review.

Steps:

1. Start Internet Explorer and type the URL for your organization's SharePoint server. The Start page will open.

2. Navigate to the publishing site. The publishing site's home page will open.

3. Navigate to the page that needs a workflow started.

4. If the editing tools are not available, click the **Settings** menu gear icon and select **Edit page**. The editing tools ribbon will be displayed.

5. Click the **Check In** button to check the document back in and enter check in comments.

6. Click the **Publish** tab. The Publish ribbon will be displayed.

7. Click the **Start a Workflow** button. The Workflows page will open.

   Note: Workflows for sites must be set up by the system administrator or someone with design rights. If you do not have any workflows available, contact the administrator and discuss what workflow templates you would like to have activated.

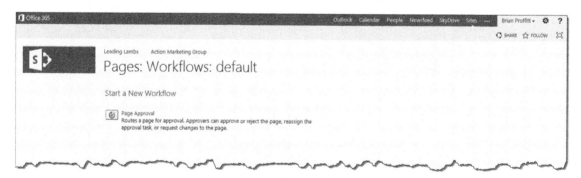

Figure 1: The Workflows Page

8. Click the **Page Approval** template link. The Start "Page Approval" page will open.

9. Fill in the pertinent information. Pay particular attention to the Due Date and Duration fields.

10. Type in the name of any users you want to follow along in the approval process in the CC field and click on the **Check Names** icon, 🐾. If the user is part of the authenticated network, their name will be underlined, which means they are authorized. If a user is not recognized, a red squiggly line will appear. You will need to correct the user name.

11. Click **Start**. The workflow will be started and the page will move to Waiting for Approval status.

Exception: If the page does not change to Waiting for Approval status, it may need to be refreshed, so the cache for the page and the page's status will be in sync. Press Ctrl+F5 in your browser to update the status of the page.

Task: Create a Custom Permission Level

Purpose: SharePoint's permission system is based on a set of atomic permissions which are grouped into permission levels like design, edit, contribute, and read. These are great when you want to assign a set of permissions that match what's in the predefined level to a group. However, when you need something that's slightly more granular, you can create your own permission level to match your exact needs. See Appendix E for more information on the atomic permissions and the oute of the box permission levels.

Example: By default the Contribute permission level has the ability to delete versions, the Action Marketing Group's compliance department wants to prevent users from doing this to ease their investigations.

Steps:

1. Start Internet Explorer and type the URL for your organization's SharePoint server. The Start page will open.

2. Navigate to the site that needs a new permission level.

   Note: For sites that inherit permissions from the parent, navigate to the parent site.

3. Select the **Settings** menu gear icon and select **Site Settings**. The Site Settings page will open.

4. In the Users and Permissions section, click the **Site permissions** link. The Permissions page will open.

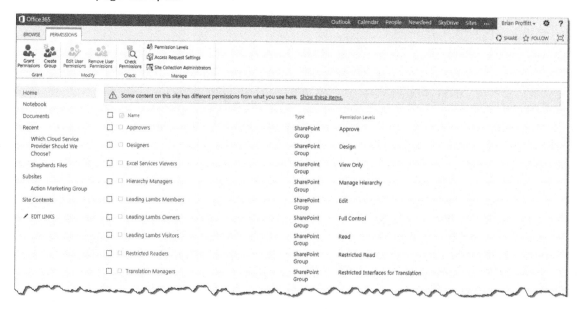

Figure 1: The Permission Tools Ribbon on the Permissions Page

5. In the ribbon click the **Permission Levels** button. The Permission Levels page will open.

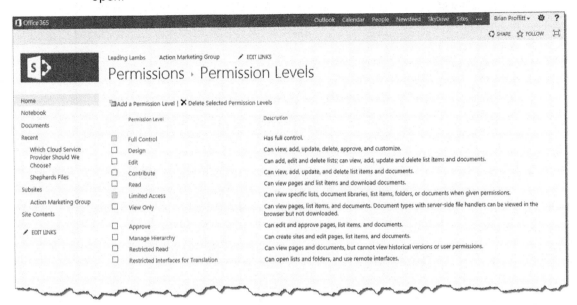

Figure 2: The Permission Levels Page

6. Click the **Add a Permission Level** link. The Add a Permission Level page will appear.

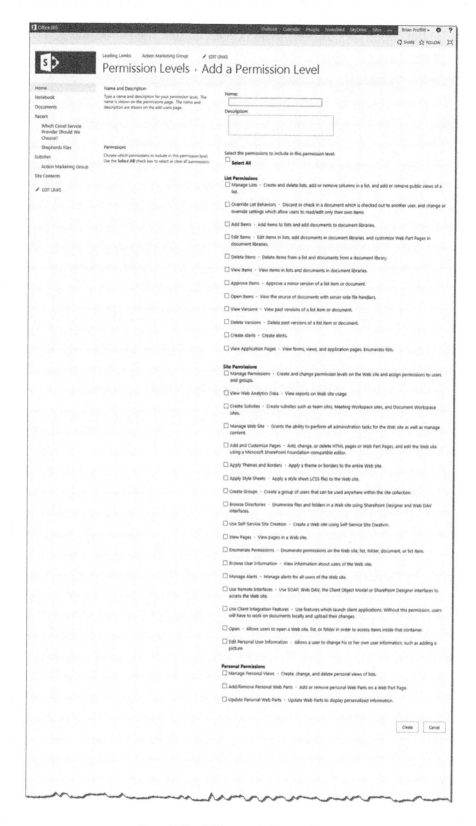

Figure 3: The Add a Permission Level Page

7. Add a Name and Description for the new permission level.

8. Select the permission options that you want to use.

9. Click **Create**. The new permission level will be created. You can now add users to this group so they can make updates to your site based on the permissions you set.

Site owners have more responsibilities and more capabilities than SharePoint site authors. Owners can create whole sites, and modify existing sites at a deeper level.

In this section, you'll learn how to:

- **Change a Site Theme**: As the owner of a site, you have the ability to make broad changes to the look and feel of your site.

- **Change a Site Logo**: When SharePoint builds a site from a template, it includes many placeholders, such as images and logos, to mark the general feel of a site.

- **Change a Site Master Page**: SharePoint site templates include a number of master page settings, which define the basic layout options for the site.

- **Add Cascading Style Sheets**: If you don't prefer what SharePoint has to offer in terms of style libraries, you can attach your own CSS document to customize the site.

- **Organize Pages in a Web Site**: As you edit a Web site, you may discover that you will need to re-organize your site to create a better flow of information and traffic.

- **Upload a User Solution to the Site Collection Solution Gallery**: Whenever you need to use a site template from another SharePoint instance, you can upload it to your SharePoint site collection.

- **Allow Users to Create Different Sub-sites**: SharePoint will, by default, limit access in a publishing site to two site templates.

- **Create a Sub-site**: If you have the appropriate permissions, you can create a new subsite fairly easily in SharePoint

- **Customize Publishing Site Navigation**: To make things very clear to site visitors, you need to make sure your navigation tools are laid out properly.

- **Add the Content Query Web Part**: All SharePoint Sites come with a number of tools to assist users, such as the Content Query Web Part.

- **Export a Web Part**: Export your Web Part for use on another page.

- **Import a Web Part**: Many SharePoint developers have created customized Web Parts that can be easily plugged in to an existing SharePoint site.

- **Add the Summary Links Web Part**: Another useful Web Part is the Summary Links Web Part, which lets you manually add links to articles and pages on your site, as well as to other sites.

Task: Change a Site Theme

Purpose: SharePoint has the capability to change the colors, fonts, and feel of the site through the use of themes. In addition to the out of the box themes provided with the product you can download and install new themes to allow you to quickly customize the look and feel of the site.

Example: The Action Marketing Group is looking for something to differentiate its confidential site. The systems administrator will reset the site to a red based theme to indicate the criticality and to differentiate it.

Steps:

1. Start Internet Explorer and type the URL for your organization's SharePoint server. The Start page will open.

2. Navigate to the site. The site's home page will open.

3. Click the **Settings** menu gear icon and select **Site Settings**. The Site Settings page will open.

Figure 1: The Site Settings Page

4. In the Look and Feel section, click the **Change the look** link. The Change the look page will open.

The SharePoint Shepherd's Guide for End Users: 2013

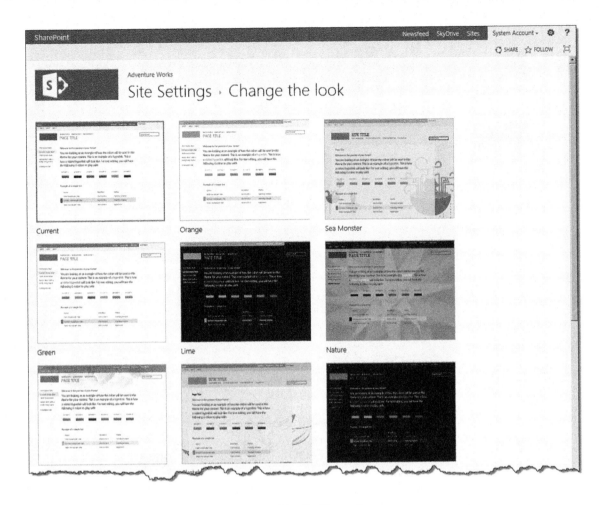

Figure 2: The Site Theme Page

5. Click any of the listed themes. The preview will change to reflect the theme's look.

6. When you have decided on a theme, click **Try it out**. The Preview page will open, with the new theme applied.

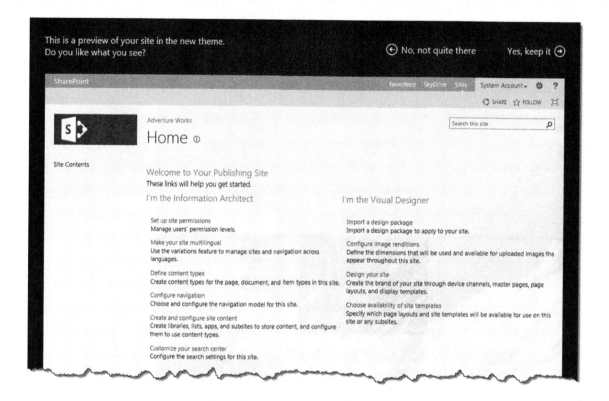

Figure 3: The Preview of the Home Page

7. If you like the theme, click **Yes, keep it**. The Site Settings page will appear, with the new theme applied.

Task: Change a Site Logo

Purpose: SharePoint provides a clean professional look – however, it starts with the default SharePoint site logo which won't match your company's brand. By replacing the site logo it's possible to quickly make a SharePoint site look like it belongs to the organization.

Example: The Action Marketing Group logo will need to be added to the site's pages.

Steps:

1. Start Internet Explorer and type the URL for your organization's SharePoint server. The Start page will open.

2. Navigate to the publishing site. The publishing site's home page will open.

3. Click the **Settings** menu gear icon and select **Site Settings**. The Site Settings page will open.

4. In the **Look and Feel** section click the **Title, description, and logo** link. The Title, Description, and Logo page will open.

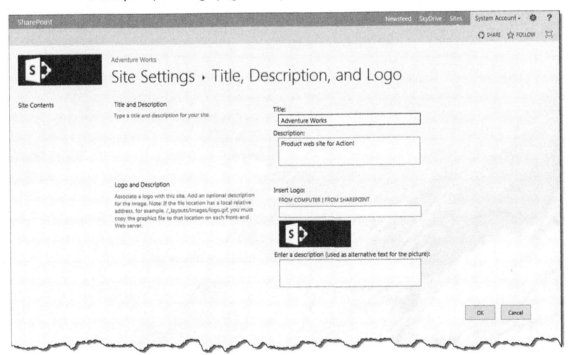

Figure 1: The Title, Description, and Logo Page

5. In the logo and description section, click the From Computer link. The Add a Document dialog box will open.

6. Click Browse. The Choose File to Upload dialog box will open.

7. Navigate to the file you want to use as a logo and select it.

8. Click **Open**. The file's path will appear in the Choose a file field.

9. Click **OK**. The image will appear in the Title, Description, and Logo page.

10. Click **OK**. The Site Settings page will open, with the new logo applied.

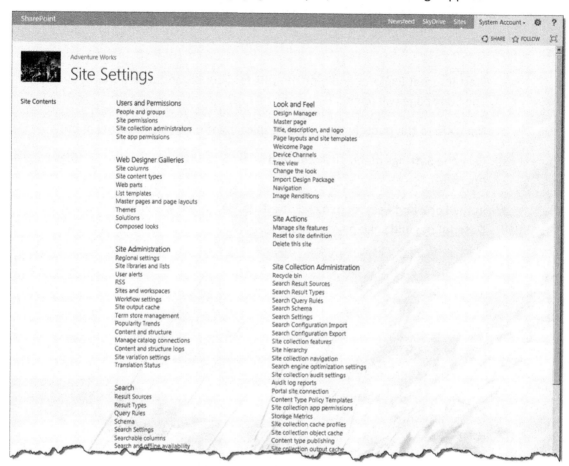

Figure 2: The New Logo Applied to the Site Settings Page

Task: Change a Site Master Page

Purpose: SharePoint master pages control the overall containers on the page which ultimately control the basic structure of the page – and therefore the site. SharePoint allows you to change master pages so that you can have a different look and feel than the out of the box definition.

Example: The Action Marketing Group had a custom master page developed and the Internet manager wants to apply it to an internal staging site.

Steps:

1. Start Internet Explorer and type the URL for your organization's SharePoint server. The Start page will open.

2. Navigate to the publishing site. The publishing site's home page\ will open.

3. Click the **Settings** menu gear icon and select **Site Settings**. The Site Settings page will open.

4. In the **Look and Feel** section, click the **Master page** link. The Site Master Page Settings page will open.

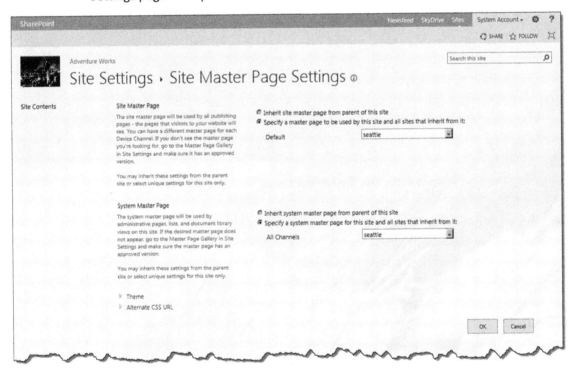

Figure 1: The Site Master Page Settings Page

5. In the Site Master Page section, confirm the **Specify a master page to be used by the site and all sites that inherit from it** option is selected.

6. In the drop down control, select the option you would like (for instance, **oslo**).

7. Click **OK**. The Site Settings page will open.

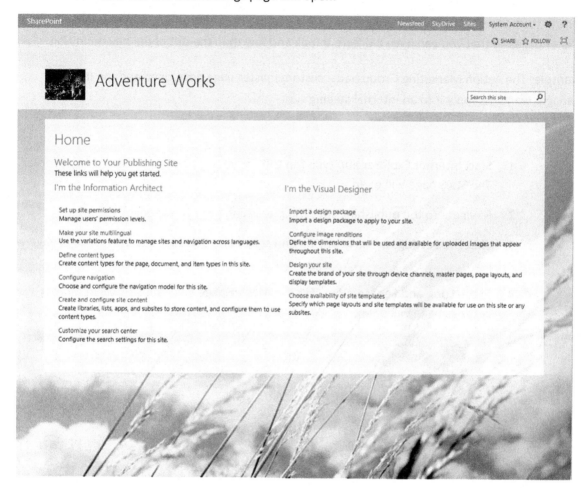

Figure 2: The New Master Page Setting Applied to the Home Page

The SharePoint Shepherd's Guide for End Users: 2013

Task: Add Cascading Style Sheets

Purpose: On the web much of the styling is handled through Cascading Style Sheets (CSS). With CSS it is possible to get a radically different look and feel because CSS can control positioning, fonts, colors, backgrounds, padding, etc. CSS works by a "last one wins" approach so SharePoint defines the standard CSS for displaying a site but also allows you to add your own CSS at the end of the list so you can override any SharePoint styling.

Example: The Action Marketing Group created a new CSS which they'll use for internal collaboration sites instead of creating a whole new master page.

Steps:

1. Start Internet Explorer and type the URL for your organization's SharePoint server. The Start page will open.

2. Navigate to the publishing site. The publishing site's home page will open.

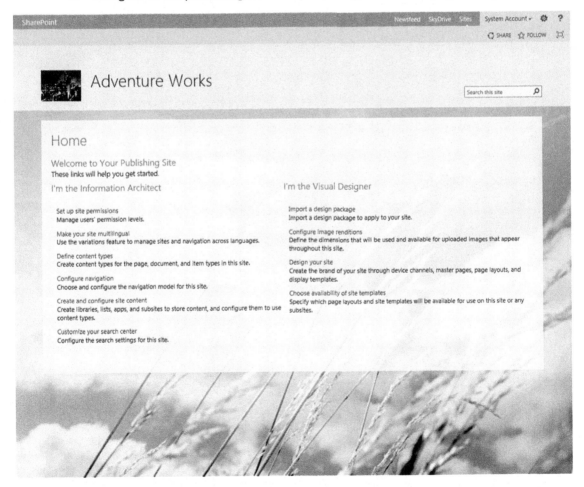

Figure 1: The Publishing Site's Home Page

3. Click the **Settings** menu gear icon and select **Site Settings**. The Site Settings page will open.

4. In the **Look and Feel** section, click the **Master page** link. The Site Master Page Settings page will open.

5. Click the **Alternate CSS URL** section heading to expand the section.

6. Click the **Specify a CSS file to be used by this publishing site and all sites that inherit from it** option.

7. Add the URL for the CSS file you would like to use, using the **Browse** button to find the file.

8. Click **OK**. The Site Settings pagewill open with the new CSS settings applied.

Task: Organize Pages in a Web Site

Purpose: Organizations change all the time. Web sites should be living and changing over time. SharePoint makes it easy to move pages in a site whether the goal is to match an organization change or to accommodate a web site structural change.

Example: The Action Marketing Group is creating a subsite for corporate information and wants to move the contact us, about us, privacy statement, etc., into the new sub-site.

Note: This procedure will only work for sites which have the publishing features enabled.

Steps:

1. Start Internet Explorer and type the URL for your organization's SharePoint server. The Start page will open.

2. Navigate to the publishing site. The publishing site's home page will open.

3. Click the **Settings** menu gear icon and select the **Site Settings** option.

4. In the Site Administration section, click the **Content and Structure** link. The Site Content and Structure page will open.

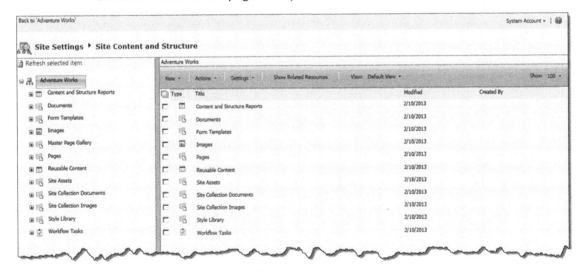

Figure 1: The Site Content and Structure Page

5. In the navigation pane, click the **Pages** folder. The contents will be displayed in the contents pane.

6. Select the checkboxes for the files you would like to move.

7. In the **Actions** menu click the **Move** option. The Move dialog box will appear.

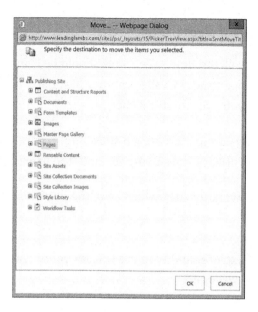

Figure 2: The Move Dialog Box

8. Click the folder for the subsite to which you want to move the files.

9. Click **OK**. The Move dialog box will close and the files will be moved to the new folder.

Task: Upload a User Solution to the Site Collection Solution Gallery

Purpose: SharePoint, since 2007, uses packages called Solutions to install custom functionality. There are two versions of solutions those which you upload to the site collection solution gallery called user solutions or sometimes sandbox solutions. SharePoint will create user solutions when you save a site as a template. If you have a user solution you can upload it into another site collection and activate it for use.

Example: The Action Marketing Group created a project management site template for use internally. They now want to use it for extranet projects and need to upload the solution to the extranet web application.

Steps:

1. Start Internet Explorer and type the URL for your organization's SharePoint server. The Start page will open.

2. Navigate to the main site from which the new site will be added. The site's home page will open.

3. Click the **Settings** menu gear icon and select **Site Settings**. The Site Settings page will open.

4. In the **Web Designer Galleries** section, click the **Solutions** link. The Solutions page will open.

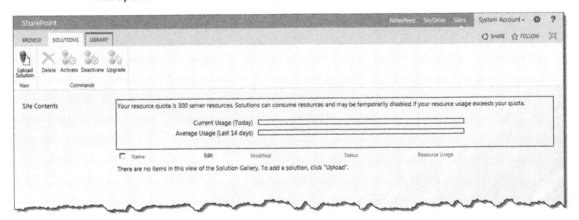

Figure 1: The Solutions Page

5. Click the **Solutions** tab. The Solutions ribbon will appear.

6. Click the **Upload Solution** button. The Add a Document dialog box will appear.

Figure 2: The Add a Document Dialog Box

7. Click **Browse**. The Choose File to Upload dialog box will open.

8. Navigate to the solution file you want to use and click **Open**. The file will appear in the Name field.

9. Click **OK**. The new solution will be uploaded. Once the solution is activated, it will be available for use.

Task: Allow Users to Create Different Subsites

Purpose: SharePoint offers a dizzying array of site templates. These templates can be daunting for content managers tying to create a structure for their content. The default behavior for publishing sites is to limit the sites that are available to be used for sub-site creation to reduce confusion and to encourage the right uses for the subsites. However, you can change which templates are available.

Example: The Action Marketing Group would like to allow content owners to create sites based off of its custom product template.

Steps:

1. Start Internet Explorer and type the URL for your organization's SharePoint server. The Start page will open.

2. Navigate to the publishing site. The publishing site's home page will open.

3. Click the **Settings** menu gear icon and select **Site Settings**. The Site Settings page will open.

4. In the **Look and Feel** section, click the **Page layouts and site templates** link. The Page Layout and Site Template Settings page will open.

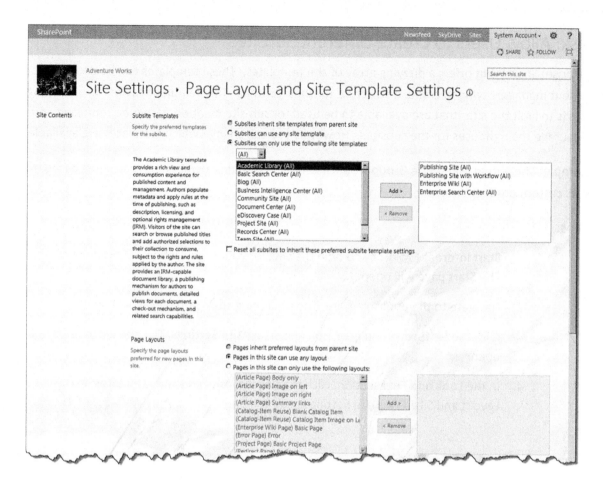

Figure 1: The Page Layout and Site Template Settings Page

5. In the **Subsite Templates** section, select the templates you want to be available and click **Add.**

6. Click **OK**. The Site Settings page will open and the template will be available when you add a subsite.

Task: Create a Subsite

Purpose: If you have the appropriate permissions, you can create a new subsite fairly easily in SharePoint. You might create a subsite to gather a collection of content into a single area, or when you want to provide some separation from the existing content.

Example: The Action Marketing Group will add a Basic Search subsite to its public site.

Steps:

1. Start Internet Explorer and type the URL for your organization's SharePoint server. The Start page will open.

2. Click the **Settings** menu gear icon and select **Site Contents**. The Site Contents page will open.

3. Click the new subsite link. The New SharePoint Site page will open.

4. In the Title field type a title for your site. The title of your site should be descriptive and can be up to about 50 letters before becoming intrusive.

5. In the Description field type a description for your site. The description is like a subtitle that will be displayed on some of the pages. It should further clarify the title so that anyone can understand the site's purpose.

6. In the URL Name field type a short, descriptive name for your search engine. This will become part of the full Web Site Address for your new subsite.

7. Click the tabs to find the templates you want and select it.

8. In the User Permissions section, select the **Use same permissions as parent site** option. You can change to unique permissions later as shown in the task "Assign Users to a Group."

9. In the Use the top link bar from the parent site field, select the **Yes** option.

10. Click **Create**. The Working on It screen will briefly appear, followed by the new site home page.

Figure 1: The New Basic Search Center Page

The SharePoint Shepherd's Guide for End Users: 2013

Task: Customize Publishing Site Navigation

Purpose: Navigation is an important component to any web site. In addition to supporting automatic creation of navigation links for global (top navigation) and local (quick launch), SharePoint allows you to manually change the navigation.

Example: The Action Marketing Group intranet manager needs to add a link to a non-SharePoint resource from the menus.

Steps:

1. Start Internet Explorer and type the URL for your organization's SharePoint server. The Start page will open.

2. Navigate to the publishing site. The publishing site's home page will open.

3. Click the **Settings** menu gear icon and select **Site Settings**. The Site Settings page will open.

4. In the **Look and Feel** section, click the **Navigation** link. The Navigation Settings page will open.

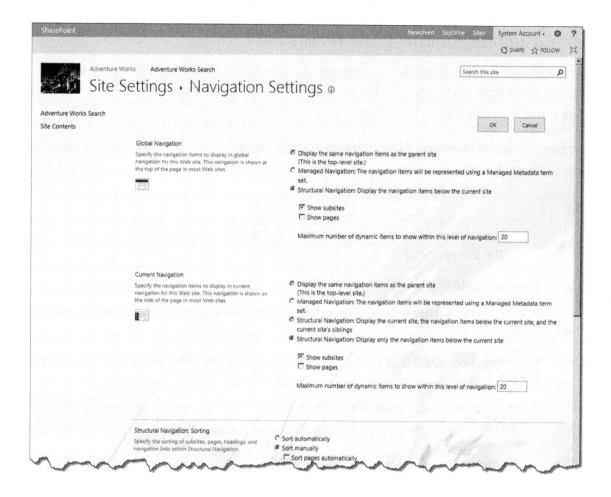

Figure 1: The Navigation Settings Page

5. In the **Sorting** section, select the **Sort manually** option.

6. In the **Structural Navigation: Editing and Sorting** section, select the **Current Navigation** folder then click **Add Link**. The Navigation Link dialog box will open.

Figure 2: The Navigation Link Dialog Box

7. Add the pertinent information, using the Browser button to find the correct URL.

8. Click **OK**. The new link will be visible in the **Navigation Editing and Sorting** section.

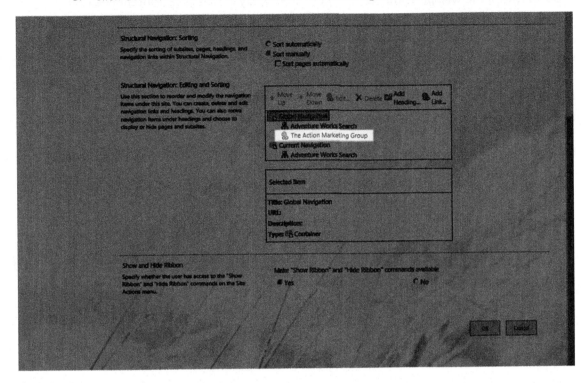

Figure 3: The New Navigation Link

9. Click the new link to select it, then click **Move Up** until the menu item is listed in the order you desire.

10. Click **OK**. The Site Settings page will open and the new link will be visible in the site's navigation menu.

Task: Add the Content Query Web Part

Purpose: One of the web parts that is used most frequently in rolling up content and displaying it on the intranet home page is the Content Query Web Part. If you want to accomplish more advanced customization, visit the "Customizing the Content Query Web Part in SharePoint" white paper at http://msdn.microsoft.com/en-us/library/ff380147.aspx.

Example: The Action Marketing Group site will add a content query Web Part to their intranet home page.

Steps:

1. Start Internet Explorer and type the URL for your organization's SharePoint server. The Start page will open.

2. Navigate to the site where you want to add the Content Query Web Part.

3. Click the **Page** tab and select the **Edit Page** button. The Page ribbon will appear and the page will open in Edit Mode.

Figure 1: The Page Ribbon and Page in Edit Mode

4. Select a zone and click **Add a Web Part**. The Add Web Parts header will open.

5. Select the **Content Rollup** folder and then click the **Content Query** Web Part. The Web Part will be selected.

6. Click **Add**. The Add Web Parts header will close and the new Web Part will appear in the selected zone.

7. Click the **open the tool pane** link. The tool pane for the Content Query Web Part will appear.

Figure 2: The Content Query Web Part Tool Pane

8. Click the **Query** expand control to expand the section, then click the **Show items from the following site and all subsites** option.

9. In the adjacent URL field enter the URL for the site.

10. Continue to fill out the remainder of the Content Query tool pane as desired.

11. Click **OK**. The Content Query Web Part Tool Pane will close and the new Web Part will be visible on the page.

Note: Follow the site approval steps to save and publish the modified page.

Task: Export a Web Part

Purpose: Customizing a web part the way you want takes time and if you want the web part to appear the same way in multiple web sites it may be easier to export the web part and import it than making the settings over and over again. Most web parts can be exported – however some web parts cannot be exported.

Example: The Action Marketing Group intranet manager has configured a Content Query Web Part and wants to use it on multiple product sites. He'll export it so that he can import it into other sites.

Steps:

1. Start Internet Explorer and type the URL for your organization's SharePoint server. The Start page will open.

2. Navigate to the site from which you want to export the Content Query Web Part.

3. Click the **Page** tab and select the **Edit Page** button. The Page ribbon will appear and the page will open in Edit Mode.

4. Hover over the title for the web part that you want to export then click the drop-down control on the right side of the title bar and click the **Export...** option. The File Download dialog box will open.

5. Click **Save**. The Save As dialog box will open.

6. Name and navigate to the folder in which you want to save the Web Part, clicking **Save**. The Web Part will be saved.

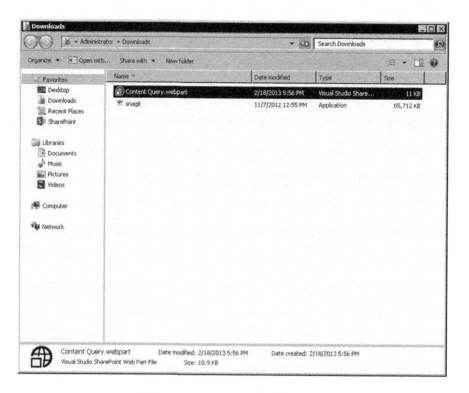

Figure 1: The Downloaded Web Part

Task: Import a Web Part

Purpose: SharePoint allows you to export a web part to save the configuration so that you can use it again. Once you have an exported web part you can import it back in on a new page in the site where you want it.

Example: The Action Marketing Group intranet manager wants to import the content query web part she's already configured to each of the product sites.

Steps:

1. Start Internet Explorer and type the URL for your organization's SharePoint server. The Start page will open.

2. Navigate to the site to add the Content Query Web Part.

3. Click the **Page** tab and select the **Edit Page** button. The Page ribbon will appear and the page will open in Edit Mode.

4. Select a zone and click **Add a Web Part**. The Add Web Parts header will open.

5. Click the **Upload a Web Part** control. The control will expand to an upload field.

Figure 1: The Upload a Web Part Control

6. Click **Browse**. The Choose File to Upload dialog box will open.

7. Navigate to the Web Part you want to upload and click **Open**. The file path and name of the folder will appear in the field.

8. Click **Upload**. The Web Part will be uploaded.

   Note: Sometimes it is necessary to click Add a Web Part again to get the web part pane to reappear after an upload.

---

9. Click **Imported Web Parts** folder and then the new Web Part. The Web Part will be selected.

10. Click **Add**. The Add Web Parts header will close and the new Web Part will appear in the selected zone.

Task: Add the Summary Links Web Part

Purpose: SharePoint also includes a Summary Links web part which allows you to add links to a page in a structured way. The value of using this web part is that when pages are moved the moves will be reflected in the web part (in most cases.) The Summary Links Web Part gives you a way to include links across the site and have them displayed in a consistent way.

Example: The Action Marketing Group site will add a Summary Links Web Part to its home page.

Steps:

1. Start Internet Explorer and type the URL for your organization's SharePoint server. The Start page will open.

2. Navigate to the site to add the Summary Links Web Part.

3. In the ribbon click the **Page** tab and select the **Edit** button. The Page ribbon will appear and the page will open in Edit Mode.

4. Select a zone and click **Add a Web Part**. The Add Web Parts pane will open.

5. Click the **Content Rollup** folder and then the Summary Links Web Part. The Web Part will be selected.

6. Click **Add**. The Add Web Parts header will close and the Summary Links Web Part will appear in the selected zone.

7. To add a new summary link, at the top of the Summary Links Web Part click **New Link**. The New Link dialog box will open.

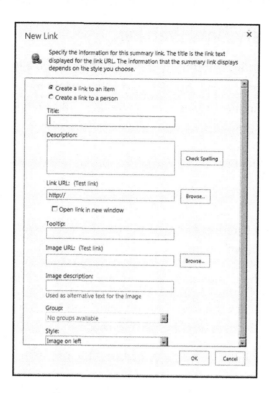

Figure 1: The New Link Dialog Box

8. Add the pertinent information about the link. You can add as much or as little information as needed.

9. Click **OK**. The new summary link will be added to the page.

Site Collection Owners will have the ability to manage entire collections of sites, which gives them the responsibility to maintain consistency in style as well as site collection efficiency.

In this section, you'll learn how to:

- **Enable Output Cache**: To counter the time it takes to query a database, and to effectively speed up the time it takes for pages to be served, Site Collection owners can implement caching.

- **Configure Site Collection Default Cache Profiles**: Once output caching is implemented on a site, the Site Collection owner can specify which profiles will apply to which kinds of site visitors.

- **Configure Output Cache Profiles**: SharePoint provides you with a few preconfigured output cache profiles to apply to your site. Each of these profiles can be tweaked to match your exact needs.

- **Add an Output Cache Profile**: Sometimes a Site Collection owner might need to create a new output cache from scratch.

- **Override the Configured Output Cache Profile**: You can set SharePoint to allow site administrators and designers to configure cache settings for individual pages.

- **Configure the Object Cache**: Object caching is another way to improve page rendering in SharePoint.

- **Flush Object Caches**: If you have made significant changes to the cache settings on your site or you suspect that the cache is invalid, it might be a good idea to purge the object and disk-based caches for your server.

- **Enable and Configure Cross-List Query Cache**: The cross-list query caching improves query performance, but only if the content of your lists or libraries is relatively unchanging.

- **Upload and Activate a Sandbox Solution**: Sandbox solutions are designed for situations where the developer of a solution isn't trusted by the central administration or the solution pertains only to a single site collection.

- **Deactivate a Sandbox Solution**: Sandbox solutions can use up a certain number of server resources and thus need to be managed accordingly.

Task: Enable Output Cache

Purpose: Whenever a user requests a page from a Web site, the request has to go through a variety of steps before the page is actually transmitted back to the user's browser. In the case of SharePoint pages, a big piece of time can be taken up by the process of checking the content database. To counter this, and to effectively speed up the time pages are served, Site Collection owners can implement caching. This allows SharePoint to keep rendered and partially rendered copies of the page on the local server disk which can be served up much quicker to the users.

Example: The Action Marketing Group site is performing slowly to the customers and the intranet manager wants to quickly increase performance by implementing output caching.

Steps:

1. Start Internet Explorer and type the URL for your organization's SharePoint server. The Start page will open.

2. Navigate to the publishing site. The publishing site's home page will open.

3. Click the **Settings** menu gear icon and select **Site Settings**. The Site Settings page will open.

4. In the **Site Collection Administration** section, click the **Site collection output cache** link. The Output Cache Settings page will open.

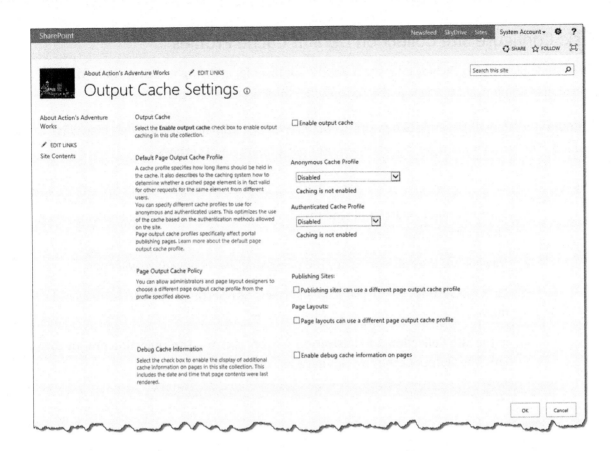

Figure 1: The Output Cache Settings Page

5. In the **Output Cache** section, select the **Enable output cache** checkbox.

6. Click **OK**. The Site Settings page will open.

Note: To disable the output cache, repeat these steps and de-select the **Enable output cache** checkbox.

Task: Configure Site Collection Default Cache Profiles

Purpose: Implementing caching on a site is good – but leveraging the right cache profile for each type of user is important to manage the consumption of disk space and performance.

Example: The Action Marketing Group site is not performing optimally even after caching was enabled. The Intranet manager is seeking a better performing set of settings.

Steps:

1. Start Internet Explorer and type the URL for your organization's SharePoint server. The Start page will open.

2. Navigate to the publishing site. The publishing site's home page will open.

3. Click the **Settings** menu gear icon and select **Site Settings**. The Site Settings page will open.

4. In the **Site Collection Administration** section, click the **Site collection output cache** link. The Output Cache Settings page will open.

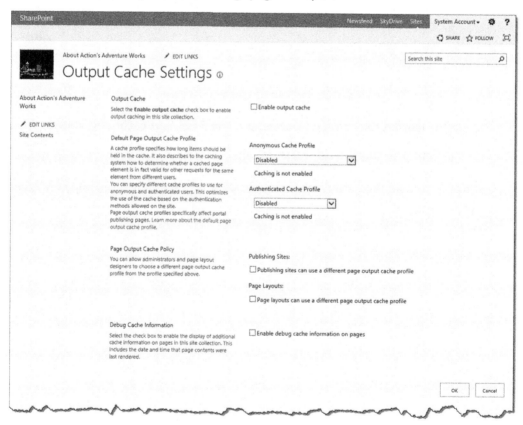

Figure 1: The Output Cache Settings Page

5. In the **Default Page Output Cache Profile** section, set the Anonymous Cache Profile field to the **Public Internet (Purely Anonymous)** option. The site will be optimized for public Internet facing sites or areas that are meant to serve the same content to all users.

6. In the **Default Page Output Cache Profile** section, set the Authenticated Cache Profile field to the **Extranet (Published Site)** option. The site will be optimized for a public extranet site with the following characteristics: authoring does not take place on the tier; only major versions of pages are deployed to the tier; and users cannot customize Web Parts on a page in the tier.

7. Click **OK**. The Site Settings page will open.

Task: Configure Output Cache Profiles

Purpose: SharePoint provides you with a few preconfigured output cache profiles to apply to your site. However, the unique needs of your site may require that you implement specific tweaks to these settings.

Example: The Action Marketing Group site cache setting for anonymous users needs its cache duration increased from 180 seconds to 360 seconds.

Steps:

1. Start Internet Explorer and type the URL for your organization's SharePoint server. The Start page will open.

2. Navigate to the publishing site. The publishing site's home page will open.

3. Click the **Settings** menu gear icon and select **Site Settings**. The Site Settings page will open.

4. In the **Site Collection Administration** section, click the **Site collection cache profiles** link. The Cache Profiles page will open.

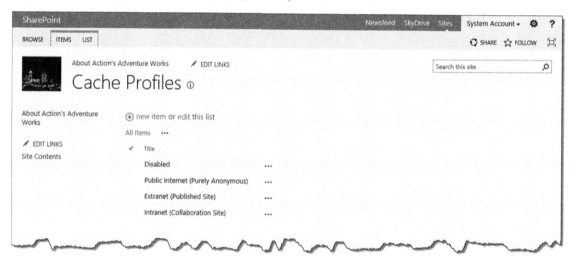

Figure 1: The Cache Profiles Page

5. Click the **Public Internet (Purely Anonymous)** link. The Public Internet (Purely Anonymous) page will open.

The SharePoint Shepherd's Guide for End Users: 2013

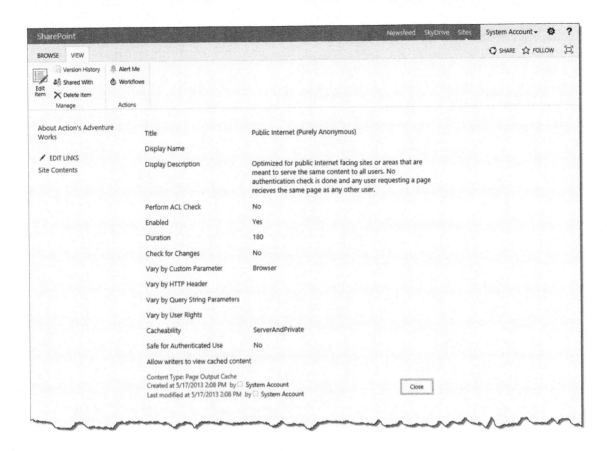

Figure 2: The Public Internet (Purely Anonymous) Page

6. Click the **Edit Item** button. The Cache Profiles editing page will change to edit mode.

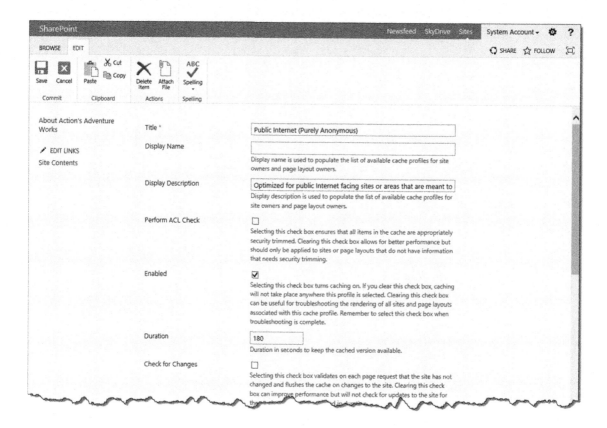

Figure 3: The Cache Profiles Page in Edit Mode

7. Make the changes necessary to customize the profile. For instance, change the Duration field to 360.

8. Click **Save**. The Cache Profiles Edit Mode page will close.

The SharePoint Shepherd's Guide for End Users: 2013

Task: Add an Output Cache Profile

Purpose: SharePoint provides you with a few preconfigured output cache profiles to apply to your site. Sometimes, however, a Site Collection owner might need to create a new output cache from scratch.

Example: The Action Marketing Group site needs a cache setting for site developers to optimize the performance for these users.

Steps:

1. Start Internet Explorer and type the URL for your organization's SharePoint server. The Start page will open.

2. Navigate to the publishing site. The publishing site's home page will open.

3. Click the **Settings** menu gear icon and select **Site Settings**. The Site Settings page will open.

4. In the **Site Collection Administration** section, click the **Site collection cache profiles** link. The Cache Profiles page will open.

5. Click the **new item** link. The New Cache Profiles page will open.

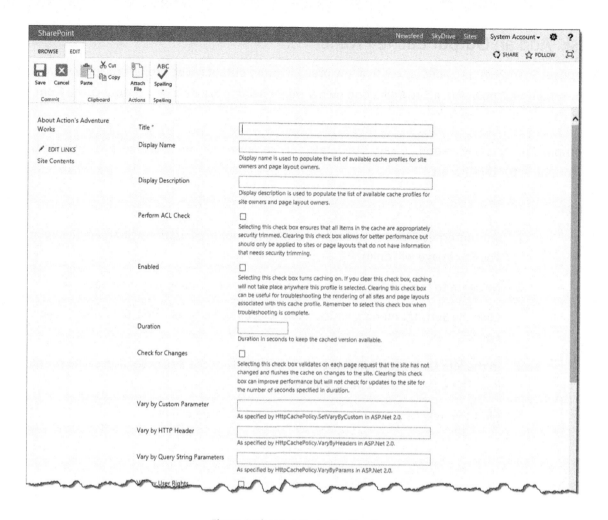

Figure 1: The New Cache Profiles Page

6.   Add the settings in the New Cache Profiles page as needed.

7.   Click **Save**. The Cache Profiles dialog box will close and the new cache profile will be added to Cache Profiles Page.

Exception: If these settings are not available, the Publishing Infrastructure site collection feature and the Publishing site feature may not be active.

Task: Override the Configured Output Cache Profile

Purpose: SharePoint's caching is very sophisticated and appropriate, however, sometimes a page may not be able to be cached appropriately due to a special circumstance or third party software. Allowing the page owner to change the caching of an individual page allows you to work around specific issues with a single page or a few pages.

Example: The Action Marketing Group site cache settings will be set by the Site Collection owner to allow cache settings to be configured by page.

Steps:

1. Start Internet Explorer and type the URL for your organization's SharePoint server. The Start page will open.

2. Navigate to the publishing site. The publishing site's home page will open.

3. Click the **Settings** menu gear icon and select **Site Settings**. The Site Settings page will open.

4. In the **Site Collection Administration** section, click the **Site collection output cache** link. The Output Cache Settings page will open.

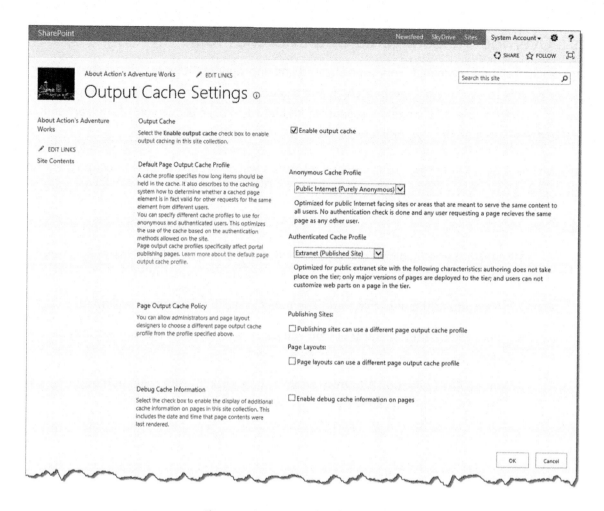

Figure 1: The Output Cache Settings Page

5. In the **Page Output Cache Policy** section, click the **Page layouts can use a different page output cache profile** checkbox.

6. Click **OK**. The Site Settings page will open.

The SharePoint Shepherd's Guide for End Users: 2013

Task: Configure the Object Cache

Purpose: SharePoint offers numerous ways to accomplish caching to improve performance including object caching. Object caching uses memory to reduce the frequency SharePoint has to go back to SQL server reducing load and improving responsiveness to the users.

Example: The Action Marketing Group wants to take better advantage of the SharePoint object cache.

Steps:

1. Start Internet Explorer and type the URL for your organization's SharePoint server. The Start page will open.

2. Navigate to the publishing site. The publishing site's home page will open.

3. Click the **Settings** menu gear icon and select **Site Settings**. The Site Settings page will open.

4. In the **Site Collection Administration** section, click the **Site collection object cache** link. The Object Cache Settings page will open.

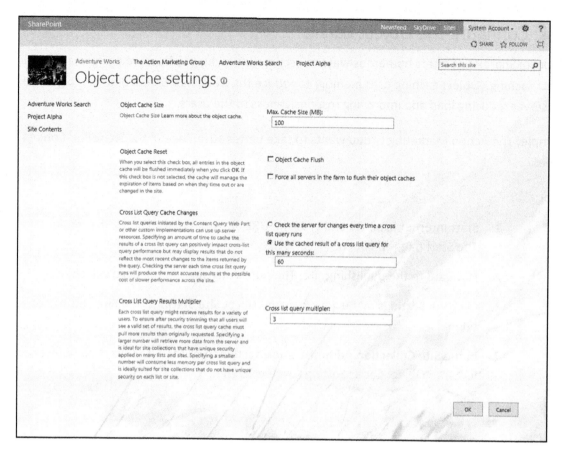

Figure 1: The Object Cache Settings Page

5. In the **Object Cache Size** section, set the Max. Cache Size (MB) field to the desired value.

6. Click **OK**. The Site Settings page will open.

Task: Flush Object Caches

Purpose: When configured SharePoint caches objects. Sometimes these caches can become corrupt. If you suspect that the cache is invalid, you can reset, or flush, the cache to ensure that you're getting current results. SharePoint enables you to do this for one server, or all servers in the SharePoint server farm.

Example: The Action Marketing Group Site Collection owner will flush the disk-based and object caches for the individual Action Group public site's server.

Steps:

1. Start Internet Explorer and type the URL for your organization's SharePoint server. The Start page will open.

2. Navigate to the publishing site. The publishing site's home page will open.

3. Click the **Settings** menu gear icon and select **Site Settings**. The Site Settings page will open.

4. In the **Site Collection Administration** section, click the **Site collection object cache** link. The Object Cache Settings page will open.

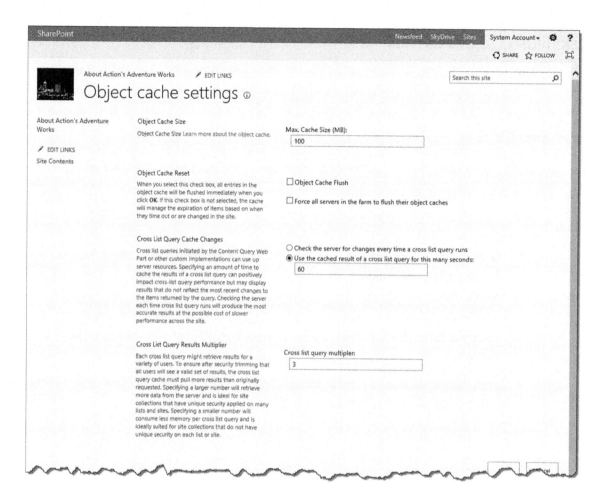

Figure 1: The Output Cache Settings Page

5. In the **Object Cache Reset** section, click the **Object Cache Flush** checkbox.

6. Click **OK**. The caches for the server will immediately be flushed and the Site Settings page will open.

Task: Enable and Configure Cross-List Query Cache

Purpose: Cross-list queries are expensive for SharePoint to execute. Most cross-list queries involve a list that rarely changes. By caching that list it's possible to improve SharePoint performance. SharePoint allows you to configure how aggressively the secondary lists will be cached.

Example: The Action Marketing Group Site Collection owner will set the query cache option to a longer cache because the site's content does not change often.

Steps:

1. Start Internet Explorer and type the URL for your organization's SharePoint server. The Start page will open.

2. Navigate to the publishing site. The publishing site's home page will open.

3. Click the **Settings** menu gear icon and select **Site Settings**. The Site Settings page will open.

4. In the **Site Collection Administration** section, click the **Site collection object cache** link. The Object Cache Settings page will open.

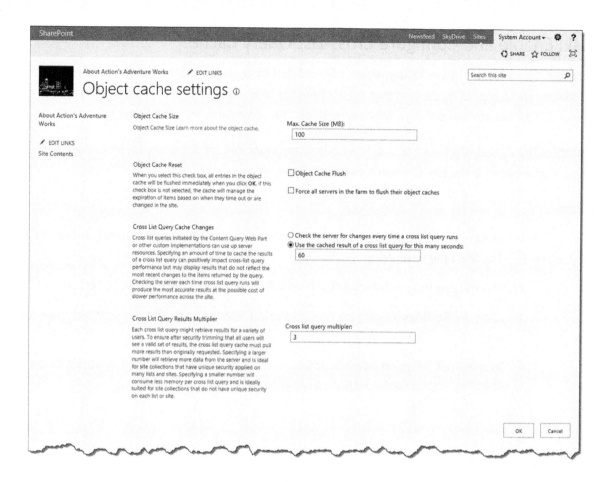

Figure 1: The Object Cache Settings Page

5. In the **Cross List Query Cache** section, click the **Check the server for changes every time a cross list query runs** option if your content changes often. Otherwise, click the **Use the cached result of a cross list query for this many seconds** option.

6. Click **OK**. The Site Settings page will open.

Task: Upload and Activate a Sandbox Solution

Purpose: SharePoint 2010 introduced a concept of Sandboxed solutions – sometimes called user solutions. These solutions are able to be uploaded and activated by site collection administrators and can be templates for lists and libraries to create – including data – or they can include code that will be run in a special "sandbox" so that it can't impact other users on the farm.

Example: The Action Marketing Group test site before implementing it in a production environment.

Steps:

1.   Start Internet Explorer and type the URL for your organization's SharePoint server. The Start page will open.

2.   Navigate to the site where the solution will be used. The site's home page will open.

3.   Click the **Settings** menu and select **Site Settings**. The Site Settings page will open.

4.   In the **Web Designer Galleries** section click the **Solutions** link. The Solutions page will open.

Figure 1: The Solutions Page

5.   Click the **Solutions** tab. The Solutions ribbon will appear.

6.   Click the **Upload Solution** button. The Add a document dialog box will appear.

Figure 2: The Add a Document Dialog Box

7. Click **Browse**. The Choose File to Upload dialog box will open.

8. Navigate to the sandbox solution file you want to use and click **Open**. The file will appear in the Name field.

9. Click **OK**. The new template will be uploaded and appear in the Solutions gallery.

10. Click the solution item to select it. A confirmation dialog box will open.

11. Click the **Activate** button. The solution will be activated.

Task: Deactivate a Sandbox Solution

Purpose: SharePoint Sandbox solutions enable functionality and when they contain code can consume resources. By deactivating a solution you can remove templates that you no longer want users to use and you can stop code from consuming resources.

Example: The Action Marketing Group has decided that the third party web part they were evaluating won't work and the intranet manager will deactivate it.

Steps:

1. Start Internet Explorer and type the URL for your organization's SharePoint server. The Start page will open.

2. Navigate to the main site from which the new sandbox site will be deactivated. The site's home page will open.

3. Click the **Settings** menu gear icon and select **Site Settings**. The Site Settings page will open.

4. In the **Web Designer Galleries** section, click the **Solutions** link. The Solutions page will open.

5. Click the solution item to select it.

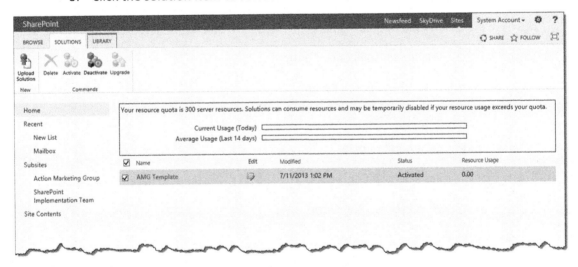

Figure 1: Selecting a Solution Item

6. Click the **Deactivate** button. After confirming the action, the sandbox solution will be deactivated.

Appendix A: Site Definitions

Purpose: There are many different kinds of sites that can be created in SharePoint. You have seen some in action throughout the tasks in this book. In this Appendix, all of the site definitions will be reviewed and displayed, to make your choices easier when it's time to create your own site.

The site definitions that can be available on the New SharePoint Site page are:

- Collaboration Sites
    - Team Site
    - Blog
    - Developer Site
    - Project Site
    - Community Site
- Enterprise Sites
    - Document Center
    - eDiscovery Center
    - Records Center
    - Business Intelligence Center
    - Enterprise Search Center
    - My Site Host
    - Community Portal
    - Basic Search Center
    - Visio Process Repository
- Publishing Sites
    - Publishing Portal
    - Enterprise Wiki
    - Product Catalog

Collaboration Sites

The five sites in this category all have the same basic purpose: to allow you and your co-workers to share and collaborate on documents to get work done more efficiently.

Team Site

A team site is a site for teams to quickly organize, author, and share information. It provides a document library, and lists for managing announcements, calendar items, tasks, and discussions.

The Team Site creates default instances of these lists and libraries:

- Documents Library
- Notebook Library
- Site Assets
- Site Pages
- Microfeed

Figure 1: Team Site

Blog Site

This is a site for a person or team to post ideas, observations, and expertise on which site visitors can comment.

The lists and libraries created in a Blog site are:

- Photo Library

- Categories

- Comments

- Links

- Posts

- Alerts

Figure 2: Blog Site

Developer Site

A site for developers to build, test and publish apps for Office.

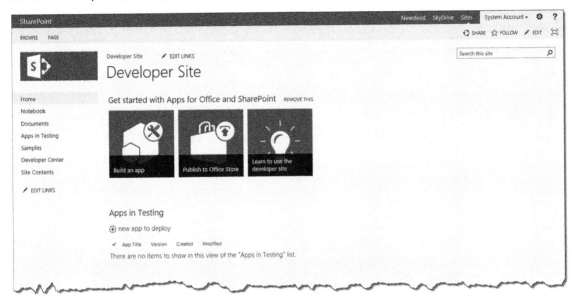

Figure 3: Developer Site

Project Site

A Project Site provides a groupware solution that enables teams to create, organize, and share information quickly and easily. It includes a Calendar, Task List, and the other basic lists included in the Team Site.

Figure 4: Project Site

Community Site

A Community site is a site for colleagues to work together and discuss relevant topics. It provides several lists geared to creating a collaborative environment. The Community site includes these lists:

- Categories

- Members

- Discussion

- Badges

- Reputation

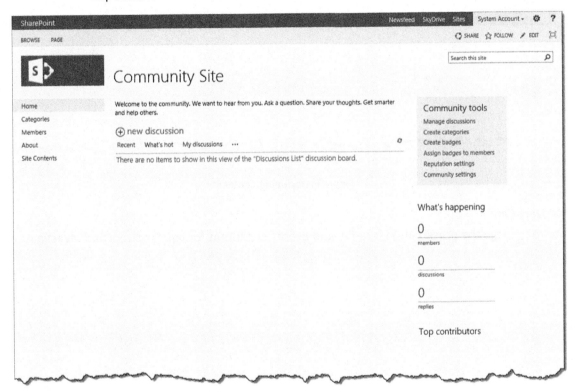

Figure 5: Community Site

Enterprise Sites

These sites contain powerful tools to help you manage your business processes no matter what size business you work in.

Document Center

Use this site to create, work on, and store documents. This site can become a collaborative repository for authoring documents within a team, or a knowledge base for documents across multiple teams.

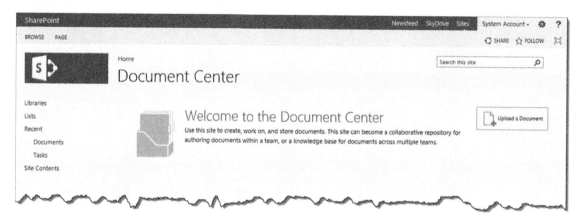

Figure 6: Document Center

eDiscovery Center

A site to manage the preservation, search, and export of content for legal matters and investigations.

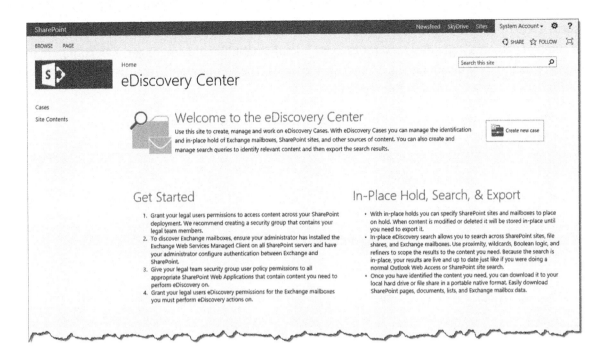

Figure 7: eDiscovery Center

Records Center

This template creates a site designed for records management. Records managers can configure the routing table to direct incoming files to specific locations. The site prevents records from being modified after they are added to the repository.

The records center creates a number of libraries and lists when it is started:

- Libraries

  o Hold Reports

  o Missing Properties

  o Records Pending Submission

  o Unclassified Records

- Lists

  o Holds

  o Records Routing

  o Records Center

  o Submitted E-Mail Records

  o Tasks

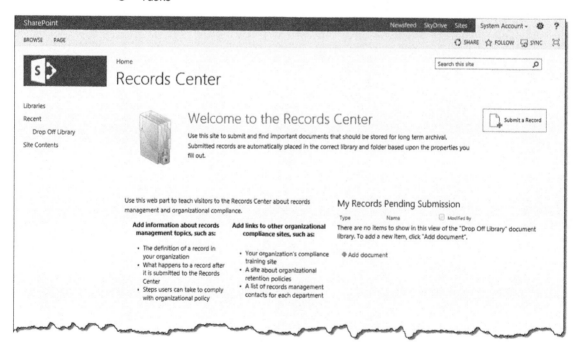

Figure 8: Records Center

Business Intelligence Center

The Business intelligence Center site helps you organize that data in a useful way and present that data as meaningful information. It uses business intelligence tools such as scorecards, dashboards, data connections, status lists, and status indicators to convey the information you need.

Enterprise Search Center

The Enterprise Search Center is a SharePoint search that includes several components, each responsible for a specific search task.

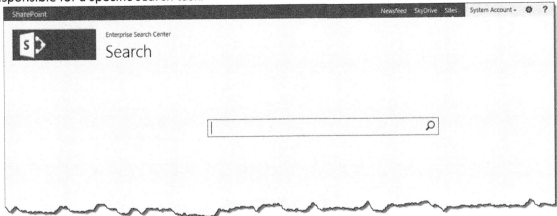

Figure 9: Enterprise Search Center

My Site Host

A site used for hosting personal sites (My Sites) and the public People Profile page. This template needs to be provisioned only once per User Profile Service Application, please consult the documentation for details.

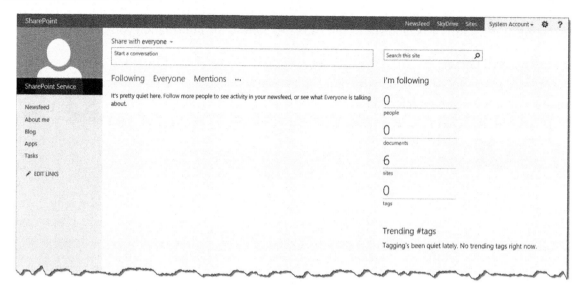

Figure 10: My Site Host

Community Portal

A site for discovering communities.

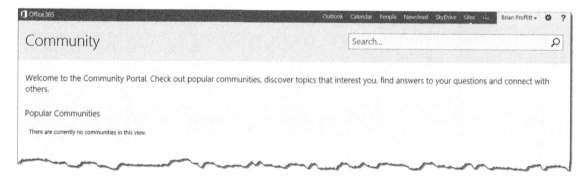

Figure 11: Community Portal

Basic Search Center

This site is for delivering a custom search experience. The site includes pages for search results and advanced searches.

Figure 12: Basic Search Center

Visio Process Repository

This is a site for teams to quickly view, share, and store Visio process diagrams. It provides a versioned document library for storing process diagrams, and lists for managing announcements, tasks, and review discussions.

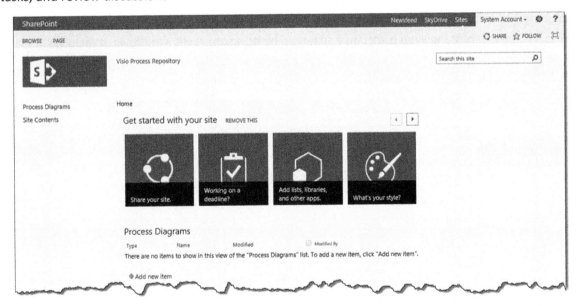

Figure 13: Visio Process Repository

Publishing Sites

The four sites in this category are for publishing custom web or wiki pages, with or without a workflow process in place.

Publishing Site

This is a blank site for expanding your Web site and quickly publishing Web pages. Contributors can work on draft versions of pages and publish them to make them visible to readers. The site includes document and image libraries for storing Web publishing assets.

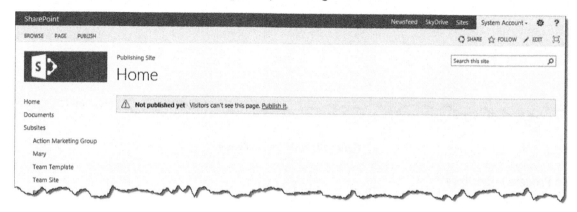

Figure 14: Publishing Site

Publishing Site with Workflow

This is a site for publishing Web pages on a schedule by using approval workflows. It includes document and image libraries for storing Web publishing assets. By default, only sites with this template can be created under this site.

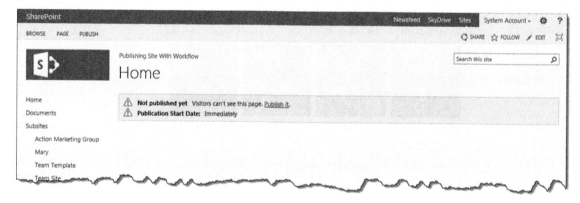

Figure 15: Publishing Site with Workflow

Enterprise Wiki

An Enterprise Wiki is a publishing site for sharing and updating large volumes of information across an enterprise.

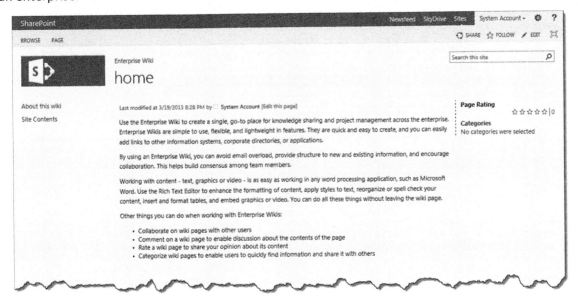

Figure 16: Enterprise Wiki

Product Catalog

A site for managing product catalog data which can be published to an internet-facing site through search. The product catalog can be configured to support product variants and multilingual product properties. The site includes admin pages for managing faceted navigation for products.

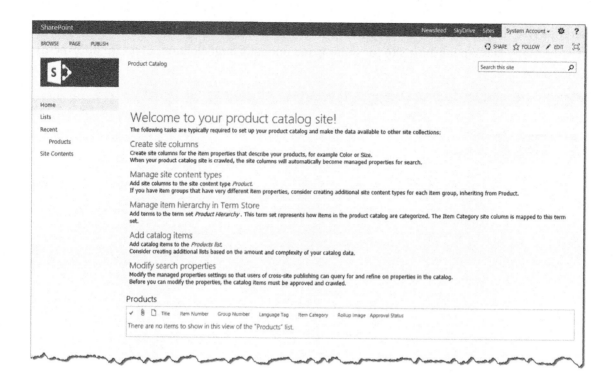

Figure 17: Product Catalog Site

Appendix B: App Definitions

Purpose: Libraries, lists, discussion boards … in SharePoint 2013, they're all some sort of app. In this Appendix, all of the apps will be reviewed and displayed, to make your choices easier when it's time to create your own list.

Libraries

Libraries are essentially lists that have one and only one file associated with each item.

Asset Library

A library for managing and sharing digital assets, such as audio, video, and other rich media files.

Figure 1: Asset Library

Data Connection Library

Create a Data Connection Library to make it easy to share files that contain information about external data connections.

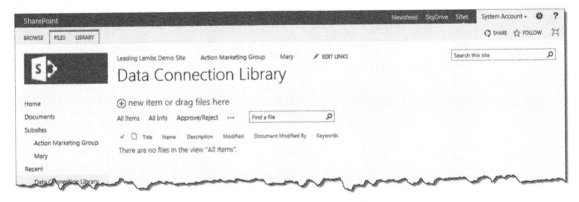

Figure 2: Data Connection Library

Document Library

Create a document library when you have a collection of documents or other files that you want to share. Document libraries support features such as folders, versioning, and check out.

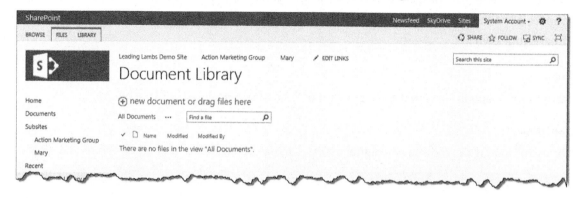

Figure 3: Document Library

Form Library

Create a form library when you have XML-based business forms, such as status reports or purchase orders, that you want to manage. These libraries are designed for use with Microsoft Office InfoPath.

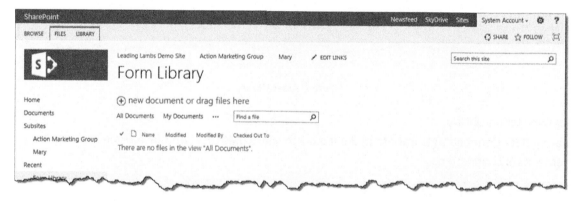

Figure 4: Form Library

Picture Library

Create a picture library when you have pictures you want to share. Picture libraries provide special features for managing and displaying pictures, such as thumbnails, download options, and a slide show.

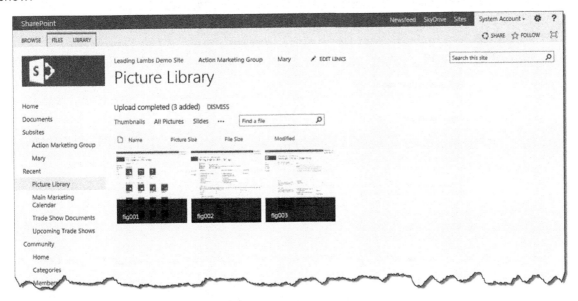

Figure 5: Picture Library

Report Library

A library designed to manage and share SQL reports.

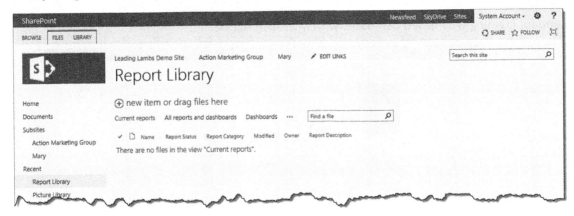

Figure 6: Report Library

Wiki Page Library

Create a Wiki page library when you want to have an interconnected collection of Wiki pages. Wiki page libraries support pictures, tables, hyperlinks, and wiki linking.

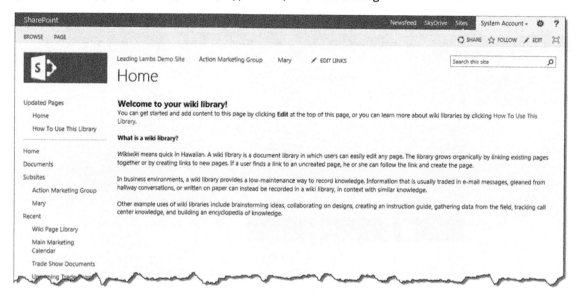

Figure 7: Wiki Page Library

Lists

Lists in this collection are designed to be used as tools to connect with your co-workers.

Access App

An app for creating web-based databases with Microsoft Access.

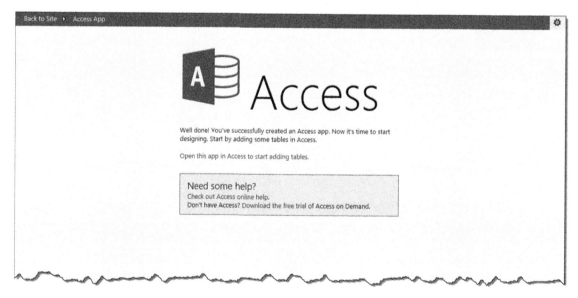

Figure 8: Access App Welcome Page

Announcements

Create an announcements list when you want a place to share news, status, and other short bits of information.

Figure 9: Announcements

Calendar

Create a calendar list when you want a calendar-based view of upcoming meetings, deadlines, and other important events. You can share information between your calendar list and Windows SharePoint Services-compatible events programs.

Figure 10: Calendar

Contacts

Create a contacts list when you want to manage information about people that your team works with, such as customers or partners. You can share information between your contacts list and Microsoft Outlook.

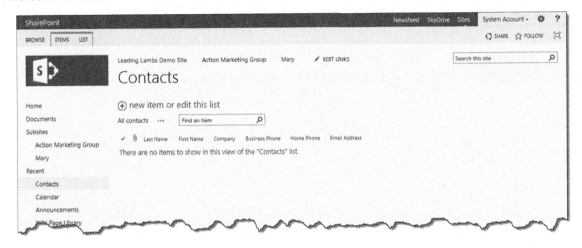

Figure 11: Contacts

Custom List

Create a custom list when you want to specify your own columns. The list opens as a Web page and lets you add or edit items one at a time. Your title field must be a single line of text, but it can be renamed. You can also add all of the columns that you want, as shown in the task "Create a List."

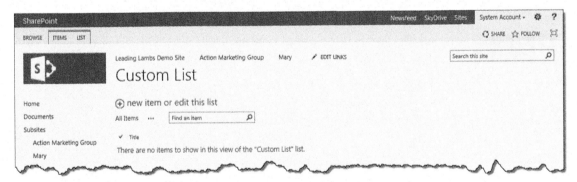

Figure 12: Custom List

Custom List in Datasheet View

Create a custom list when you want to specify your own columns, just like a regular custom list. In this case, the list opens in a spreadsheet-like environment for convenient data entry, editing, and formatting. It requires Microsoft Access and a browser with ActiveX control support.

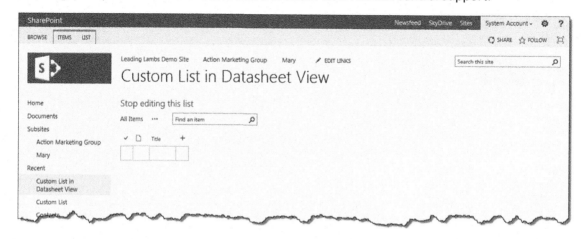

Figure 13: Custom List in Datasheet View

Discussion Board

Create a discussion board when you want to provide a place for newsgroup-style discussions. Discussion boards provide features for managing discussion threads and ensuring that only approved posts appear.

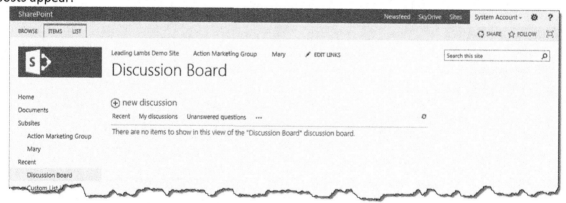

Figure 14: Discussion Board

External List

Create an external list to view your data in an External Data list.

The SharePoint Shepherd's Guide for End Users: 2013

Import Spreadsheet

Import a spreadsheet when you want to create a list that has the same columns and content as an existing spreadsheet. Importing a spreadsheet requires Microsoft Excel.

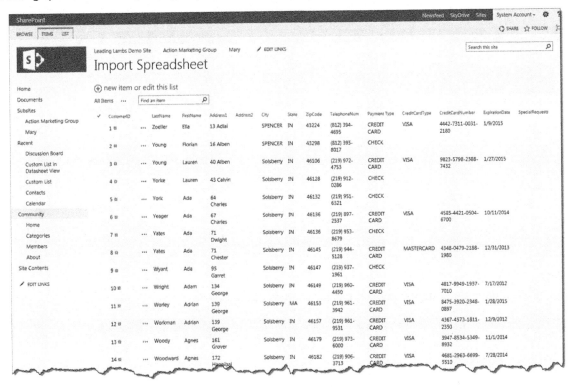

Figure 15: Import Spreadsheet

Issue Tracking

Create an issue tracking list when you want to manage a set of issues or problems. You can assign, prioritize, and follow the progress of issues from start to finish. Another key feature is that you can relate issues to one another, which makes it easier to create logical progressions of work to be done.

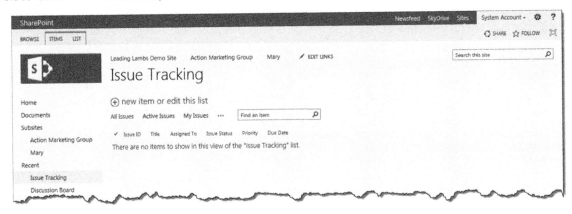

Figure 16: Issue Tracking

Promoted Links

Create a promoted links list when you have links to Web pages or other resources that you want to share. This list can also the source for the tile icons web part view similar to the Welcome Page when a new site is created.

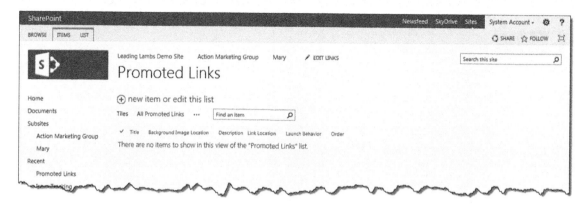

Figure 17: Promoted Links

Survey

A list for conducting and managing surveys for team members.

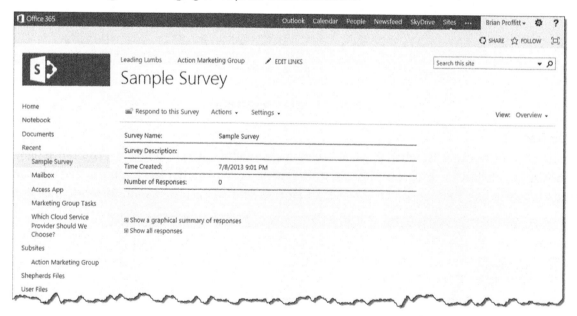

Figure 18: Survey List

Tasks

Create a tasks list when you want to track a group of work items that you or your team needs to complete.

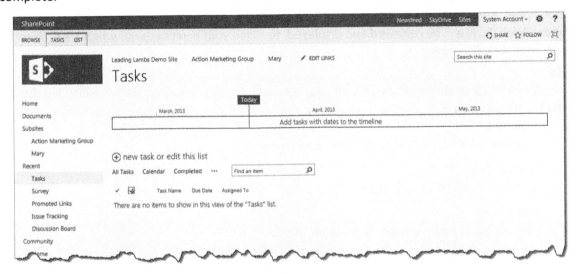

Figure 19: Tasks

When you create a Web Parts page, you can easily insert content from almost any list made available in SharePoint. There are also some specialized content Web Parts. In this Appendix, the most common Web Parts will be reviewed and displayed, to make your choices easier when it's time to create your Web Parts page.

Apps

Not only can whole pages be created for an app, but some app functionality can be inserted within a section of a page.

Calendar
The Calendar app can track dates on a web page.

Documents
List documents on a web page.

MicroFeed
Display alerts and messages from other users.

Site Assets
List components and tools on your site.

Tasks
List the things that need to be done.

Blog

Web Parts for adding blogging capabilities to a page.

Blog Archives
Provides quick links to older blog posts.

Blog Notifications
Provides quick links to register for blog posts notifications using Alerts or RSS feed.

Blog Tools
Provides blog owners and administrators with quick links to common settings pages and content lists for managing a blog site.

Business Data

Connect to your data easily with these Web Parts.

Business Data Actions
Displays a list of actions from Business Data Connectivity.

Business Data Connectivity Filter
Filters the contents of Web Parts using a list of values from the Business Data Connectivity.

Business Data Item
Displays one item from a data source in Business Data Connectivity.

Business Data Item Builder
Creates a Business Data item from parameters in the query string and provides it to other Web Parts.

Business Data List
Displays a list of items from a data source in Business Data Connectivity.

Business Data List Related List
Displays a list of items related to one or more parent items from a data source in Business Data Connectivity.

Excel Web Access
Use the Excel Web Access Web Part to interact with an Excel workbook as a Web page.

Indicator Details
Displays the details of a single Status Indicator. Status Indicators display an important measure for an organization and may be obtained from other data sources including SharePoint lists, Excel workbooks, and SQL Server 2005 Analysis Services KPIs.

Status List
Shows a list of Status Indicators. Status Indicators display important measures for your organization, and show how your organization is performing with respect to your goals.

Visio Web Access
Enables viewing and refreshing of Visio Web Drawings.

Community
Introduce collaborative features to any web page.

About this Community
This Web Part displays the community description and other properties, like established date. This Web Part will work on Community sites or any other site that has Community Features turned on.

Join
Provides the ability for non-members of a community site to join the community. The button hides itself if the user is already a member. This Web Part will work on Community sites or any other site that has Community Features turned on.

My Membership
Displays reputation and membership information for the current visitor of a community site. This Web Part will work on Community sites or any other site that has Community Features turned on.

Tools
Provides community owners and administrators with quick links to common settings pages and content lists for managing a community site. This Web Part will work on Community sites or any other site that has Community Features turned on.

What's Happening
Displays the number of members, topics and replies within a community site. This Web Part will work on Community sites or any other site that has Community Features turned on.

Content Rollup
Web Parts in this category can aggregate content from a variety of sources.

Categories

Displays categories from the Site Directory.

Content Query
Displays a dynamic view of content from your site.

Content Search
Content Search Web Part will allow you to show items that are results of a search query you specify. When you add it to the page, this Web Part will show recently modified items from the current site. You can change this setting to show items from another site or list by editing the Web Part and changing its search criteria. As new content is discovered by search, this Web Part will display an updated list of items each time the page is viewed. Depending on the search configuration, there may be a delay between when the content is modified and when it appears.

Project Summary
Displays information about a project in an easy to read overview.

Relevant Documents
Displays documents that are relevant to the current user.

RSS Viewer
Displays an RSS feed

Site Aggregator
Displays sites of your choice.

Sites In Category
Displays sites from the Site Directory within a specific category.

Summary Links
Allows authors to create links that can be grouped and styled.

Table of Contents
Displays the navigation hierarchy of your site.

Term Property
Displays the specified property of a Term.

Timeline
Use this timeline to show a high level view of data from another Web Part or tasks list.

WSRP Viewer
Displays portlets from Web sites using WSRP 1.1.

XML Viewer
Transforms XML data using XSL and shows the results.

Document Sets
Manage document sets in your SharePoint site.

Document Set Contents
Displays the contents of the Document Set.

Document Set Properties

Displays the properties of the Document Set.

Filters

Add filter controls to your SharePoint pages.

Apply Filters Button

Add this button to a page so users can decide when to apply their filter choices. Otherwise, each filter is applied when its value is changed.

Choice Filter

Filters the contents of Web Parts using a list of values entered by the page author.

Current User Filter

Filters the contents of Web Parts by using properties of the current user.

Date Filter

Filters the contents of Web Parts by allowing users to enter or pick a date.

Page Field Filter

Filters the contents of Web Parts using information about the current page.

Query String (URL) Filter

Filters the contents of Web Parts using values passed via the query string.

SharePoint List Filter

Filters the contents of Web Parts by using a list of values.

SQL Server Analysis Services Filter

Filters the contents of Web Parts using a list of values from SQL Server Analysis Services cubes.

Text Filter

Filters the contents of Web Parts by allowing users to enter a text value.

Forms

Web Parts in this category build Web page forms for users.

HTML Form

Connects simple form controls to other Web Parts.

InfoPath Form

Use this Web Part to display an InfoPath browser-enabled form.

Media and Content

Web Parts in this category display a variety of multimedia content.

Content Editor

Allows authors to enter rich text content.

Get Started With Your Site

This Web Part displays a set of tiles with common SharePoint actions.

Image Viewer

Displays a specified image.

Media

Use to embed media clips (video and audio) in a Web page.

Page Viewer
Displays another Web page on this Web page. The other Web page is presented in an IFrame.

Picture Library Slideshow
Use to display a slideshow of images and photos from a picture library.

Script Editor
This Web Part displays a set of tiles with common SharePoint actions.

Silverlight
A Web Part to display a Silverlight application.

Search
Web Parts that help determine search results.

Refinement
This Web Part helps the users to refine search results.

Search Box
Displays a search box that allows users to search for information.

Search Navigation
This Web Part helps the users to navigate among search verticals.

Search Results
Displays the search results and the properties associated with them.

Taxonomy Refinement Panel
This Web Part helps the user to refine search results on term set data. To use this Web Part, you must also have a Search Data Provider Web Part on this page and use Managed Navigation.

Search-Driven Content
Web Parts that produce content lists based on content type.

Catalog-Item Reuse
Use this Web Part to reuse or republish the content of an item from a catalog.

Items Matching a Tag
This Web Part will show items that are tagged with a term.

Pages
This Web Part will show any items that are derived from the Pages content type.

Pictures
This Web Part will show any items that are derived from the Picture or Image content type.

Popular Items
This Web Part will show items that have been recently viewed by many users.

Recently Changed Items

This Web Part will show items that have been modified recently. This can help site users track the latest activity on a site or a library.

Recommended Items
This Web Part will show content recommendations based on usage patterns for the current page.

Videos
This Web Part will show any items that are derived from the Video content type. It will sort items by number of views.

Web Pages
This Web Part will show any items that are derived from the Page content type.

Wiki Pages
This Web Part will show any items that are derived from the Wiki Page content type.

Social Collaboration
Web Parts in this category enable user to engage in collaborative and social activities.

Contact Details
Displays details about a contact for this page or site.

Note Board
Enable users to leave short, publicly-viewable notes about this page.

Organization Browser
This Web Part displays each person in the reporting chain in an interactive view optimized for browsing organization charts.

Site Users
Use the Site Users Web Part to see a list of the site users and their online status.

Tag Cloud
Displays the most popular subjects being tagged inside your organization.

User Tasks
Displays tasks that are assigned to the current user.

Purpose: When you create a new view of an app in SharePoint, you are given a choice of six default views. In this Appendix, these views will be reviewed and displayed, to make your choices easier when it's time to customize the way you look at a list.

Standard

View data on a Web page. This view displays a standard data grid type view of the data, as seen on most Web pages and sites.

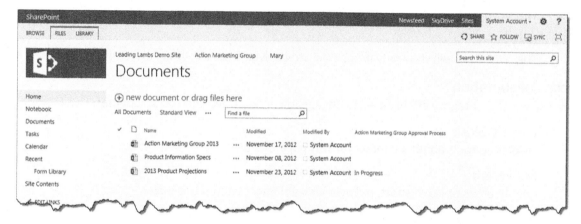

Figure 1: Standard View

Calendar

View data as a daily, weekly, or monthly calendar.

Figure 2: Calendar View

Gantt

View list items in a Gantt chart to see a graphical representation of the items related over time.

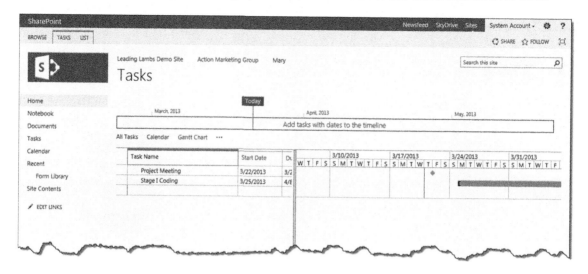

Figure 3: Gantt View

Datasheet

View data in an editable spreadsheet format that is convenient for bulk editing and quick customization. This view requires the use of an ActiveX-capable browser and Microsoft Access.

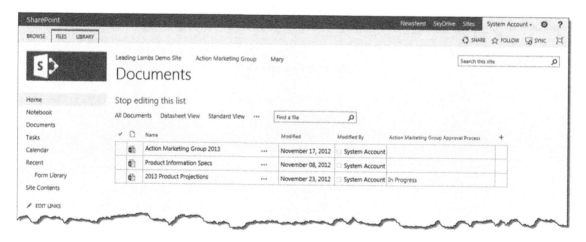

Figure 4: Datasheet View

Access

Start Microsoft Office Access to create forms and reports that are based on this list.

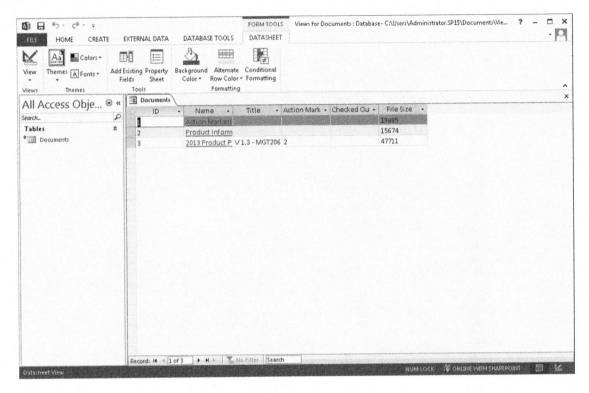

Figure 5: Access View

Custom View in SharePoint Designer

Start SharePoint Designer to create a new view for this list with capabilities such as conditional formatting.

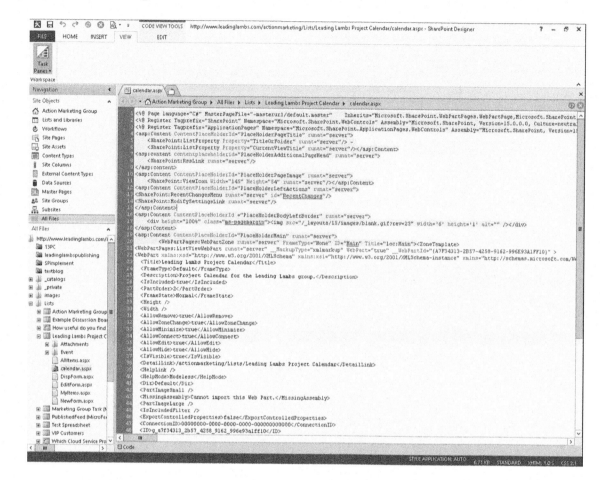

Figure 6: SharePoint Designer View

Appendix E: Permissions in SharePoint

Purpose: To keep documents secure in SharePoint, there are a number of permission levels that can be assigned to individual users or user groups. You can also manage permissions for a user or group at the site level, at the individual list item level, and everywhere in between within SharePoint. In this Appendix, the definitions of the various default permission levels in SharePoint are listed.

> **Note:** SharePoint administrators can define additional permission levels, so there may be other permission levels defined for your organization's sites.

Permission Levels

	Name in browser	Description	*Visitors (Restricted Read)	*Members (Contribute)	*Owners (Full Control)	Designers (Design)	Approvers (Approve)	Hierarchy Managers (Manage Hierarchy)
Create	Add Items	Add items to lists, add documents to document libraries, and add Web discussion comments.		✓	✓	✓	✓	✓
Read	Browse Directories	Enumerate files and folders in a Web site using Microsoft Office SharePoint Designer 2007 and WebDAV interfaces.		✓	✓	✓	✓	✓
Read	Enumerate Permissions	Enumerate permissions on the Web site, list, folder, document, or list item.			✓			✓
Read	Open	Allow users to open a Web site, list, or folder to	✓	✓	✓	✓	✓	✓

		access items inside that container.						
	Open Items	View the source of documents with server-side file handlers.	✔	✔	✔	✔	✔	✔
	View Application Pages	View forms, views, and application pages, and enumerate lists.	✔	✔	✔	✔	✔	✔
	View Items	View items in lists, documents in document libraries, and view Web discussion comments.	✔	✔	✔	✔	✔	✔
	View Pages	View pages in a Web site.	✔	✔	✔	✔	✔	✔
	View Versions	View past versions of a list item or document.	✔	✔	✔	✔	✔	✔
Update	Approve Items	Approve a minor version of a list item or document.			✔	✔	✔	
	Edit Items	Edit items in lists, edit documents in document libraries, edit Web discussion comments in documents, and customize Web Part Pages in document libraries.		✔	✔	✔	✔	✔
	Override Checkout	Discard or check in a document which is checked			✔	✔	✔	✔

		out to another user.						
Delete	Delete Items	Delete items from a list, documents from a document library, and Web discussion comments in documents.		✓	✓	✓	✓	✓
	Delete Versions	Delete past versions of a list item or document.		✓	✓	✓	✓	✓
Email	Create Alerts	Create e-mail alerts.	✓	✓	✓	✓	✓	✓
	Manage Alerts	Manage alerts for all users of the Web site.			✓			✓
Personalize	Edit Personal User Information	Allows a user to change his or her user information, such as adding a picture.		✓	✓	✓	✓	✓
	Manage Personal Views	Create, change, and delete personal views of lists.		✓	✓	✓	✓	✓
	Add/Remove Personal Web Parts	Add or remove personal Web Parts on a Web Part Page.		✓	✓	✓	✓	✓
	Update Personal Web Parts	Update Web Parts to display personalized information.		✓	✓	✓	✓	✓
Program	Use Remote Interfaes	Use SOAP, WebDAV, or Microsoft Office SharePoint Designer interfaces to	✓	✓	✓	✓	✓	✓

Category	Permission	Description						
		access the Web site.						
	Use Client Integration Features	Use features that launch client applications; otherwise, users must work on documents locally and upload changes.	✓	✓	✓	✓	✓	✓
Security	Create Groups	Create a group of users that can be used anywhere within the site collection.			✓			
	Manage Permissions	Create and change permission levels on the Web site and assign permissions to users and groups.			✓			✓
Structure	Create Subsite	Create subsites such as team sites, Meeting Workspace sites, and Document Workspace sites.			✓			✓
	Manage Lists	Create and delete lists, add or remove columns in a list, and add or remove public views of a list.			✓			✓

	Manage Web Site	Grant the ability to perform all administration tasks for the Web site as well as manage content. Activate, deactivate, or edit properties of Web site scoped Features through the object model or through the user interface (UI). When granted on the root Web site of a site collection, activate, deactivate, or edit properties of site collection scoped Features through the object model.			✓			✓
	Add and Customize Pages	Add, change, or delete HTML pages or Web Part Pages, and edit the Web site using a Windows SharePoint Services–compatible editor.			✓	✓		✓
Style	Apply Theme and Border	Apply a theme or borders to the entire Web site.			✓	✓		
	Apply Style Sheets	Apply a style sheet (.css file) to the Web site.			✓	✓		
Misc.	Browse User Information	View information	✓	✓	✓	✓	✓	✓

		about users of the Web site.						
View Web Analytics Data	View reports on Web site usage.			✔			✔

Get access to more helpful resources, quick reference materials, and SharePoint tips and tricks. Sign up at tinyurl.com/followtheshepherd.

Appendix F: Exploring the SharePoint Interface

Purpose: SharePoint 2013 has been sleekly redesigned to emulate many of the interface features found in Office 2013 and Office 365 applications. While many of the interface controls are self-explanatory, a quick visual primer on the various interface tools and controls should prove helpful.

Figure 1: SharePoint Interface Elements

 The Ribbon

These links are actually tabs for different sets of controls that are relevant to where you are. When you click one of the links, the appropriate set of controls will appear. If you want the ribbon to go away, click browse.

User Menu

This menu contains navigation and action that pertains to you. You can use About Me to navigate to your personal My Site. Sign Out signs you out of SharePoint, and Personalize this Page allows you to change your personal view of a page.

Settings

The settings menu is the primary place to take action on the site and the current page. You can change the site settings, add an app, a page, or review the site contents. Additionally most other action settings will appear in this menu or lead you to pages which allow you to control the site.

Quick Access Toolbar

In the Quick Access Toolbar you'll find actions that you can perform in the context of where you're at – these same actions are on the ribbon but here you can access them in one click. The common actions are:

Share the site with someone inside the organization – or externally if allowed.

Add this site, library, etc., to your newsfeed so you will see updates automatically.

Synchronize the files in this site or library to your computer using SkyDrive Pro.

Edit the contents of this page including changing web and app parts.

Focus on content by minimizing the navigation and chrome in the display to allow more space for the content.

Suite Bar

The Suite Bar allows you to navigate between the various applications in your organization – or on Office 365. Your IT systems administrator controls these options.

Top Navigation Bar

The top navigation bar is "big picture" navigation in your site or set of sites. Like highways they move you between different large areas in your SharePoint space. You, or your site administrator, control these options.

Quick Launch

Local navigation is handled in the Quick Launch area. This may include links that you add to the area manually as well as recent links. This is where you navigate to the site, list, or library containing the precise content you are looking for.

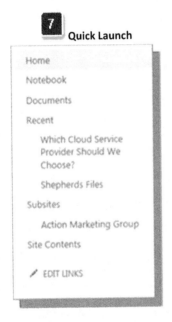

Home

Notebook

Documents

Recent

    Which Cloud Service Provider Should We Choose?

    Shepherds Files

Subsites

    Action Marketing Group

Site Contents

✎ EDIT LINKS

Ellipsis Control

These three dots indicate that there is more information available that has been 'hidden" for brevity. In SharePoint, whenever you see the three dots of an ellipsis, you can click it to get more items or more information about the current item. On a document, the ellipsis will lead you to a hover panel with more information and a preview of the document.

Contact Card

Cody Leaderbrand
Available - Video Capable

Start Video Call
Share Desktop
Tag for Presence Alerts
Pin to Frequent Contacts
Add to Quick Contacts

Hovering over any name will cause the contact card for that person to appear. If you and the other person are logged into Lync you'll get presence information and an opportunity to contact them via email, chat, or phone. Even more options are available in the drop down.

Get access to more helpful resources, quick reference materials, and SharePoint tips and tricks. Sign up at tinyurl.com/followtheshepherd.

Index

Follow the Shepherd and

Receive a Free User Interface Quick Reference

Thank you for purchasing the SharePoint Shepherd's Guide for End Users: 2013 (if this was a gift, then, well, thanks for being thorough and reading all the way to the last page), we hope you found the book informative and helpful.

Looking for more tools to help make the most of SharePoint?

Go to tinyurl.com/FollowTheShepherd and sign up to **receive a FREE User Interface Quick Reference. The User Interface Quick Reference is a handy tool that you'll want to keep within reach – it explains the most commonly used SharePoint Navigation and Action Controls.** You'll also receive the Shepherd's monthly newsletters packed with more tips to help you achieve greater productivity and efficiency with SharePoint. Use the code: FREEQR.

Your feedback is welcome. We're always looking to hear about the challenges you are facing. Drop us a note at Shepherd@SharePointShepherd.com to let us know the challenges you're facing in your SharePoint environment.

CPSIA information can be obtained
at www.ICGtesting.com
Printed in the USA
BVOW10s1054170817

492246BV00003B/43/P